Communicating Power and Gender

Deborah J. Borisoff

James W. Chesebro

WAVELAND
PRESS, INC.

Long Grove, Illinois

For information about this book, contact:
   Waveland Press, Inc.
   4180 IL Route 83, Suite 101
   Long Grove, IL 60047-9580
   (847) 634-0081
   info@waveland.com
   www.waveland.com

Contents

4 *Early Socialization in the Home:*   **103**
Influencing Gendered Scripts

5 *The Educational Landscape:*   **125**
Connecting Gender and Identity

Introduction

*A*s the title *Communicating Power and Gender* suggests, this volume would appear to be relatively narrow in scope, examining the relationships between two concepts, *gender* and *power*, as they are linked and transformed by the human communication process. Yet, this link is only apparently narrow. As soon as we ask about the relationships between gender and power, a host of associations spins out, crossing different social, cultural, historical, political, and even racial, cross-cultural, and societal spheres. Moreover, these relationships and associations are not fixed; they can and do change over time, just as social mores and cultural values continually change.

Accordingly, in this introduction, we seek to accomplish four ends. First, we define what we mean by the terms *gender* and *power* as well as *communication*. Second, these definitions provide us with a foundation for a highly selective review of four historical volumes that we believe have shaped how we understand the relationships among gender, power, and communication. Third, we also want to argue that conditions we face today support—indeed, require—that we extend the historical foundation that has been previously developed. We are convinced that current circumstances are generating new kinds of relationships and issues. We want to provide a brief rationale for why we once again approach the relationships between gender and power in this volume today. Fourth and finally, this introduction concludes by previewing how this volume is organized, and the role and function of each of the six chapters within the book. We begin, then, by first considering what we mean by the words *gender, power,* and *communication.*

Defining Gender, Power, and Communication

As we deal with the words *gender* and *power*, we need to recognize initially that fixed and enduring definitions of these concepts simply do

1

not exist. When we admit that various meanings exist for these words for different groups, we are more likely to remain flexible and even seek out the variations and transformations that have and can exist when people use these terms. Indeed, recognizing the changing ways in which the terms are used is a wonderful part of the decision to observe and study how gender and power are communicated.

With these qualifiers in mind, we can begin by defining *gender*. To do so, we need to recognize and employ a distinction between sex and sexuality (see, e.g., Tannen, 2006, p. 116).

While it would be nice if the term remained stable, the word *sex* itself has gained and transformed in meaning over time. For example, today we frequently hear the word *sex* used to refer to the act of sexual intercourse (e.g., "They had sex"). However, in its more technical and scientific sense, the word *sex* is used to refer to biological characteristics and more precisely biological differences. In this regard, sex refers to two groups of people or organisms—males and females—distinguished by certain structural, functional, and behavioral characteristics that are most frequently associated with the various elements and dimensions of reproduction of the species. The word *gender* does not really fit within the broader category of *sex*. *Gender* has far different meanings than the biological framework implied by the word *sex*.

To deal with gender more properly, we need to view it as a subpart or one element of the broader category of sexuality. Sexuality recognizes the power of human creativity and the symbolic abilities of people when they encounter and have to deal with biological distinctions such as male and female. Broadly speaking, sexuality recognizes the biology of people, but it highlights the social and psychological characteristics and attributes that people give or attribute to sex. These social and psychological characteristics and attributes transform questions of mere biological sex—male and female—into questions of sexuality or gender. When the biological differences between male and female shift to the social meanings that people give to biological differences, questions of gender emerge, and these gender differences actually require the use of different words. Hence, we begin to deal with gender when we employ terms such as *masculine* and *feminine*. Such gender terminologies are profoundly dynamic and open-ended terms that vary dramatically as you move from one culture to another. For example, Chesebro and Fuse (2001) identified some 10 different dimensions that college students in the United States associated with and used to define *masculinity*. However, college students who were born and raised in Korea did not use these 10 dimensions to define how they used the word *masculinity* in Korea. In all, gender attributions—such as masculine and feminine— vary tremendously from one culture to another as well as from one historical era to another, from one class to another, and—we believe—even from one racial grouping to another and even from one economic class to another. Such recognitions make the study of gender a flagrantly open area of investigation, capable of revealing so much about the diversity and differences among different groupings of people. Indeed, we suspect that the different ways in which people use terms such as *gender*—and as we shall shortly see, even *power*—can ultimately become apt focal points for recognizing how and why people organize themselves in different ways in terms of historical, social, and cultural eras.

From our focus on gender, we can make a shift and ask how and what gender has to do with questions of power. Power, of course, can take many forms. Money can create power; titles and positions can convey and create a sense of power; physical properties can give people power; and, even something as vague and transitory as popularity can give an individual power over others. In all of these cases, power involves the belief that some can control others, influence and shape the reactions of others, or have authority over others. In all of these cases, power is the physical, psychological, social, cultural, political, religious, legal, or even symbolic ability to act, produce, or control how people do things, how things are done, and often affects the outcomes or effects of human efforts and processes. In this view, power is always with us. When people act together, they must necessarily organize how things are done. As soon as they organize, some priorities are established while other goals are ignored, some procedures are specified and approved while others are not, and some actual processes and outcomes are prized and encouraged while others are neglected or defined and cast as undesirable. All of these actions create power relationships, hierarchies, and systems. People are constantly seeking adjustments in existing systems, or even during the creation of new systems, that are more responsive to their ever-changing and evolving needs and values.

We are left with the notion of *communication*, a key and essential term employed throughout this volume. A rich and useful variety of philosophies and models of communication exist, but we evoke here a definition that seems extremely direct and useful for our purposes in this volume. The *International Encyclopedia of Communications* (1989) provides an apt point for clarifying communication:

> The study of communications focuses on a process fundamental to the development of humans and human society—interaction through messages. By means of communication we share ideas and information, live in infinitely varied cultures, and extend knowledge and imagination far beyond the scope of personal experience. (p. 358)

With "interaction through messages" as our focus, in this volume, we focus on the complexities of factors affecting interactions and that ultimately convey meanings or convey messages to others. Thus, in our view, communication is a decisive variable affecting how gender and power are ultimately related, perceived, understood, and acted on.

Interactions through messages thus define and determine how and why people define and link gender and power as they do. As a point of departure in this exploration, we begin with the historical foundation that influenced the messages linking gender and power at the end of the twentieth century and ultimately has shaped how gender and power have been linked during the first decade of the twenty-first century.

A Historical Foundation for Examining Gender and Power as a Communication Process

Any number of schemes have been employed to describe the interrelationships among gender and power. For example, Brunell (2008) has suggested that feminism is an appropriate heading for examining how gender and power are related. In this context, she has argued for three "waves" of feminism. The first wave of feminism (1848–1920) focused "primarily on obtaining the full legal personhood and the political enfranchisement of women" (p. 196). The second wave of feminism (1963–1991) "continued these struggles through the ultimately unsuccessful push for an Equal Rights Amendment to the U.S. Constitution" and the "founding of durable political organizations" such as the National Organization for Women (NOW) (p. 196). And the third wave of feminism, often associated with the creation of the 1997 Third Wave Foundation,

> grew up with the expectation of achievement and examples of female success as well as an awareness of barriers. They chose to battle sexism by standing sexist symbols on their heads, to fight patriarchy with irony, to answer violence with stories of survival, and to combat continued exclusion with grass-roots activism and radical democracy. Rather than becoming part of the machine, third wavers took steps to both sabotage and rebuild the machine itself. (p. 197)

At certain times, this three wave framework can be extremely useful. It is likely to be useful when a decisively radical ideological posture is adopted, and when movement perspective or orientation functions as the controlling framework for initiating political actions. However, our concerns are broader. We are intrigued by actions, not only of political radicals, but also by liberals, conservatives, and reactionaries. Moreover, we think it vitally important to pay attention to and recognize the transformations occurring in all of the major social and societal institutions within the United States. Accordingly, we think a historical foundation can be more useful at this point in time.

Indeed, we can reasonably drop back and examine some of the principles that began some 60 years ago. Specifically, while fully recognizing how incomplete our treatment is, we do think that four previously published volumes deserve specific recognition here. Typical of a host of statements about gender and power relationships, these volumes introduce key concepts that are an essential part of the controversies and issues that have made the study of the relationships between gender and power so significant and enduring. In the context of this introduction, we use the analysis of these four volumes as a foundation for isolating some critical principles that allow us to begin our treatment of how gender and power are communicated.

Our historical treatment of the contemporary political culture begins, then, with a discussion of the interrelationships between gender and power that emerged, reflected, and captured gender and power issues in the second half of the twentieth century. At the same time, you will notice how this analysis and discussion continues to shape how we think about the communication of gender and power in the United States today.

Simone de Beauvoir's *The Second Sex*

Our point of departure is the early 1950s. In the early 1950s, television was just beginning to dominate and characterize the American culture. Television series such as *I Love Lucy*, *The Honeymooners*, *Lassie*, *Walt Disney*, *The Mickey Mouse Club*, *Superman*, and *The Twilight Zone* directed attention in the United States away from issues and questions of oppression. However, in sharp contrast to the emerging world that television created for the American people, an alternative perspective was outlined by Simone de Beauvoir in her 1953 volume *The Second Sex*. Born in 1909, Simone de Beauvoir obtained her PhD from the Sorbonne and taught until 1943. In association with Jean-Paul Sartre, she was a leader among French intellectuals. In 1947, she gained attention when her four-month lecture tour included the United States. *The Second Sex* represented a definitive analysis by Beauvoir of the role and destiny of women in ancient and modern times. While a complete exploration of *The Second Sex* is beyond our ability here, we can note that Beauvoir's point of departure in this volume vigorously denies that a woman's biology or sex should determine her social roles and functions. Her voice is clear enough in the first paragraph of her volume:

> Woman? Very simple, say the fanciers of simple formulas: she is a womb, an ovary; she is a female—this word is sufficient to define her. In the mouth of a man the epithet *female* has the sound of an insult, yet he is not ashamed of his animal nature; on the contrary, he is proud if someone says of him: "He is a male!" The term "female" is derogatory not because it emphasizes woman's animality, but because it imprisons her in her sex; and if this sex seems to man to be contemptible and inimical even to harmless dumb animals, it is evidently because of the uneasy hostility stirred up in him by woman. Nevertheless he wishes to find in biology a justification for this sentiment. The word *female* brings up in his mind a saraband of imagery—a vast, round ovum engulfs and castrates the

agile spermatozoon; the monstrous and swollen termite queen rules over the enslaved males; the female praying mantis and the spider, satiated with love, crush and devour their partners; the bitch in heat runs through the alleys, trailing behind her a wake of depraved odors; the she-monkey presents her posterior immodestly and then steals away with hypocritical coquetry; and the most superb wild beasts—the lioness, the panther—bed down slavishly under the imperial embrace of the male. Females sluggish, eager, artful, stupid, callous, lustful, ferocious, abased—man projects them all at once upon woman. And the fact is that she is a female. But if we are willing to stop thinking in platitudes, two questions are immediately posed: what does the female denote in the animal kingdom? And what particular kind of female is manifest in woman? (pp. 3–4)

Beauvoir concludes her volume with a "Conclusion" that focuses on the power relationships between men and women in which she specifically calls for a shift from dominance to equality, but with the recognition that traditional forms of "femininity" can confound, if not block, this transformation:

Now the attitude of the male creates a new conflict: it is with a bad grace that the man lets her go. He is very pleased to remain the sovereign subject, the absolute superior, the essential being; he refuses to accept his companion as an equal in any concrete way. She replies to his lack of confidence in her by assuming an aggressive attitude. It is no longer a question of a war between individuals each shut in his or her sphere: a caste claiming its rights goes over the top and it is resisted by the privileged caste. . . . The "feminine" woman in making herself prey tries to reduce man, also, to her carnal passivity; she occupies herself in catching him in her trap, in enchaining him by means of the desire she arouses in him in submissively making herself a thing. The emancipated woman, on the contrary, wants to be active, a taker, and refuses the passivity man means to impose on her. (pp. 717–718)

Beauvoir ends her analysis by suggesting that males and females will always be different, but nonetheless—while the concept may be difficult—these sex differences can be equally respected and constitute the foundation for how all people are treated:

To begin with, there will always be certain differences between man and woman; her eroticism, and therefore her sexual world, have a special form of their own and therefore cannot fail to engender a sensuality, a sensitivity, of a special nature. This means that her relationships to her own body, to that of the male, to the child, will never be identical with those the male bears to his own body, to that of the female, and to the child; those who make much of "equality in difference" could not with good grace refuse to grant me the possible existence of differences in equality. (p. 731)

And, Beauvoir ends her analysis with what is—for some—the paradoxical notion that females are both simultaneously dependent upon but also independent of males. In other words, at some points and in some circumstances, both males and females are interdependent and must function together as an interacting unit. At certain times and in certain situations, females must be recognized, appreciated, and valued as independent.

> To emancipate woman is to refuse to confine her to the relations she bears to man, not to deny them to her; let her have her independent existence and she will continue none the less to exist for him *also*: mutually recognizing each other as subject, each will yet remain for the other an *other*. The reciprocity of their relations will not do away with the miracles—desire, possession, love, dream, adventure—worked by the division of human beings into two separate categories; and the words that move us—giving, conquering, uniting—will not lose their meaning. (p. 731)

Kate Millett's *Sexual Politics*

While literally thousands of volumes and essays extended the analysis provided by Beauvoir's 1953 treatise, almost twenty years later, Kate Millett authored *Sexual Politics* in 1970. The dust jacket of the book proclaimed that her book would provide "A surprising examination of society's most arbitrary folly." Indeed, Millett does deal with an explicit "theory of sexual politics," a perspective that forces her to specifically ask if "the relationship between the sexes can be viewed in a political light at all?" (p. 23). In other words, Millett particularly asked how power can and should be viewed as a linking concept between males and females. As she put it, "This essay does not define the political as that relatively narrow and exclusive world of meetings, chairmen, and parties. The term 'politics' shall refer to power-structured relationships, arrangements whereby one group of persons is controlled by another" (p. 23). In her view, "the entire notion of power *over* others should be banished" (p. 24).

These preliminary observations led Millett to argue that a "theory of patriarchy" exists in which "sex is a status category with political implications" (p. 24). And, "the principles of patriarchy appear to be twofold: male shall dominate female, elder male shall dominate younger" (p. 25). This theory of patriarchy has functioned as an ideology that was intended to socialize each sex, providing social characteristics arbitrarily associated with each sex. Hence, males became masculine insofar as they displayed "aggression, intelligence, force, and efficacy" while females became "feminine" when they displayed "passivity, ignorance, docility, 'virtue,' and ineffectuality" (p. 26). With these characteristics came "appropriate" social roles in which "domestic service and attendance upon infants" were assigned to females and social roles associated with "human achievement, interest, and ambition to the male" (p. 26). These social roles implicitly gave males more "status" than females, and those with "higher status tend to adopt mastery, largely because they are first encouraged to develop temperaments of dominance" (p. 26).

While Millett's view of patriarchy appears oppressive and virtually impossible to change short of a massive social revolution, the foundations for social change exist within her view of sexual politics. Noting that any patriarchy is ultimately a social and symbolic construction by human beings, Millett aptly concluded that, "Male supremacy, like other political creeds, does not finally reside in physical strength but in the acceptance of a value system which is not biological" (p. 27). As human beings, while it may require a focused attention and perception as well as a marked effort to undergo change, we are fully capable of shifting and transforming the values that dominate and control us.

Vivian Gornick and Barbara K. Moran's *Woman in Sexist Society: Studies in Power and Powerlessness*

While Millett's analysis predominantly provided a literary critique of the writings of six male writers, Gornick and Moran (1971) focused their analysis upon the far more concrete, material, and tangible, isolating issues and experiences affecting the everyday lives of women. In this regard, the personal experiences of diverse women are treated as potentially political issues that can be shared by all women. Hence, *Woman in Sexist Society* provides a collection of 33 different women, a collection treated as a "class" (p. xviii), a class that "is just about the last category of humans on earth to challenge civilized life for her humanity" (p. xvi).

In more concrete terms, Gornick and Moran reported that in 1966, white women were making 68% of the salary of white males. And, underscoring the fact that discrimination against women was intimately linked with racism, they reported that black women were making 44% of the salary of white males. In this regard, in the first quarter of 2010, the U.S. Department of Labor (2010b) reported that women's median wages were 78% of men's income. And, while some upward adjustment toward income equality is evident (from 68% in 1966 to 78% in 2010), a class-based form of discrimination based upon sexism continues to exist, and women's pay relative to men's rose rapidly from 1980 to 1990 (from 60.2% to 71.6%), and less rapidly from 1990 to 2004 (from 71.6% to 76.5%) ("For Young Earners," 2007). For Gornick and Moran, such income disparities are but one of a host of concrete and practical issues that shapes the everyday lives of women.

Gornick and Moran ultimately argued for a broader framework that aptly shapes any discussion of the relationships between power and gender. They maintain that the condition of woman is determined by her biology rather than her social capabilities and competencies. In their view, the controlling perspective must ultimately be viewed as a form of sexism:

> This book is a collection of essays gathered together for the purpose of demonstrating that woman's condition, here and now, is the result of a slowly formed, deeply entrenched, extraordinarily pervasive cultural (and therefore political) decision that—even in a generation when man landed on the moon—woman shall remain a person defined not by the struggling development of her brain or her will or her spirit, but rather by her childbearing properties and her status as companion to men who make, and do, rule the earth. Though she is a cherished object in her society, she shall remain an object rather than becoming a subject; though she is exposed to education, wealth, and independence, apparently exactly as though she were an autonomous being and the equal of men, every genuine influence in her life is actually teaching her that she may educate herself only in order to be a more fit companion to her husband. (pp. xix–xx)

When all of these diverse attitudes are integrated and given a single label, Gornick and Moran concluded that, "This is the substance of sexism" (p. xx). More pervasively, they maintained that, "Sexism, like any other cultural characteristic, lives through institutions—those that blindly perpetuate it and those that depend upon it for their very life" (p. xxi).

Judith Lorber's *Gender Inequality: Feminist Theories and Politics*

Shifting from the rhetoric of the early 1970s, Lorber offered a broader and more comprehensive sense of the scope of thought that is possible when gender and power are examined as interacting concepts. Lorber specifically sought to reflect the wide diversity of thought that is possible about the analysis of gender and power. As she put it, "What I have tried to do . . . is, first, to show that there is a variety of feminist theories, and how the various theories diverge and converge." As others have done before her, Lorber sought to reflect the voices of some 25 different authors who have dealt with the issues involved in linking gender and power.

However, Lorber's controlling framework or structure for examining these diverse voices is far more central to our concerns here. Lorber argued that 11 different approaches to feminism are possible. Some of these approaches are grouped as "reform" oriented. Within this "reform" category, Lorber includes "liberal feminism," "Marxist and Socialist feminism," and "development feminism." An additional four approaches were identified as forms of "resistance," and they include the writings associated with "radical feminism," "lesbian feminism," "psychoanalytic feminism," and "standpoint feminism." The last four approaches are identified as explicit efforts at "rebellion," and they include "multiracial feminism," "men's feminism," "social construction feminism," and "postmodern feminism and queer theory."

Once the entire array of approaches to feminism are recognized in such a form, i.e., as a political label, the term *feminism* itself can easily seem—at best—vague. For some, the term itself simply fails to capture, with accuracy and power, the precise efforts of any specific analysis or political action. In one sense, the recognition of such a diverse set of approaches actually, we think, discourages others (due to "an information overload") from exploring the relationships among gender, power, and communication. Accordingly, while we have found Lorber's analysis useful, we actually avoid adopting any one of these approaches in the six chapters that follow here. We certainly do not deny that a political ideology can affect how we would react to specific issues, but for our purposes here, we believe that we ultimately adopt a *communication perspective*, seeking to describe, interpret, and evaluate the various ways in which others have forged symbolic relationships and ultimately behavioral and political agendas about the relationships between gender and power.

Interim Conclusions

In all, these four historical volumes have, at least, sensitized us to situations where gender and power are involved. However, as we examine the sequence of events that define and shape our contemporary culture, we are increasingly convinced that gender and power issues must also now be understood in two other ways. First, gender and power issues must be understood, not only in terms of the American culture, but also globally. Second, beyond this new global placement of gender and power issues, the sociocultural context of gender itself has also been reassessed, and it must also be viewed as related to other social systems. Both of these changes in the way in which gender and power are considered are reflected on in some detail here.

First, as we see contemporary gender and power events, we believe that the scope of gender and power issues is also changing. Gender and power issues increasingly involve more than merely the events within the United States. Reacting to the development of a wide array of digital communication technologies, Thomas L. Friedman (2007), in his book *The World Is Flat*, has aptly argued that social, trade, cultural, and information barriers among nation-states are being reduced, making those who were once "foreigners" neighbors and part of the environment in which we exist on a daily basis. Marshall McLuhan (1964) aptly argued that we now live in a global village. In part because of the comprehensive, global, and constant flow of information in which we now exist, we are simply aware of what happens to others throughout the world, and those actions become part of how we think and react to others and how we perceive and define ourselves. This global perspective has changed how we understand and think about gender and power issues.

Second, as we examine current events, it is increasingly clear to us that questions of gender and power are now essentially, intimately, and necessarily linked to other social issues. In our view, gender questions are profoundly affected by other forms of discrimination such as race, age, sexual preference, economic class, and even political ideology.

We have already considered how an extremely vivid example of gender discrimination becomes even more problematic when racial questions are involved. U.S. Department of Labor statistics show that gender and race have a discriminatory effect on wages. Here is a less obvious, but just as revealing, example of gender and racial issues. In December of 2009, Annise Parker was recently elected the mayor of the city of Houston, Texas. In covering the election results, *The New York Times* had a series of choices to make in how it characterized the election. Rather than focus on the fact that a woman had been elected mayor to one of the largest cities in the United States, the *Times'* headline proclaimed: "Houston Is Largest City to Elect Openly Gay Mayor" (McKinley, 2009). In this case, either gender or sexual preference—or both—could be cast and treated as equally important and relevant when reporting the election results, for the question is not simply the gender of the candidate but also the sexual preference of the candidate. Ultimately, however, the *Times* elected to make a choice between gender and sexual preference. It cast the fact that Parker was a lesbian to be the far more critical news.

Interrelationships among sex roles, race, and sexual preference also exist, and they have been explored in some extremely vivid, if not dramatic, ways. For example, in *On the Down Low: A Journey into the Lives of "Straight" Black Men Who Sleep with Men*, J. L. King (2004) examines the consequences and implications of a closeted culture of sex between black men who lead "straight" lives. In this case, the variables involved include masculinity, sexual preference, and race. Indeed, certain concepts—such as "straight" black men who sleep with men—increase the complexity of dealing with traditional notions of "masculinity" and "femininity."

In an even more complicated situation, the distinctions between male and female—which have been held by some to be the most enduring and biologically grounded categories—are now confounded. The issue is articulated by Kate Bornstein in her 1994 volume *Gender Outlaw: On Men, Women, and the Rest of Us*. She has reported that, "I know I'm not a man . . . and I've come to the conclusion that I'm probably not a woman either. . . . The trouble is we're living in a world that insists we be one or the other." Bornstein identifies herself as a "transsexual lesbian whose female lover is becoming a man" (p. 3). Indeed, concepts such as *androgyny, transsexual, transgender,* and *bisexual* play havoc with the categories of *male* and *female* if we treat male and female as discrete, comprehensive, and exclusive bipolar categories.

Indeed, seeking to develop a philosophy in which all people possess the characteristics or nature of both males and females, Kaplan (1976) seriously suggested that sex-role stereotypes might be eliminated if both males and females more clearly adopted "a psychology of androgyny" whenever possible.

From a broader perspective, the various links among gender, race, sexual preference, class, age, and even religious discrimination have also been vividly articulated by several third-wave feminists. Indeed, for this group, an alternative conception of personhood itself is beginning to emerge in which gender issues—it is argued—must be assessed in terms of related questions of race, sexual preference, economic class, age, religion, and even political ideology. As Brunell (2008) has noted:

> Influenced by the postmodern movement in the academy, third-wave feminists have sought to question, reclaim, and redefine the ideas, words, and media that have transmitted ideas about womanhood, gender, sexuality, femininity, and masculinity, among other things. There has been a decided shift in favour of viewing gender as existing along a continuum. Each person is not simply male or female but rather is seen as possessing, expressing, and suppressing the full range of traits commonly associated with males or females. (p. 197)

Beyond the perspective outlined by Brunell, a host of others have also identified critical links between gender and other forms of discrimination (e.g., see Lake, Conway, & Whitney, 2005; Marcus, 2009, p. 16; Morin & Taylor, 2008). In this view, then, questions of gender do not and cannot exist independent of other factors that influence groups and society. For example, a female's gender can influence the income she can achieve, but other factors—such as her race, sexual preference, class, and age—also shape what a woman can achieve within society.

As we examine contemporary events, then, our view of gender and power is shaped by the global environment in which we exist, and by the fact that gender itself can be necessarily linked to other questions such as race, sexual preference, age, and class. Our view of contemporary events are shaped by these relatively new perspectives of gender and power.

Gender and Power Issues in the Second Half of the Year 2009

We are certainly aware that improvements and gains have occurred in how males and females communicate. Those adjustments are to be celebrated. At the same time, we continue to believe that tremendous room exists for improvement. We do wish we could report that the kind of gender-based discrimination Beauvoir reported no longer existed, and we do wish we could report that our society has now granted equal respect for gender-based differences. But, we do not think such claims would be accurate and appropriate. However, we would like to report that the patriarchal system Millett perceived has been eliminated. We would like to suggest—but we cannot—that all of the forms of sexism recorded in Gornick and Moran's volume no longer existed. While we cannot do this, we would like to report that coherent and complementary actions now unify the diverse structure and various political agendas of the various political groups examined by Lorber. While remarkable progress has certainly occurred in all of these areas, we continue to believe that we must renew and continue to mark circumstances and events that require positive and corrective social actions on the part of all of us.

We want to illustrate our argument at this point. To do so, we decided to follow some of the major events that occurred during the last half of the year 2009, as they were reported by various national and international news agencies. The events recorded are vivid, if not dramatic, and they ultimately suggest that we have no choice but to pay attention to and seek to redress some of the overwhelming gender and power issues dominating the national and international scene today. These events virtually cross all of the chapters in this volume, and as you consider each chapter in the balance of this book, a foundation exists for dealing with these events. Accordingly, at this juncture, we have opted simply to list the events as they occurred from July 1, 2009 through the end of December 2009. Actually, we also think the events are so self-evident that they require no comment from us. We will let the reporting speak for itself.

- **Losing Confidence in Marriage** (Kay S. Hymowitz, July 3–5, 2009, *The Wall Street Journal*): " . . . marriage is suffering a full-scale crisis in consumer confidence. . . . Marital breakdown is not rampant across the land. It is concentrated among low-income and black couples. . . . More than one-fifth of marriages break up within five years. The median age at first divorce is 30.5 for males and 29 for females. The risk of break-up goes up after one year of marriage and peaks at 4½ years. . . . The essence of the marriage vow is to stay still. But as a group, Americans are an especially flighty bunch, always looking for a better opportunity, a bigger home, a second chance. We're no less fidgety in our mating habits, as Andrew Cherlin demonstrates in his recent book, *Marriage-Go-Round*. Americans divorce and 'repartner' far more than do people in other Western countries, either by remarrying or shacking up. True, the educated classes are less inclined to actually hop on the go-round. But that does not mean that they don't hear the barker calling: You can start over, you can do better."

- **Does Broadway Need Women?** (Terry Teachout, July 25, 2009, *The Wall Street Journal*): "Not only are there roughly twice as many male playwrights as female playwrights in America, but they also write more plays per capita. . . . The one play by a woman, Ms. Reza's, was, sure enough, one of the biggest hits of the year. . . . What does this analysis show? That when it comes to straight plays, Broadway almost always plays it safe—and next to no 'safe' plays have been written by women. . . . That's not just gender speaking: It's the unwelcome sound of cold, hard common sense."

- **Latest Tragic Symbol of Unhealed Congo: Male Rape Victims** (Jeffrey Gettleman, August 5, 2009, *The New York Times*): ". . . the sexual violence against men is yet another way for armed groups to humiliate and demoralize Congolese communities into submission . . . possibly includes hundreds of victims . . . more than 10 percent of its cases in June were men . . . for the men involved, aid workers say, it is even harder to bounce back. 'Men's identity is so connected to power and control . . . in a place where homosexuality is so taboo, the rapes carry an extra dose of shame. . . . The people in my village say: 'You are no longer a man. Those in the bush made you their wife.' . . . Humiliation is often so severe that male rape victims come forward only if they have urgent health problems, like stomach swelling or continuous bleeding. . . . Castrations also seem to be increasing, with more butchered men showing up at major hospitals."

- **The Women's Crusade** (Nicholas D. Kristof and Sheryl WuDunn, August 23, 2009, *The New York Times Magazine*): "The oppression of women worldwide is the human rights cause of our time. And their liberation could help solve many of the world's problems from poverty to child mortality to terrorism. A 21st-century manifesto. . . . In Burundi, which is one of the poorest countries in the world, Goretti Nyabenda used to be largely a prisoner in her hut. In keeping with tradition in the region where she lived, she could not leave without the permission of her husband, Bernard. Her interactions with Bernard consisted in good part of being beaten by him. 'I was wretched,' she remembers. Then Goretti joined an empowerment program run by CARE, taking out a $2 microloan to buy fertilizer. The result was an excellent crop of potatoes worth $7.50—and Goretti began to build a small business as a farmer, goat breeder and banana-beer brewer. . . . Today Goretti is no longer beaten, and she comes and goes freely. . . . In India, a 'bride burning' takes place approximately once every two hours, to punish a woman for an inadequate dowry or to eliminate her so a man can remarry—but these rarely constitute news. . . . The U.N. has estimated that there are 5 thousand honor killings a year, the majority in the Muslim world."

- **The High Price of Being a Gay Couple** (Tara Siegel Bernard and Ron Lieber, October 3, 2009, *The New York Times*): ". . . for years, we've heard from gay couples about all the extra health, legal and other costs they bear. So we set out to determine what they were and to come up with a round number—a couple's lifetime cost of being gay. . . . We looked at benefits that routinely go to married heterosexual couples, but not to gay couples, like certain Social Security payments. We plotted out the cost of health insurance for couples whose employers don't offer it to domestic partners. Even tax preparation can cost more, since gay couples have to file two sets of returns. Still, many couples may come out ahead in one area: they owe less in income taxes because they're not hit with the so-called marriage penalty. Our goal was to create a hypothetical gay couple whose situations would be similar to a heterosexual couple's. . . . Here's what we came up with. In our worst case, the couple's lifetime cost of being gay was $467,562. But the number fell to $41,196 in the best case for a couple with significantly better health insurance, plus lower taxes and other costs. . . . Nearly all the extra costs that gay couples face would be erased if the federal government legalized same-sex marriage."

- **The New Gender Gap** (Lisa Belkin, October 4, 2009, *The New York Times Magazine*): "Women are doing better in the recession—because men are doing worse. . . . [Women] have gone from holding 34.9 percent of all jobs 40 years ago to 49.8 percent today. . . . Under other circumstances, that would be cause for celebration. But women have gained this latest bit of ground mostly because men have lost it—78 percent of the jobs lost during this recession were held by men. So not only is it unseemly to rejoice over a larger share of a smaller pie, it is also unsettling to face the fact that so much of the history of women in the workplace (both their leaps forward and their slips back) is a reaction to what was happening to men."

- **In a Guinea Seized by Violence, Women as Prey** (Adam Nossiter, October 6, 2009, *The New York Times*): "Cell phone snapshots, ugly and hard to refute, are circulating here and feeding rage: they show that women were the particular targets of the Guinean soldiers who suppressed a political demonstration at a stadium here last week, with victims and witnesses describing rapes, beatings, and acts of intentional humiliation. . . . The exact number of women who were abused is not known. Because of the shame associated with sexual violence in this West African country, victims are reluctant to speak, and local doctors refused to do so. Victims who told of the attacks would not provide their names because they were afraid of retribution."

- **House Votes to Expand Hate Crime Definition** (Carl Hulse, October 9, 2009, *The New York Times*): "The House voted Thursday to expand the definition of violent federal hate crimes to those committed because of a victim's sexual orientation, a step that would extend new protection to lesbian, gay and transgendered people."

- **Rape Troubles Nearly All in South Africa** (Christine Delmeiren, October 22, 2009, The Gallup Poll): "A Gallup survey of South Africa conducted March 21–April 7, 2009, reaffirms the extent to which the issue of rape plagues the country—with 97% of residents calling it a major problem. . . . In a recent survey conducted by South Africa's Medical Research Council in KwaZula-Natal and Eastern Cape provinces, one in four men admitted to having raped someone, and nearly half said they had attacked more than one victim. . . . There's a general belief within the country that most rape cases go unreported because of the stigma and shame attached to it. . . . Men's attitude toward women is at the root of the problem, which reveals a deeply rooted culture of violence against women, and gender inequality."

- **Soul-Searching in Turkey After a Gay Man Is Killed** (Dan Bilefsky, November 26, 2009, *The New York Times*): "For Ahmet Yildiz, a stocky and affable 26-year-old, the choice to live openly as a gay man proved deadly. Prosecutors say his own father hunted him down, traveling more than 600 miles from his hometown to shoot his son in an old neighborhood of Istanbul. Mr. Yildiz was killed 16 months ago, the victim of what sociologists say is the first gay honor killing in Turkey to surface publicly. . . . His body remained unclaimed by his family, a grievous fate under Muslim custom."

- **CBS Is Criticized for Blurring of Video** (Dave Itzkoff, November 28, 2009, *The New York Times*): "An appearance by the singer Adam Lambert on *The Early Show,* the CBS morning program, on Wednesday had led to further complaints from those who say Mr. Lambert has been subjected to a double standard. At issue is a video package that was used to introduce the interview with Mr. Lambert, the *American Idol* finalist who gave a sexually charged performance at the American Music Awards on Sunday. When CBS rebroadcast a clip from that show, it blurred a scene of Mr. Lambert kissing his male keyboardist. But it did not blur a scene of Madonna and Britney Spears kissing at the 2003 MTV Video Music Awards."

- **Questions for Martha Nussbaum: Gross National Politics** (Interview by Deborah Solomon, December 13, 2009, *The New York Times Magazine*): "What is it that makes people think that a same-sex couple living next door would . . . taint their own marriage? . . . At some level, disgust is still operating. . . . What becomes really bad is the projective kind [of disgust], meaning projecting smelliness, sliminess and stickiness onto a group of people who are then stigmatized and regarded as inferior."

- **Menopause, as Brought to You by Big Pharma** (Natasha Singer and Duff Wilson, December 13, 2009, *The New York Times*): "Millions of American women in the 1990s were told they could help their bodies ward off major illness by taking menopausal hormone drugs. . . . Ms. Barton, . . . is one of more than 13,000 people who have sued Wyeth over the last seven years, claiming in courts across the country that its menopause drugs caused breast cancer and other problems."

- **Houston Is Largest City to Elect Openly Gay Mayor** (James C. McKinley Jr., December 13, 2009, *The New York Times*): "Houston became the largest city in the United States to elect an openly gay mayor on Saturday night, as voters gave a solid victory to the city controller, Annise Parker. . . . 'Tonight the voters of Houston have opened the door to history,' she said, standing by her partner of 19 years, Kathy Hubbard, and their three adopted children."

- **U.N. Website Details Peacekeeper Sex Abuse Claims** (Reuters, December 24, 2009, *The New York Times*): "The United Nations unveiled a website on Thursday aimed at improving transparency about sexual misconduct allegations and other charges leveled against members of its missions. The website (http://cdu.unlb.org/) tracks the number of alleged offenses by U.N. personnel over the last three years, collected from political and peacekeeping missions across the globe. . . . In one case, a 14-year-old Congolese girl said she was paid two eggs in return for having sex with a soldier."

- **A Peril in War Zones: Sexual Abuse by Fellow G.I.'s** (Steven Lee Myers, December 28, 2009, *The New York Times*): "Sexual harassment and sexual assault, which the military now defines broadly to include not only rape but also crimes like groping and stalking, continue to afflict the ranks, and by some measures are rising within the United States military. . . . The strains of combat, close quarters in remote locations, tension and even boredom can create conditions for abuse, even as they hinder medical care for victims and legal proceedings against those who attack them. . . . A Pentagon-appointed task force, in a report released this month, pointedly criticized the military's effort to prevent sexual abuse, citing the 'unique stresses' of deployments in places like Camp Taji. 'Some military personnel indicated that predators may believe they will not be held accountable for their misconduct during deployment because commanders' focus on the mission overshadow other concerns,' the report said."

Certainly, we believe that the events reported between July and December of 2009 dramatically reveal why gender and power issues constitute such a significant force in our culture and the world today. Moreover, based upon the Pew Research Center's July 1, 2010 report of 22 nation states throughout the world, we would add that we believe these events appear typical of what we know about gender issues in significant areas of the globe. Based upon its April 7 to May 8, 2010 survey by the Pew Research Center's Global Attitudes Project, the Pew Research Center (2010) concluded,

> while egalitarian sentiments are pervasive, they are less than robust; when economically challenging times arrive, many feel men should be given preferential treatment over women in the search for employment.
>
> This is especially true in the predominantly Muslim countries surveyed as well as in India, China, South Korea and Nigeria. In these countries, solid majorities agree that women should be able to work outside the home; yet, most also agree that men should have more right to a job than women when jobs are scarce. For example, about six-in-ten in Egypt (61%) and Jordan (58%) say women should have the right to work outside the home, but even larger shares (75% and 68%, respectively) say the priority should be for men to have jobs. (p. 1)

Overall, in terms of three areas, the Pew Research Center's data are particularly vivid.

1. In terms of achieving equal rights, "When respondents who favor gender equality are asked whether their country has made most of the changes needed to give women equal rights with men or if more changes are needed to achieve that goal, majorities in 18 of 22 countries say the latter" (p. 13).

2. In terms of who has a better life—men or women—the majorities or pluralities in 10 of 22 nations say "men have the better life in their countries." In 10 others, more respondents volunteer that there are no differences. "Only in Japan and South Korea do pluralities say that life is better for women in their countries (47% and 49%, respectively)" (p. 14).

3. In terms of inequality in job opportunities, the Pew Research Center's findings are particularly clear: "The view that men get more opportunities than women for jobs that pay well, even when women are as qualified for the job, is widespread in most of the countries surveyed, particularly those that are wealthy or have recently experienced substantial economic growth" (p. 14).

In all, we are left with particularly vivid examples between July and December of 2009 that suggest that gender and power issues are overwhelmingly significant, and when broader surveys across significant nation-states are considered, a confirming set of findings appear. As we observed at the outset of this analysis, we have no choice but to pay attention to and seek to redress some of the overwhelming gender and power issues dominating the national and international scene today.

As we have viewed and comprehended these events, among several other reactions, we have certainly concluded that as a people, we live in a society and world that are intensely and dramatically affected by how the relationships between gender and power are understood and acted upon. We are also at the point where we must now decide how we are to perceive, comprehend, and respond to and deal with contemporary events that we encounter on a daily basis. We hope that this volume will be a useful tool in that process.

Organization of This Book

This book is divided into six chapters.

We begin with more fundamental and definitional issues related to the examination of gender, power, and communication.

- **Chapter 1, The Stereotype: Fiction or Fact**, examines why and how people necessarily generalize with verbal and nonverbal languages, when these generalizations begin to function as ineffective, if not harmful, stereotyping, and concludes by suggesting ways in which gender stereotypes in communication have changed.

- **Chapter 2, Verbal and Nonverbal Communication by Gender in Face-to-Face Communication**, explores how the major forms of communication can be useful in understanding how gender influences communication and how gender-based communication can be more sensitively, usefully, and effectively employed.

In chapters 3 through 6, we consider four situations or contexts shaping and influencing gender socialization and sex-role constructions.

- **Chapter 3, Mediated Communication and Gender Roles**, examines how sex roles are portrayed in different media systems. Attention is specifically given to how feminine and masculine roles are constructed and displayed on television and in movies and music, as well as how sex roles are presumed, if not encouraged, in various Internet contexts such as video games and social network websites.

- **Chapter 4, Early Socialization in the Home: Influencing Gendered Scripts**, focuses upon the nuclear family and early childhood development as a stage where sex roles are fashioned and constructed. In this context, early messages have a profound influence on how children learn the gendered traits, roles, and scripts that may ultimately influence their aspirations as adults.

- **Chapter 5, The Educational Landscape: Connecting Gender and Identity**, examines how parents and teachers contribute to creating different learning experiences for females and males that may influence academic performance. Identity gaps in the curriculum as well as strategies to develop a more inclusive learning climate aimed at closing the achievement gap also are explored.

- **Chapter 6, Gendered Scripts: Women and Men in the Workplace**, examines how assumptions about roles, traits, and behaviors influence career paths, the interview process, salaries, mentoring, workplace interactions, and work/life choices. Included as well are recent initiatives and recommendations for change that impact women and other underrepresented members of the workforce. Throughout the chapter, examples from the field are provided for discussion.

We hope you view these chapters as explorations, possibilities that influence all of us, and which ultimately invite each of us to make decisions about who we are as individuals, how we wish to redefine our own sense of the inner self as well as what we wish to convey to others, and how we will and will not function as communicators in the diverse situations we continually encounter. In our experience, examining and exploring how communication is employed to link gender and power can create a child-like sense of wonderment in us. It can disappoint. It can infuriate. It can make us smile at the human condition. It can make us shake our head in concern. But, it continues to always be an adventure. We hope you can share that adventure with us in the chapters that follow.

SUGGESTED ACTIVITIES

1. How Genders Are and Should Be Distinguished

How we define words and how we distinguish one word from another is critical in any discussion of power and gender. In this introduction, a distinction has been drawn between the words *sex* and *gender*. It has been suggested that the word *sex* should be reserved for discussions about biology and traits and characteristics that stem directly from biological functions. Hence, the ability to give birth to a child falls with the domain of the category sex, because it stems directly from a biological function directly reserved to females, not males. Likewise, the ability to generate and transmit sperm is a biological function of males, not females. However, a host of other characteristics used to distinguish women and men appear to be related to the social and psychological characteristics attributed by people through customs and language to either men or women. Hence, when we say that "men are the breadwinners of a family," we are reflecting that a cultural and societal system says what males ought to do. But, the attribution is not linked to the biology of males. It is a solely social attribution that is assigned to men. In terms of a classroom discussion, address the following:

a. Focus on your favorite television show and determine what gender roles or functions are assigned to females and which are assigned to males. For example, does the announcer of the program have a male voice? In general, are male voices predominantly used as announcers? Why? What other functions are normally assigned predominantly to either males or to females on popular television shows? For example, for a long time, males were always the doctor on medical shows while women were always the nurses. Is that still true?

b. What is the origin of the gender attributes currently given to men and women? To what degree are religious institutions involved in defining these attributes? To what degree are schools involved in "defining" what is the province or domain of men and women? To what degree are families involved in reinforcing certain functions and characteristics of people as either female or male?

c. In the United States, do you believe that there are changes occurring in the notions of sex as biological and gender as sociocultural? What about in the distinctions between sex as biological and gender as sociocultural? For example, with the recognition of sex changes as an option for individuals, do we need to reconsider the idea that sex is always or predominantly determined biologically?

2. *Feminism* **as a Dynamic and Changing Political Force for Mobilizing Responses**

In this introduction, we noted that many people believe that feminism has undergone transformations. Some people believe that the "first wave" of feminism focused on legal and voting rights for women, the "second wave" emphasized constitutional equality for men and women, and the "third wave" of feminism has focused on attacking and denying the philosophy and institutional forms of patriarchy. Has there been a counterattack on feminism? As some have argued, has the media systematically sought to diminish the value of feminism? If the three waves of feminism have succeeded in their goals, why don't all younger women embrace feminism as a self-description? What forces, institutions, and/or groups seek to undermine the meaning and acceptance of feminism? Do the diverse forms of feminism identified by Judith Lorber reflect the diversity of women, but also diminish the power of women as a political force and movement?

3. **The Origins of Discrimination and Domination**

   In a class discussion, examine the meaning of sexual discrimination and domination. This discussion can easily begin if someone volunteers to relate an example of sexual discrimination or domination they have personally encountered. Or, reexamine how the different feminist authors discussed in the introduction have made a host of different claims about the origins of discrimination against women. What are the motives for such discrimination? Simone de Beauvoir argued that the demeaning of all female sexual functions was carried out in order to control women more effectively. Is the desire to control women the origin of discrimination against women? Is this form of control and discrimination what other feminists have used to refer to the idea that males seek to dominate women?

4. **Personal Documents as a Source of Gender Symbol-Using**

   Select a "document" you value as helpful and useful to you. Such a document might include the Bible, a work of fiction you have particularly enjoyed, a recording or music video you find involving, a popular movie, or even a game, toy, or doll that you played with as a child. In other words, select a "document" that has conveyed specific meanings to you that has been instructive and inspiring. Examine the specific words of the "document." Does it employ words or nonverbal images that refer to *men, women, male,* and/or *female*? Does it show men and women doing things? Are there any patterns or regularities to what men and women do in this "document?" Do you think that either men or women are assumed to have more power or more control over others and the circumstances found in the portrayals in this "document?" What attributes are persistently associated with males that are not associated with females? What attributes are persistently associated with females that are not associated with males? Report your findings to others in your class.

The Stereotype
Fiction or Fact

Webster's New Collegiate Dictionary directly and simply maintains that a stereotype is "a standardized mental picture that is held in common by members of a group and that represents an oversimplified opinion, prejudiced attitude, or uncritical judgment" (2003). In one sense, such a definition seems simple enough, for a stereotype can be viewed merely as an ill-informed generalization applied to an entire group. However, despite our ability to give such generalizations a dismissive label such as stereotypes, stereotypes can have power. Certainly, viewing stereotypes as the statements and actions of bigots does not eliminate the power of a stereotype. Indeed, sometimes stereotypes can be humorous, and they may also reflect partial truths that require time and energy if they are to be unpacked to reveal the misleading nature of the generalization. For example, we might believe that "men are slobs, women are neat." If the distinction initially strikes you as humorous, you might not examine the logical implications of the distinction. Moreover, if we think about it, we know that not every man is a slob and not every woman is neat. People often disagree about what tidiness and orderliness are, or we may not even be sure what the words *slob* and *neat* actually mean. Indeed, Alyn and Phillips (2010) have recently cautioned us that the stereotype "men are slobs, women are neat" is but one of several "gender lies that damage relationships."

In this chapter, we want to begin by noting some of the problems that exist when we seek to identify certain statements and behaviors as stereotypes. Following this discussion, the stereotypes attributed to females (femininity) and males (masculinity) are surveyed. Finally, we end this chapter by identifying the emergence of androgyny as a significant concept for dealing with the characteristics shared by females and males. We begin, then, by recognizing some of the problems that exist whenever we want to use the term *stereotype* in a critical fashion.

Stereotype as an Awkward Term

In terms of how people normally and typically communicate, stereotypes in general and sex-role stereotypes in particular are particularly difficult to isolate for several reasons.

First, people have a "natural" tendency to generalize and to believe that they are using inclusive and neutral language. The human use of words themselves can be viewed as the core of this issue. In this view, the use of any word—either in oral or written form—involves the use of a generalization. The word *mother*, for example, refers to a group of females who have reproduced. Yet, the word carries far more connotations than just the biological function of some women. The word may also carry additional associations such as *caring*, *protective*, *loving*, and perhaps even *domineering*. When you use the word *mother*, what images come to your mind? While you may only be thinking about a word, nonetheless an image may immediately and vividly come to your mind. You may be convinced that your image of mothers is not an oversimplified opinion, affective attitude, or uncritical judgment. Nonetheless, upon reflection, you might readily admit that your view of the category of *mother* necessarily is a standardized—and therefore oversimplified—mental picture that reflects your emotional and uncritical experiences and conclusions about mothers. Such an image is a stereotype. Hence, if we return to the definition of a stereotype provided earlier, you will remember that a stereotype occurs any time one highlights and emphasizes a "standardized mental picture" as its core object. In this sense, virtually all language-using involves a generalization process that can invoke standardized mental pictures.

Second, the use of stereotypes no longer automatically leads people to believe they have made an error in judgment or that they are even offensive to others in a way that requires an adjustment in their behaviors. The charge that "you have stereotyped" is now frequently placed within the popular culture context about what is "politically correct." Any discussion of stereotyping—especially sex-role stereotyping—now exists within a hotly contested debate regarding the backlash against the quest to be "politically correct."

While being "politically correct" first occurred in the Supreme Court *Chisholm v. Georgia* decision in 1793, being "politically correct" entered the United States' popular culture during the 1960s radical movement. For example, in 1970, Bambara had thoughtfully argued that a "man cannot be politically correct and a chauvinist" at the same time (in Aufderheide, 1992, p. 73). By the 1990s, "politically correct" was used in a pejorative sense, viewed as more ironic and with disapproval. In this regard, "pcp," or "politically correct people," have been viewed by some as excessively moral, dishonest, as well as politically and ideologically excessive. Indeed, especially as hosted by the controversial and ironic comedian Bill Maher, the 1997–2002 television talk show *Politically Incorrect* challenged conventions about what was offensive and appropriate characterizations of any group, especially sex-role generalizations. In other words, identifying stereotypes as politically incorrect may actually have created a boomerang effect. Accordingly, rather than diminishing the power and use of the stereotype, the very people who identify the stereotypes that others use may themselves become the object of scorn.

The problematic nature of stereotyping has persistently affected communication scholars, researchers, and teachers. We think it useful to illustrate some of the problems these groups have encountered when they have identified and discussed stereotypes. We think a historical example can be particularly useful, for the implicit "advice" involved in identifying characteristics as stereotypes is often more obvious when some time and distance exists between when people act and when people reflect upon their actions. In other words, sometimes our best efforts to *describe* differences between male and female communicators can, itself, be stereotypical. Our example takes us back some thirty years. In their 1978 volume *Sex Differences in Human Communication*, Eakins and Eakins identified five "communication strategies" distinguishing males and females.

1. Tag Questions: Used more frequently by women, a tag question is "in-between a statement and a question," such as "you know what I mean?" at the end of a statement. Particularly, Eakins and Eakins maintained that:

> A tag question is less assertive than an outright statement such as "Jill wore my clown suit." . . . It is useful for in-between situations where an outright question is not appropriate and where a yes/no question is not fitting either. (p. 39)

> The tag question is a tool of politeness. . . . In situations where feelings are strong and persons with opposing views threaten to clash head-on, the use of this device is obvious. It can help avoid conflict and unpleasant confrontation. But the same device can be a burden as well as a boon to women. It becomes a burden when, because of its obliqueness, the tag question robs communication of force in situations that require vigor and directness. The talker may give the impression that she is not really sure of herself. Overuse of tags puts the speaker in the position of constantly looking to someone else for confirmation or approval of her ideas. She avoids committing herself and never directly reveals or takes a stand on her own views. (p. 41)

While Eakins and Eakins do admit that there is a "paucity of research on the appearance of tag questions in conversation," as cast here, the tag question becomes "evidence" for the claim that women, as communicators, are more likely to be polite than direct, honest, and decisive. Likewise, the tag question means that women avoid commitments, refuse to state their opinion, and neglect to articulate and take a stand on their own views.

Yet, in our view, tag questions can be perceived in dramatically different ways. Tag questions such as "isn't it?" or "you know what I mean?" can also—we think—be an invitation for others to become involved, to encourage others to express their opinions, to encourage others to state their views, and to determine whether or not there is agreement. In this view, a tag question prevents monologue, and it encourages interaction and dialogue. Cast in this fashion, the tag question need not be viewed as a strategy of the polite, it also can be viewed as a way to encourage others to be involved. Indeed, rather than avoiding disagreement and conflict, tag questions can also be perceived as ways to open up a conversation to differences.

2. Qualifiers: "Another technique that seems to be employed in women's language," argued Eakins and Eakins, "more often than in men's is the use of softening, mitigating, or qualifying words and phrases. These are additions to our utterances that can soften or blunt the impact of what we say. They are used to avert or avoid negative or unwanted reactions to our words, and they seem to make our statements less absolute in tone. We use these devices in the beginnings, endings, and sprinkled throughout our utterances: *well, let's see, perhaps, possibly, I suppose, I think, it seems to me, you know,* and so on" (p. 43). More specifically, Eakins and Eakins suggest the "force" of statements can be noted when a qualifier is not used and when it is added: "You shouldn't do that" or "*Perhaps* you shouldn't do that."

At the same time, we have an alternative view of qualifiers. Eakins and Eakins specifically maintained that qualifiers are a way of "softening" and "mitigating" words. Or, as Eakins and Eakins also maintained, a qualifier "makes the speech sound more tentative" (p. 43). Yet, as we see it, qualifiers can also be perceived and understood as a way of recognizing the contingencies of life, that there are unknown forces that can exist when choices are made, and qualifiers are one way of taking responsibility for a claim being made. In this context, we can return to the statements "You shouldn't do that" and "Perhaps you shouldn't do that." Rather than maintain that the difference between these two statements is the degree of "force" being used, one might see the difference as urging caution in action simply because a variety of alternatives might also be considered, particularly when acting decisively. In other words, qualifiers can merely be a way of letting a person know that caution may be appropriate.

3. Lengthening of Requests: "Another useful verbal strategy that women employ is the mode of politeness," maintained Eakins and Eakins, "the lengthening of orders and request through the addition of extra particles. Generally, the shorter a request, the more force or compulsion it conveys. The longer a request, the less it seems to press agreement or compliance on the hearer, to imply threat of consequences for noncompliance, or to suggest a position of superiority or power for the speaker" (p. 46). Eakins and Eakins provided this example:

Gender Emphasis	Examples	Eakins and Eakins' Explanation
Masculine	"Water the dog."	Overt order. Implies the right to enforce obedience.
Feminine	"Please water the dog."	Request. Implies decision is left up to the hearer.

In this case, the explanation provided by Eakins and Eakins appears inappropriate, if not unnecessarily aggressive and hostile: It is simply unclear why an overt order is apt and why a more polite form of the verbal statement must or should be used to establish superiority or power for the speaker. It seems dubious to us why threats of consequences for noncompliance must be invoked or why a position of superiority or power should be established to achieve goals. Indeed, it would seem to us that force, compulsion, threats, and power should generally never be the preferred or desired mode for interactions, especially in everyday male-female interactions. Perhaps an unknown immediate urgency or unstated circumstance exists that would require the use of force and power to achieve a desired result. However, as we see such situations, sex-role stereotypes in interpersonal communication should avoid—if at all possible—the use of force, compulsion, threats, and power.

4. Fillers: "Fillers used in talk include such verbalizations as *uhm*, *well*, *like*, *you know*," noted Eakins and Eakins. They continued, "In a study of female-male conversational interactions, females were found to use a much higher proportion of fillers than males. Females used fewest fillers in female-female conversations, although they still surpassed males in the use of this device" (pp. 47–48). When explaining the use of fillers by women, Eakins and Eakins noted that, "Women who do take the initiative more in conversations may feel guilty because of their past socializations to docility and their awareness of society's norms of talk for women. Perhaps to offset or play down their taking the initiative, some women try still to give some signs of 'proper' nonassertiveness or submissiveness. Use of fillers and hesitations such as *uhm*, *well*, and so forth may serve as one such sign" (p. 48).

We have no doubt that fillers are used, and we expect that women may use them more frequently than men in some cases. However, we also suspect that the motivations of women have been changing over the last three decades. We are no longer confident that the primary reason women use fillers should be reduced down to "guilt" (even Eakins and Eakins provide no evidence for such a claim). Likewise, we are no longer confident that women are now goaded and motivated by their prior "docility" training (again, even Eakins and Eakins provide no evidence for such a claim). Additionally, we believe that society's norms for women's talk is now changing. As women attain levels of education that exceed those of men—especially in terms of higher education—the demands for the kinds of communication women are expected to use is, we believe, changing (see chapter 5 for details regarding these changing norms). Finally, we would note that fillers may have an alternative function. Rather than them being viewed as signs of submission, we also anticipate that some women may use fillers to conceal and hide the fact that they are, indeed, taking control of a set of circumstances, for we also think that males have been "trained" or socialized to understand that when they hear fillers used, they need not be alarmed or alert, for the use of fillers by women means that women are adopting more nonassertive or submissive roles. In this sense, we can imagine that fillers could be used as a deception strategy to disarm males while initiating control over a situation.

5. Suiting Style and Situation: Eakins and Eakins conclude their description of the communication strategies of females and males by offering two primary conclusions: (1) "Women's speech tends to be more person-centered and concerned with interpersonal matters" while (2) "Men's speech tends to be more centered around external things and is more apt to involve straight factual communication" (p. 48). Eakins and Eakins conclude that the person-centered and event-centered approaches can be viewed as two possible conversational styles in which "women are seen to use more of style 1, although some occasionally resort to style 2. More men adopt style 2" (p. 48).

We should note that we are not convinced that the "person-centered" and "event-centered" distinction is an altogether meaningful one. We are more likely to view these approaches as strategies for dealing with issues in ways that seem appropriate to the situation. However, there is simply no question that women always have a wide range of options rather than just one style or that they should always use just one conversational style. Likewise, males should employ whatever strategy is most effective for articulating what they mean. Eakins and Eakins aptly summarized the point:

> The damage comes when women and men cannot readily switch from one style to the other to meet the demands of the situation. To be consistently tied to one style or general mode of talk just because of one's sex limits one as a human being. It predestines the woman or man to a one-sidedness and narrowness in communication. We hope today's children can be encouraged and taught to use both styles early in their communication training. (p. 49)

We suspect, and even anticipate, that descriptions of the differences in the ways women and men communicate can far too easily become tomorrow's stereotypes. The issue here is the decision to try to provide any sociocultural generalizations about all members of one sex.

Given such issues, how should we think of stereotypes so that the term *stereotype* can become a more critical and useful term? At a minimum, Chesebro and Fuse (2001, p. 217) have argued that stereotyping occurs under four conditions: (1) When one feature of a group is used as if it is the only characteristic of the group; (2) When one feature of a group is used as if it is a full description of the group; (3) When a universal social characteristic is used as if it is a description of only one group; and (4) When a universal social characteristic is used to distinguish or separate one group from another. With this in mind, as we examine some of the contemporary sex-role stereotypes in our next unit of this chapter, we also suggest the following:

First, a stereotype is an unwarranted characteristic or attribute given to all members of a group. In terms of sex-role stereotyping, a stereotype ascribes a characteristic or attribute to the entire group of females or to the entire group of males. Going back some 25 years, in their 1986 book *Communication between the Sexes: Sex Differences and Sex-Role Stereotypes*, Stewart, Cooper, and Friedley stated, "we are concerned with sex differences and sex-role stereotypes that affect communication in various contexts" (p. 8). They specifically noted that sex-role stereotyping occurs whenever a person is "being categorized as male and female," and when a sense exists that a person is "either *male* or *female.*" In this regard, argued Stewart, Cooper, and Friedley, "we are categorized or we categorize others as *masculine* or *feminine.* This social grouping is based on stereotypical perceptions of qualities belonging to males and females, or *sex-role stereotyping*" (p. 4).

Second, as we examine what others have identified as sex-roles and sex-role stereotypes, the dynamic nature of these concepts is striking. Sex roles can dramatically change from one generation to the next, and sex-role stereotypes themselves can change rapidly and decisively.

Third, we do think that virtually every sex-role generalization and sex-role stereotype should automatically be viewed with suspicion and perhaps even as "unwarranted." Whenever a characteristic is attributed to all females or to all males, we are immediately cautious, for we personally know of no single social characteristic that is shared by all females or by all males in all social contexts and sociocultural systems. In other words, our initial reaction is that every sex-role stereotype is not only a generalization, but probably an unwarranted generalization.

Fourth, we can control and react to ourselves and to others whenever a sex-role stereotype is invoked, especially a generalization that encourages us to think, talk, and behave in one way rather than another simply and only because of our gender.

Sex-Role Stereotypes:
Feminine and Masculine Preconceptions

For a significant group of people, perhaps the vast majority of those throughout the world, generalizations about women and men are critical, if not central, to how they identify and respond to individuals. Frequently these generalizations are assumptions about entire classes of people that simply are without merit. Yet, the generalizations continue. These stereotypes gain power if people believe that a single set of beliefs, attitudes, and behavioral standards exist for all women under the heading of *femininity* and for all men under the heading of *masculinity*. For example, boys and young men are frequently told: "Be a man!" The statement is actually a command, for it is not said to encourage analytical thought about the meaning and value of the statement. It is a "given," an enduring and universal value for all boys, young men, and older men. In this review, femininity and masculinity become close to being an informal ideology, if not a religion, for these concepts contain standards that merely and simply exist, and, for all of us, they are so readily adopted in an almost subconscious fashion. Indeed, femininity and masculinity are clusters of learned values, attitudes, and behaviors during early childhood from parents and relatives, they are reinforced in schools, and they ultimately achieve their full meaning in virtually all social systems.

Feminine Stereotypes

In considering these modes of sexuality, we begin with the preconceptions that guide and regulate feminine stereotypes.

In 1998, Borisoff and Merrill identified four feminine stereotypes that we believe continue to dominate and control interpersonal communication in the American culture. Each of these stereotypes deserves individual attention.

First, **a feminine woman is soft spoken.** As Borisoff and Merrill (1998) have explained: "Women, like children, have been taught that it is preferable for them to be seen rather than to be heard. When heard, female voices are apt to be considered abrasive or displeasing and their words devoid of serious meaning" (p. 10). In the most extreme case, an articulate, direct, vivid female speaker—especially the woman who makes a leadership bid in a group—is a "bitch." The analogy to an animal is intended to be decisive and to block all additional efforts on the part of the woman. If not a "bitch," the articulate, direct, and vivid female speaker is "carping, brassy, nagging, shrill, strident, or grating" (p. 10). And, as Borisoff and Merrill have explained, "Many women have internalized this socially imposed stereotype; in many cases, a deeply rooted reticence to speaking out precludes them from expressing themselves in any public setting, rather than risking being judged in such negative terms" (p. 10).

Second, **a feminine woman is self-effacing.** A person becomes self-effacing when they become part of the background. In other words, the self-effacing individual "drops back," becomes a follower, and lets others step forward and provide guidance and directions for how circumstances and events should be handled and controlled. In terms of specific communication tactics, Borisoff and Merrill (1998, p. 10) have reported that self-effacing strategies include the use of disclaimers ("This may not be right, but . . ."), weak particulars ("Dear me," "Goodness," etc.), and tag questions ("The book was good, wasn't it?"). In other words, in the jargon of the day, a self-effacing woman learns to "talk like a lady." Or, as Borisoff and Merrill have aptly put it,

> one of the ways women may perform their femininity is to adopt communication strategies that are hyperpolite, constructed to please others by minimizing one's own skills, rather than to risk antagonizing one's (presumably male/more powerful) audience. When women do adopt these tactics, the perception of women's relative weakness as communicators is confirmed. (p. 11)

Third, **a feminine woman is compliant.** As a communicator, a compliant woman engages in "'self-trivializing messages' that register the speaker's insecurity, doubt, and eagerness to please" (Borisoff & Merrill, 1998, p. 11). Specifically, "the compliant woman demonstrates her submissiveness" by allowing "herself to be interrupted," moves "out of the way when someone approaches her," smiles "often to assure the good will of others," and maintains "eye contact and listens attentively when others speak," but "averts her eyes when she is the focus of attention." In all, the "less powerful tend to employ verbal and nonverbal tactics calculated to appease rather than to threaten their listeners" (p. 11).

Fourth, **a feminine woman is emotional and subjective.** Borisoff and Merrill (1998, p. 11) have argued that, "This aspect of the feminine stereotype directly affects the female speaker's credibility. A speaker is considered credible when she or he can demonstrate competence, dynamism, consistency, and coorientation with an audience." Within a patriarchal dichotomy (see the introduction), objectivity and reason are associated with a male's external reliance on "facts" while subjectivity and feelings are associated with a female's subjective experience (p. 11). Borisoff and Merrill conclude this analysis by quoting Simone de Beauvoir (1953), who wrote that the "representation of the world, like the world itself, is the work of men. They describe it from their own point of view, which they confuse with the absolute truth" (p. 133).

Masculine Stereotypes

In 2001, Chesebro and Fuse defined masculinity in this fashion: "From a communication perspective, masculinity is the study of the discourses and the effects of the discourses generated by men, unifying men, and revealing the identity and characteristics men ascribe to themselves, others, and their environment." With this conception in mind, Chesebro and Fuse surveyed the published literature for the characteristics attributed to *masculinity, femininity, androgyny* (high masculinity and high femininity), and *undifferentiated* (low masculinity and low femininity). Based upon this review of the literature, as well as several different drafts of a questionnaire and several focus group interactions designed to determine how meaningful each question on the questionnaire was, Chesebro and Fuse distributed a "perceived masculinity" questionnaire to a representative sample of 562 undergraduate college males and females across the United States to determine the characteristics they attributed to masculinity. They concluded that college students employed ten different factors when they used the term *masculinity*. Here these ten variables are used as an operational definition of masculinity as well as the variables that define the stereotypes that cluster with masculinity when the concept is used by undergraduate college students in the United States today. In the following these variables are individually examined.

A masculine male possesses physiological energy. In addition to mere physical power and the demonstration of this physical power, college students believe that for a man to be perceived as "masculine," he must be "aggressive," "assertive," "competitive," "dominant," and "forceful." As college students saw it, a masculine man was defined, in part, by his body, his physiological energy, and any displays of such features were shaped and understood in terms of "experiences in the American society." Within a communication interaction, we would necessarily expect that a man perceived as masculine would employ a dominant voice (perhaps louder than necessary), not expect to be interrupted, use explicit and decisive hand gestures, and even occupy more physical space within an environment than others.

A masculine male possesses a bodily shape and size appropriate to the traditional male. Specifically, body shape and the quality of the voice were viewed as critical to the overall physical construction of a male when he was perceived as "masculine." Hence, manliness was consistently associated with more facial hair, a deeper voice, certain genitals, larger body sizes, a higher ratio of muscle to fat, and greater upper-body strength. These physical attributes were associated with masculinity at extremely early ages and in formal environments such as schools. While we explore this issue in greater detail in chapter 5, teachers rank boys who are "tall-broad" or "short-broad" as "significantly more masculine than boys who are tall-thin or short-thin" (Biller, 1968; also see several confirming studies: Biller & Liebman, 1971; Doyle & Paludi, 1985; LaVoie & Andrews, 1976). Within a communication interaction, a man perceived as masculine would literally be larger, possess a deeper voice, perhaps have a mustache or beard, and possess a noticeable chest.

A masculine male is more adaptive and enacts and can function proficiently in certain gender-specific sociocultural roles. Involving a cluster of both social and sexual behaviors, masculine men were thought to be in control more often than others, respondents believed they should achieve more and have a greater variety of sexual satisfaction in sexual interactions, have more sexual encounters with more people, be a sports fan, identify with a sports team and even display the name and insignia of their favorite sports team, and intensely dislike rival sports teams. Within communication interactions, masculine males would display and even wear the symbols associated with a favorite team (e.g., Peyton Manning's blue and white number 18 jersey), function as the focal point for group interactions, and perhaps even define his social agenda by his contacts in terms of opposite sex partners.

A masculine man has an idealized view of what masculinity is. Based upon television and newspaper advertisements, as well as standards within a man's local, immediate, and national culture, men are aware of what is defined as masculine, ideal forms of masculinity, and the degree to which others treat him as meeting this standard of masculinity. More generally, sociologists Lindesmith, Strauss, and Denzin (1999, p. 267) have reported that, "no society fails to embody in its practices and language the fundamental biological distinctions between the sexes. . . . Femininity and masculinity are socially defined terms added to these sex classes." While it probably goes without saying, men must enact certain roles if they are to be viewed as masculine. In this regard, Franklin (1984, p. 130) has maintained that a particular man's behavior is subjectively compared by others to some idealized "prototypical male." In many cases, these ideal masculine images are derived from the media or from sports.

A masculine male is heterosexual, displays heterosexuality, and is more masculine than his partner. As Franklin (1984) has directly put it, "For many people, the single factor determining a man's masculinity more than any other is his choice of a sexual partner . . . if a male chooses another male as a sexual partner, many people will automatically question his masculinity" (p. 130). In this regard, as Franklin has concluded, even the selection of a female sexual partner must reinforce a man's heterosexuality if he is to be perceived as masculine: "a man who chooses a masculine female sexual partner may differ only minimally from a male who chooses a masculine sexual partner" (p. 131). In this regard, perhaps the most vivid stereotype of a classic "straight guy" would be an oversized football player with a feminine cheerleader as his "girlfriend."

A masculine male is self-conscious and aware of his own sexuality as a man. For a man to believe he is masculine, he must believe that what he thinks and does reflects a socially understood conception of a masculine man, and others he encounters must—in one fashion or another—confirm that self-conception. As Franklin (1984) has aptly noted, "a male's perception of himself is critical in determining his gender. Does he think that he is highly masculine, moderately masculine, or minimally masculine?" (p. 131). Franklin has observed that "most men tend to rank themselves somewhat below their prototypes of masculinity but with sufficient distance from femininity." Hence, men perceiving themselves as masculine report that they think of themselves as masculine, that their friends and parents treat them as masculine, and that even strangers treat them as masculine. In this regard, as communicators, masculine men are likely to use more physical space on public transportation (e.g., their legs are spread apart and they literally take more space than others), have a larger area around them when chatting with friends, and are seldom interrupted when they tell a story.

A masculine male is perceived as neither young nor old, but past adolescence while not yet past middle age. A male's age can affect how masculine he is and how masculine others view him. Two groups of males—the young and the old—are placed at the greatest disadvantage because of how age and masculinity are and are not related by others. Indeed, boys are normally not classified as masculine or feminine until they begin to approach puberty. Likewise, elderly men are seldom viewed as active sexual agents. Indeed, Sheehy (1998, pp. 185–186) has reported that "most men in middle life do experience some lapses in virility and vitality" that can be appropriately identified as a "male middle-life pause," and specifically that, "52 percent of healthy American men between ages 40 and 70 can expect to experience some degree of impotence." Even if sexual activity is not affected, nonetheless younger and older men lack a degree of masculinity predominantly because of the social and symbolic constructions of others (and even of boys and older men themselves).

A masculine male possesses certain racial and nationality characteristics. Racial and nationality stereotypes are employed to define and characterize what is and is not masculine. For example, some people believe that African-American men are more masculine than white men and white men are more masculine than Asian men because—in this hierarchy—those at the top of the hierarchy are assumed to have larger penises and more potency in terms of procreation. While there is no evidence to sustain such beliefs, nonetheless masculinity is a social and symbolic construct that is influenced by forms and degrees of racism. At the same time, race may be employed to define a dimension of masculinity in a far more constructive fashion. For example, the scope, significance, and issues involved within black masculinity—particularly for African-American men—were revealed in events defining the October 16, 1995 Million Man March in Washington, DC. Designed to promote personal responsibility and community involvement, the march was an "emotional celebration for thousands of black men" (Franken, 1995) as well as an effort to devise ways in which individual black men might deal with crime, voting issues, poverty, children, and even genocide within their communities. In a similar fashion, the influence of racism has affected how Asian men understand and define their own sense of masculinity. For example, Han (2000) has maintained that Asian-American men are perceived and understood as "asexual, undersexed, and desexualized. Their masculinity tightly bound by these stereotypes, as women's feet once were in China, Asian American men hardly have their space to claim and define manhood" (pp. 206–207).

Race and nationality were identified as powerful variables in the masculinity literature review conducted by Chesebro and Fuse (2001):

> our sample was predominantly white and young. While our literature review suggested that race and masculinity can be powerfully related under certain conditions, our exploration here suggested that unless a more racially and age-diverse population is targeted and used in a formal survey, these items may not reveal a race-masculinity relationship. (p. 243)

A masculine male is lustful. When defining lustfulness, Chesebro and Fuse (2001, p. 269) employed four standards: (1) how often a man has sex, (2) the degree to which a man is orgasm (rather than romantically) oriented, (3) the degree to which bodily stimulation is genital (rather than full body), and (4) the degree to which erotic touching or foreplay are preferred. In this regard, while lusting can rob a man of his reason and thereby diminish his masculinity, nonetheless lust focuses attention upon the man himself, for it is a form of self-indulgence, an intense longing, and a decision to be ruled by one's own passion. More specifically, for men, Kay (2000) has argued that:

> Questions about sex are intimately linked to questions of power. For men, the connections between sex and power show themselves in an assortment of ways: the portrayal of sex as a competitive game; a matter of "scoring" and "bases"; and the image of sex as an intrinsically desirable commodity, a reward offered to those who achieve, or who at least buy the right car; the valorization of the always-hard, always-ready dick. (p. xvii)

In this view, a man becomes more masculine as he is more lustful. Indeed, as Kay (2000, p. xviii) has concluded, lustful men are ultimately "unemotional sexual predators."

A masculine male displays forms of male eroticism. Pope, Phillips, and Olivardia (2000) believe that the foundation for an erotic conception of masculinity can be traced back to 1965 when *Cosmopolitan* changed its editorial policy to include an open discussion of sex with men within its pages. They also report that 1965 is the year when the Gold's Gym chain began. Within this framework, they also note that penile-lengthening cosmetic surgery was first performed in 1970, *Playgirl* began in 1973, and in 1976 Hair Club for Men made its debut as well as the image of the gym-built Rocky Balboa (the movie *Rocky* ultimately generated $115 million worldwide). In addition, it should be noted that the Chippendale male dancers began in 1978, and in 1982, "muscleman" movies such as *Conan the Barbarian* and *First Blood* appeared. And, in 1981, Calvin Klein initiated a series of ads of men posing only in white Calvin Klein underwear, an advertising campaign that continues today. Included in this erotic imagery, an entire host of products have been designed to make men more erotic, such as the development of grooming (e.g., fragrances and deodorants, hair coloring and hair restoration systems), physical development (e.g., exercise and stomach muscle machines), clothing (both revealing and concealing), and cosmetic surgery products. Based upon a content analysis of one week's worth of major network television programming involving some 505 television programs, Lin (1997) found that

> both men and women were depicted largely in stereotypical "traditional roles," with men viewed as "beefcake," and no more likely than women to be presented in stereotypical product-model relations, as both genders appear equally in a nonfunctional, decorative, or function role in relation to the products they endorsed. (p. 237)

All of these findings suggest to us that it is at least worth exploring the notion that masculinity itself may be undergoing a transformation for some men in which products designed to create a more erotic image for men are simultaneously viewed as providing a form of more acceptable, less aggressive, and pleasurable kind of masculinity.

Changing Conceptions of Sexuality: The Emergence of Androgyny

As is true of virtually all social mores and norms, human interactions and communication continually change. We may value some of these changes while we disapprove of and seek to eliminate other changes. Sex-role changes are particularly sensitive issues for many people, and any change is likely to be examined with suspicion. Since the late 1960s, a host of changes in sex roles has been noted. For example, employing measures of assertiveness, Twenge (2001) has argued that women's scores on assertiveness and dominance scales have increased from 1968 through 1993. She has concluded that, "women's scores have increased enough that many recent samples show no sex differences in assertiveness." While men's scores have not been demonstrated to change, for women this change in assertiveness and dominance constitutes a "social change" that is "internalized in the form of a personality trait" (p. 133).

In a broader context, Ivy and Backlund (1994, p. 58) have observed that "in traditional views of development," sex roles are cast as either "male or female." In this conception, the masculine "involves instrumental or task-oriented competence," and it "includes such traits as assertiveness, self-expansion, self-protection, and a general orientation of self *against* the world." In contrast, "femininity is viewed as expressive or relationship-oriented," whose "corresponding traits include nurturance and concern for others, emphasis on relationships and the expression of feelings, and a general orientation of self *within* the world." Ivy and Backlund (1994, p. 58) have concluded that these "traditional views" perpetuate "the male-female dichotomy and limit individuals' options in terms of variations in identities."

Indeed, in our view, it is now extremely difficult to find anyone who wants to only be "task-oriented" or "relationship-oriented." At least in the popular parlance, most people now seem to seek a balance between the instrumental and the expressive. In other words, in our experience, people seem to prefer that a task-orientation approach occur within a context of concern for others.

One of the first efforts to establish an alternative to the male-female and related masculinity-femininity bipolar framework was provided by Sandra L. Bem in 1974. Bem argued that, "Both in psychology and in society at large, masculinity and femininity have long been conceptualized as bipolar ends of a single continuum; accordingly, a person has had to be either masculine or feminine, but not both" (p. 155). Employing a term that has upset many, Bem continued her line of thought and proposed that, "many individuals might be 'androgynous'; that is, they *might* be *both* masculine and feminine, *both* assertive and yielding, *both* instrumental and expressive—depending on the situational appropriateness of these various behaviors" (p. 155). Therefore some individuals might be androgynous, while other individuals might continue to be explicitly and strongly masculine or feminine. At the same time, she reasoned, even strongly sex-typed individuals might find it reasonable and effective to limit their solely masculine or feminine sex roles under certain conditions. As Bem argued, "strongly sex-typed individuals might be seriously limited in the range of behaviors available to them as they move from situation to situation" (p. 155).

To establish her claims, in a preliminary condition, Bem compiled a list of "approximately 200 personality characteristics" that "seemed to be both positive in value and either masculine or feminine." She also

compiled a list of 200 characteristics that "seemed to be neither masculine nor feminine"—or gender "neutral"—of which "half were positive in value and half were negative" (p. 156). Using these 400
characteristics, individuals were asked to evaluate the desirability
(using a seven point Likert-type scale from 1, "not at all desirable," to
7, "extremely desirable") of each characteristic for both men and
women (e.g., "In American society, how desirable is it for a man to be
truthful?" "In American society, how desirable is it for a woman to be
sincere?"). Using these ratings, a characteristic was qualified as masculine, for example, only if a statistically significant amount of both
males and females applied it to men, but not to women. The same criteria were used to differentiate feminine characteristics. In the final
compilation, 20 personality traits made up the masculinity scale, 20
made up the femininity scale, and 20 were selected for the social desirability scale. The traits for this scale were "independently judged by
both males and females to be no more desirable for one sex than for
the other" (p. 157). Table 1.1 provides the complete list of these 60
characteristics classified as "masculine items," "feminine items," or
"neutral items."

**Table 1.1   Items for the Masculinity, Femininity, and Social Desirability
Scales of the Bem Sex-Role Inventory (BSRI)**

Masculine Items	Feminine Items	Neutral Items
49. Acts as a leader	11. Affectionate	51. Adaptable
46. Aggressive	5. Cheerful	36. Conceited
58. Ambitious	50. Childlike	9. Conscientious
22. Analytical	32. Compassionate	60. Conventional
13. Assertive	53. Does not use harsh language	45. Friendly
10. Athletic	35. Eager to soothe hurt feelings	15. Humorous
55. Competitive	20. Feminine	3. Helpful
4. Defends own beliefs	14. Flatterable	48. Inefficient
37. Dominant	59. Gentle	24. Jealous
19. Forceful	47. Gullible	39. Likable
25. Has leadership abilities	56. Loves children	6. Moody
7. Independent	17. Loyal	21. Reliable
52. Individualistic	26. Sensitive to the needs of others	30. Secretive
31. Makes decisions easily	8. Shy	33. Sincere
40. Masculine	38. Soft spoken	42. Solemn
1. Self-reliant	23. Sympathetic	57. Tactful
34. Self-sufficient	44. Tender	12. Theatrical
16. Strong personality	29. Understanding	27. Truthful
43. Willing to take a stand	41. Warm	18. Unpredictable
28. Willing to take risks	2. Yielding	54. Unsystematic

From: Bem (1974).

Table 1.2   Independent Sexuality Dimensions

Mode of Sexuality	Operational Definitions of Terms on the BSRI
Masculine	High on Masculinity and Low on Femininity
Feminine	High on Femininity and Low on Masculinity
Undifferentiated	Low on Masculinity and Low on Femininity
Androgynous	High on Masculinity and High on Femininity

At two different universities, on a seven point Likert-type scale, a total of 917 undergraduate male and female college students (61% were males) was asked to determine how well each of the 60 masculine, feminine, and neutral personality characteristics given described him- or herself. The results of these self-assessments were classified as either "masculine," "feminine," "undifferentiated," or "androgynous." The definitions of these categories are provided in table 1.2.

Among a host of conclusions and implications, Bem established that more than masculine and feminine modes of sexuality existed. She additionally established that masculine and feminine are not bipolar terms along a single continuum. Sexuality, in the context provided by Bem, could also involve undifferentiated and androgynous modes of sexuality. In all, the world of sex roles changed dramatically, becoming a multidimensional set of options and possibilities for all individuals based on circumstances and personal preferences. For some, androgyny itself can be a confusing, if not upsetting, attribute. Seeking to create a more receptive attitude about androgyny, Ivy and Backlund (1994) suggest:

> Let's explore . . . [the] androgyny concept within gender-role transcendence a bit further. It may make the concept more understandable if you envision a continuum with masculinity placed toward one end, femininity toward the other end, and androgyny in the middle. You don't lose masculine traits or behaviors if you become androgynous, or somehow become masculine if you move away from the feminine pole. Androgyny is an intermix of the feminine and the masculine. Some androgynous individuals may have more masculine than feminine traits, and vice versa. (pp. 59–60)

Another way to think of androgyny is to perceive it as one of four options or choices that might be selected in any given situation. In some cases, you may decide that a more masculine approach is required and likely to be the most effective strategy. In other cases, a more feminine strategy will be the best choice. In yet another set of circumstances, an androgynous approach—in which both masculine and feminine traits are employed—will function the best. And, finally, in some cases, a sex-role emphasis might be completely inappropriate, you may decide that a more undifferentiated approach will produce the most positive outcome. In other words, rather than believing that individuals are inherently one sex role or another at all times and in all places, we can become more effective communicators when we begin to view sex roles as a choice or option, just as we consciously consider, select, and judge any other kind of strategy for its effectiveness.

In terms of communication practices, we do think an increasing number of people are learning to adopt a rich array of masculine and feminine traits depending upon the people and circumstances they encounter. For example, the Pew Research Center (2008) reported—based upon a representative sample of 2,250 adults living in the continental United States—that people now perceive women as more effective leaders than men. Identifying key traits associated with effective leadership (see table 1.3), people decisively believe that women are more likely to possess these traits.

The terms the Pew Research Center employed to characterize leadership can easily be equated to the cluster of terms that Bem used. In regard to the qualities wanted in leadership, you will notice that the traits reflect an androgynous rather than either a masculine or feminine perspective. This androgynous leadership style is composed of masculine traits (decisive or makes decisions easily, willing to take a stand,

Table 1.3   Men or Women: Who's the Better Leader?

Leadership Trait[a]	% Saying This Trait Is More True of	
	Men	Women
Honest	20%	50%
Intelligent	14%	38%
Hardworking	28%	28%
Decisive	44%	33%
Ambitious	34%	34%
Compassionate	5%	80%
Outgoing	28%	47%
Creative	11%	62%

[a] Traits listed in order of the public's ranking of their importance to leadership. "Equally true" and "don't know" responses are not shown.

From: Pew Research Center (2008).

willing to take risks, assertive, intelligent, or analytical), feminine traits (compassionate, outgoing, sensitive to the needs of others, understanding, warm, eager to soothe hurt feelings), and gender-neutral traits (honest, hardworking, creative). As defined by the Pew Research Center, women are more likely to display this combination of personality traits. Therefore, when women perform androgynously in leadership roles, they are viewed as the "better leader."

Likewise, women continue to occupy the dominant leadership position in the home, but a wider variety of sex-role strategies are employed. Morin and Cohen (2008) have reported that "in 43% of all couples it's the woman who makes decisions in more areas [at home] than the man. By contrast, men make more of the decisions in only about a quarter (26%) of all couples. And about three-in-ten couples (31%) split decision-making responsibilities equally" (p. 1).

Diana Lee (2005) has reported that "androgyny seems to have found its way to global mainstream." Among those representing this androgynous style, Lee includes Michael Jackson, David Beckham, Angelina Jolie, Boy George, David Bowie, Prince, Sharon Stone, Milla Jovovich, and Uma Thurman. In her view, androgyny combines "both masculinity and femininity as traits of a unified gender that defies social roles and psychological attributes." While some have argued that an androgynous system will make men and women "interchangeable," suppress "physicality," make men "neuter" themselves, and make "ambitious women postpone procreation" (Paglia, 2010), we are not as negative, and we think a host of equally valid alternatives are also possible, including the individualization of men and women beyond gender categories.

In all, as we suggest throughout the book, people are more likely to become more effective communicators if they can condition and train themselves to view the application of sex roles as an opportunity to make choices and develop strategies that can be judged as more or less effective depending upon the people and circumstances encountered. As Bem (1974) put it some 35 years ago, "In a society where rigid sex-role differentiation has already outlived its utility, perhaps the androgynous person will come to define a more human standard of psychological health" (p. 162).

Conclusion

Any discussion of sex-role stereotypes will necessarily encounter a host of problems. Human language in and of itself encourages people to create and use categories, of which stereotypes are an apropos example. Moreover, the attack on political correctness has implicitly been an attack on those who argue against sex-role stereotypes. Finally, sex-role stereotypes themselves are subject to change and can often be viewed in more than one way. With these precautions in mind, we have isolated what we believe to be four stereotypes of female communication and 10 stereotypes of male communication. We concluded this chapter by suggesting that androgyny could be perceived as a method for increasing the range, and ultimately the effectiveness, of sex-role communication strategies.

SUGGESTED ACTIVITIES

1. **Field Study Designed to Reveal Gender Use in Everyday Groups**
   Form a team of 3 to 5 students from your class, and then conduct a field study of any group that you wish, or is conveniently and readily available to you. You should be intrigued by how this group communicates, and you should be able to identify how this group can influence the lives of its members or even those beyond the group. For example, say a member of your team is part of a fraternity. How men in a fraternity talk about women when only other men are around might be extremely informative about all-male groups. As part of the fraternity, your team member can function as a participant-observer in such all-male conversations, recording any relevant data with a focus on what generalizations the group employed when distinguishing women. The results can then be examined and interpreted by all members of the team. The same procedures also could be employed to discover how all-women groups discuss men. Your team should report the results of its investigation back to your class.

2. **Reconsider Male and Female Communication Patterns**
   In terms of a classroom discussion, consider each of the five "communication strategies" described by Eakins and Eakins that distinguish male and female speech and communication. After considering each of these communication strategies one-by-one, determine if one gender is more likely to use one of these strategies more frequently than the other. Do exceptions exist for each of these generalizations? Are there any patterns of communication that men use more frequently than women? Are there some activities (e.g., sports) where certain words and concepts are used more frequently by one gender than the other? If there are gender distinctions in communication, are such distinctions a sign of discrimination or power differences between the genders?

3. **Are Feminine Stereotypes Always Harmful?**
   In a classroom discussion or after students are divided into groups, review the four feminine stereotypes identified in this chapter. If women are more soft-spoken, self-effacing, compliant, and emotional than men, do women suffer or reduce their own effectiveness in terms of effective and persuasive communication? Do some of these stereotypes even discourage women from com-

municating at all? When responding to these questions, provide examples or "evidence" of your position from the public domain by using events involving media personalities, politicians, and so forth so that your classmates are able to identify with them.

4. **Do Masculine Stereotypes Describe Only Men?**
   In a classroom discussion or after students are divided into groups of five to six, review the ten masculine stereotypes that were identified in this chapter. Drawing examples from the public domain (such as television, films, and the Internet) to establish your claim, do men use each of these stereotypes more than women? Have women used some of these stereotypes with effective or positive outcomes?

5. **Compare a Vernacular Definition of the Word *Androgyny* and Its Internet Meanings**
   In a 2–3 page research paper, identify the range of meanings given to the word *androgyny*. First, locate a dictionary and itemize each of the specific attributes the dictionary gives for the word *androgyny*. When you have isolated these specific attributes, do a Google search for the word *androgyny*. Go through the search results one by one, and see how many of the dictionary's attributes are used, but also note any attributes not found in the dictionary.

6. **Personal Contemplation and Self-Conception Exercise**
   As an exercise in self-discovery (done, we would recommend, when you are alone, have some free time, and are in a self-exploratory mood), one by one go through all 60 of the words included in table 1.1. Being as honest as you can about yourself, circle in *red* all of those words that best describe you. Go through these words again, but this time, being as honest as you can, circle in *blue* all of those words that people assume about you when they communicate with you.

   a. Are some words circled in both red and blue? Are these the personality characteristics that you find the safest to use when you communicate with your friends?

   b. In terms of the words circled only in red, do you think these are traits you conceal from your friends? In terms of the words circled only in blue, do you think these are traits you think your friends would like you to display and employ more frequently?

   c. Based upon the items you circled in red, do you predominantly perceive yourself as masculine, feminine, or neutral? Based upon the items you circled in blue, do your friends predominantly perceive you as masculine, feminine, or neutral? Based upon the items circles in both red and blue, are you predominantly masculine, feminine, or neutral when communicating with others?

Verbal and Nonverbal Face-to-Face Communication by Gender

*F*ace-to-face communication is an extremely complex and dynamic process. In terms of complexity, the number of variables involved in the process goes far beyond what you would expect the average person to monitor and act upon. In terms of its dynamic nature, as relationships change (due to circumstances and the level of involvement and intimacy), verbal and nonverbal communication change. It is unclear how conscious and aware most people are of how verbal and nonverbal communication changes occur. If we add in the fact that men and women process both the variables and the levels of intimacy differently, the entire communication process seems overwhelming, at least mysterious, if not virtually impossible to dissect in reasonable and useable ways.

In response to the complexity and dynamic nature of verbal and nonverbal communication when used by men and women, we have divided this chapter into two parts. In the first part, we identify the basic ten elements or the grammar of verbal and nonverbal communication. In part two, we focus on the process of verbal and nonverbal communication between men and women, and we suggest how the ten elements change and recombine in different ways as relationships evolve and transform as they pass through different stages of the interpersonal communication process. We begin, then, with a delineation of the ten basic elements or the grammar of verbal and nonverbal communication.

Basic Elements or Structural Features of Verbal and Nonverbal Communication

In a quest to simplify and provide an overview of the ten basic elements of verbal and nonverbal communication, we begin by noting that

45

the two areas—verbal and nonverbal communication—vary tremendously in terms of their social impact upon people. While there are some variations among the findings, in general, nonverbal communication repeatedly has been established as more powerful than verbal communication in terms of face-to-face communication.

In one of the landmark studies of nonverbal communication, Mehrabian (1968, pp. 52–55) argued that words or linguistic content accounted for only 7% of the meanings conveyed to others, that vocal quality accounted for some 38% of the meanings conveyed to others, and that facial expression accounted for 55% of the meanings conveyed to others. In sum, if vocal quality is treated as a nonverbal factor, the content of words or linguistics accounts for only 7% of social meanings conveyed to others, while nonverbal communication accounts for 93% of what people perceive from their speaking partners.

In a related study, Burgoon, Buller, and Woodall (1989) excluded vocal quality from their definition of nonverbal communication, and they found that nonverbal communication accounted for 60 to 65% of the meanings communicated to others. They also found that nonverbal communication becomes even more powerful and important when the context for communication becomes more emotional.

If verbal and nonverbal communication do affect people differently or do have different impacts on people, one might also ask: *How do verbal and nonverbal communications function differently for people?* Many have proposed distinctions intended to suggest extremely different functions or roles. Table 2.1 provides several of these distinctions. Do you agree with them?

Table 2.1   Traditional Distinctions between the Functions of Verbal and Nonverbal Communication

Verbal Communication Functions

1. Conveys precise information
2. Provides the content for channels of communication
3. Reveals ideas
4. Content-centered

Nonverbal Communication Functions

1. Conveys ambiguous context cues
2. Opens up the channels of communication
3. Reveals emotions
4. People-centered

We have to admit that we do have major reservations about each of these distinctions. However, we are inviting you to consider how valid and reliable they may be. Based upon your experiences in face-to-face interactions, do you believe they are true most of the time? Some of the time? Or, do you believe that verbal and nonverbal communication cannot be distinguished in terms of their functions, because verbal and nonverbal communication overlap dramatically in how they affect people?

We encourage you to consider these distinctions now, formulate your own ideas about these differences, and then when you have finished this chapter, return to these distinctions and decide anew how and why you value or dismiss each one.

Other studies have reported that we are simply not as conscious and aware of our reactions to nonverbal communication. We do not study nonverbal communication systematically nor do we engage in the kinds of exercises and practices that might build our skills in using and reacting to nonverbal communication. Some have suggested that certain nonverbal emotions, such as happiness, can be more readily recognized (55% to 100% accuracy) than other emotions, such as surprise (38% to 86% accuracy) and sadness (19% to 88% accuracy). We might conclude that because people react with wide variation to nonverbal communication there is—at the very least—less social agreement about its purpose, and therefore, we cannot expect it to be as useful and meaningful in terms of its ability to convey what we intend as other modes of communication.

With these notions in mind, we want to provide a framework for considering verbal and nonverbal communication in a systematic fashion, and as a set of basic elements in the face-to-face communication process. More formally, others would note that we are articulating the basic grammar of verbal and nonverbal communication. Certainly, our effort here is to identify a basic and enduring structure that accounts for the major factors or variables found when people communicate in face-to-face encounters. Table 2.2 provides an overview of these elements, however, they deserve separate attention. We consider each of them in order here.

Linguistics

Traditionally focusing on human language and speech, linguistics is the study of the units, structure, processes, and modifications of oral language use. Five forms of linguistic analysis exist: (1) **Phonetics and phonology** is the study of speech sounds, including articulation and acoustics as well as speech classes such as pitch, stress, and tone; (2) **Morphology** is the study of the internal structure of words (e.g., books = book + s); (3) **Syntax** is the study of combinations of words into larger units such as sentences and texts; (4) **Semantics** is the study of the meaning of speech forms (signs and symbols) in terms of

Table 2.2   Verbal and Nonverbal Elements in Face-to-Face Communication

Variable	Definition
Linguistics	Linguistics is the study of speech production, construction, modifications, and changes (such as articulation, speaking rate, pitch, stress, and tone).
Haptics	Haptics is the study of touching as a variable affecting communication.
Oculesics	Oculesics is the study of eye contact as a variable affecting communication.
Aromatics	Aromatics is the study of smell as a variable affecting communication.
Proxemics	Proxemics is the study of space manipulation as a variable affecting communication.
Vocalistics	Vocalistics is the study of verbal and linguistic acts as a variable affecting communication.
Chronemics	Chronemics is the study of time as a variable affecting communication.
Kinesics	Kinesics is the study of body movement as a variable affecting communication.
Objectics	Objectics is the study of the use of objects as variables affecting communication.
Coloristics	Coloristics is the study of hue, brightness, and saturation of light as variables affecting communication.

context; and (5) **Pragmatics** is the study of the uses to which language can be put to effect, influence, and persuade people (see Gardner, 1983, pp. 73–79; Swiggers, 1989, p. 432).

As an area of study, linguistics focuses our attention on oral speech sounds as a variable affecting human communication. Given the large number of specific factors involved in the area of linguistics, a rich variety of studies have been done, especially regarding gender studies. For example, sex differences in terms of pitch has more to do with social interpretation than physiological production (Graddol & Swann, 1989). Others have suggested that detectable vocal differences by gender can be used to mark linguistic intelligence. In this regard, Spender (1985, p. 38) has argued that pitch is "an index for the measurement of women's language inferiority." For others, such as Gardner (1983, p. 76), detecting and reacting to the sounds of words can be a measure of one's ability to communicate through poetry and music.

In terms of offering a semantic and pragmatic analysis of women as speakers, Bizzell and Herzberg (1990, p. 670) provide a perspective that cannot be ignored: "From the days of ancient Greece, women were generally discouraged from speaking in public and, except in a few cases, from obtaining the kind of education that informed such performances by men. Indeed, few women achieved literacy; in seventeenth-century England, according to social historian David Cressy, only 20 percent of women were sufficiently literate to sign their names" (see Campbell, 1989a, 1989b). More precisely, when pragmatic analyses assess the perceived persuasiveness of male and female speakers, gender is demonstrated to be a powerful factor. In the legal world, for example, Reinard (2002, p. 546) has argued that, "some research suggests that male attorneys have greater trial success than do female lawyers" even though the "male attorney's physical attractiveness did not influence verdicts." In other kinds of cases, especially rape cases, if the defensive lawyer is a woman, juries apparently assume that the case against the defendant is not particularly strong, for defendants represented by female attorneys are acquitted 71% of the time compared to a 49% acquittal rate if the defending attorney is male (Reinard, 2002, p. 547).

Haptics

In terms of gender studies, the role of touching in the communication process is revealing and significant. Women, particularly when they are enacting an extremely feminine role, are likely to use touch far more frequently than a "traditional" or masculine man. Indeed, the average woman touches someone an average of twelve times a day whereas the average male touches someone only eight times a day (Kotulak, 1985). In contrast to what occurs in most other cultures, most of the touching behavior in the United States is opposite sex touching. In this context, you might want to ask if this kind of touching reflects and reinforces traditional dominant/submissive roles among men and women.

Oculesics

Oculesics draw our attention to the eye itself and the various roles that eye contact can play in terms of gender communication. Certainly, various types of eye contact can be specified. People can *gaze*, surveying and treating all elements of their environment with relative importance. Gazing, of course, can also be perceived as a way of avoiding any specific person within an environment. Beyond gazing, one can *stare* at another person, in which the uninterrupted focus presumes a level of intimacy that many find—especially at the outset of a relationship—extremely uncomfortable. And, in some clubs, *cruising* can be viewed as a combination of both gazing and staring, a process of maintaining one's options but also periodically employing stares to determine if a positive response is received. McCroskey (2006) has reported:

> Heterosexual courtship behavior of Americans depends heavily on eye contact in the early stages. In particular, the male will tend to establish what is sometimes referred to as the "courtship stare" with the female. This overlong, direct eye contact communicates strong interest on the part of the male. It says to the female, "I am interested in you; are you interested in me?" If the female turns

away, the answer is no. If she smiles or in some other way indicates approval of the male, the answer is yes. Meaningful verbal communication can begin at this point. (p. 138)

Aromatics

Women are explicit about the smells they convey to others, with different perfumes for different social situations (work versus dating situations). Moreover, when we discussed male eroticism in chapter 1, we observed that men are increasingly finding perfumes—often relabeled "aftershave" or "cologne"—to be an important way of attracting sexual attention.

Proxemics

Manipulating space can dramatically affect human communication. The physical space between people can be manipulated, with 18 or fewer inches perceived as a form of intimacy, 1½ to 3 feet perceived as a friendship distance, 3 to 5 feet as a more social mode of interaction, and 5 or more feet for more public and formal modes of interaction. Likewise, the angles and inclinations between two people can affect a relationship. A male boss standing over a seated female employee reinforces formality as well as a form of dominance, all of which is likely to inhibit and reduce the number of creative and useful comments an employee is likely to offer.

Space manipulations can be a powerful way of influencing communication processes and their outcomes. The distance between two people as well as the physical arrangement of furniture can be decisive in how people do and do not respond to others. In North America, perhaps as a form of nonverbal aggression, men enter the "private space" of women more frequently than women enter the "private space" of men (Hall, 1984). And, in general, women are encouraged to sit eagerly on the edge of a chair, leaning forward, conveying the image that they are at the ever-ready in terms of engaging in verbal communication (Borisoff & Merrill, 1998, p. 53).

Vocalistics

While we have already explored some of the social implications of the use of speech variations (or linguistics), vocal qualities can exert a profound influence over how people view and react to each other. If a man's first contact with a woman is on the telephone, and if her voice is deep, husky, and slowly paced, he is very likely to believe she is sexy but also overweight. A foundation for such observations can exist when we examine the variables affecting vocalistics. Leathers (1986) has suggested that the sound of a voice is affected by its loudness, pitch, rate of speech, vocal quality, clarity of pronunciation, intonation pattern, and use of silence.

Chronemics

We certainly have widely diverse reactions to how different people in different positions manipulate time. For example, even if you have made your appointment a month ahead of time, you might easily wait for a doctor in his office for 20 to 30 minutes without a negative reaction. Time can even be a variable in terms of speaking rate. An extremely slow speaker might be perceived as mentally disadvantaged. In some cultures, social events begin one to two hours after the announced beginning time. Indeed, entire schemes for discussing time have been devised, such as *arrival time, waiting time, business time, social time*, and so forth. Within a culture, there are different expectations about how interactions will be conducted as well as the content of interactions depending upon when and where people are communicating.

Even the awareness of time can convey an attitude to others. For example, if someone is chatting with you and checks his or her wrist watch, you may have the sense that you are less important and probably even blocking or interfering with another future meeting. Or, especially in interpersonal communication, the length of a relationship— measured in years or even decades—can be perceived as an indication of its significance.

Kinesics

One of the most extensively studied forms of nonverbal communication, kinesics is the study of body movements as a variable affecting human communication. According to Ekman and Friesen (1969), there are five kinds of body movement: (1) **Emblems**—physical movements that have direct verbal translations in a culture (e.g., thumbs up); (2) **Illustrators**—physical visualization of verbal statements (e.g., "The table is this high"); (3) **Regulators**—using physical movements as signs of transitions in an interaction (e.g., moving toward a door when a conversation is ending); (4) **Affect Displays**—facial expressions that convey emotions; and (5) **Adapters**—physical actions to change that reflect a bodily condition (e.g., to scratch what itches). While it may now be changing, a traditional analysis of kinesics in terms of sex roles would hold that men use bodily movements to regulate and control power and dominance within a relationship while women convey senses of powerlessness and submissiveness with their bodily movements.

Objectics

While the use of specific objects can be analyzed (e.g., the kind of car a man drives can be a reflection of his attitudes about people), we are particularly intrigued by the labeling system for overall styles of clothing (e.g., formal, sporting, clubbing, etc.). But, the study of the objects used to convey and reinforce masculinity and femininity can be decisive and certainly depends upon the culture in which we exist. In some subcultures in the United States, for example, a man is perceived to be more masculine if he carries no objects with him (i.e., he is completely independent of all social emblems and regulators). In contrast, both males and females carry backpacks and books on a college campus, and in combination with certain types of clothing, these objects help to create the image of what we call a "student." Yet, even on a college campus, men and women use certain objects that convey and reinforce images of masculinity and femininity. What are the objects you have noted on your campus that convey masculinity and femininity? Are there some objects (such as blue jeans) that are treated as gender-neutral or androgynous?

Coloristics

The selection of certain hues, levels of brightness, and saturation of light elicits different responses in people, thereby affecting human communication. Certainly, there are some "traditional" colors that are "understood" to be appropriate for certain occasions. Dark colors are worn at a funeral while brides normally wear white or lighter colors (signifying cheerfulness and happiness) at weddings.

Advertising provides us with a rich variety of the sense of what colors mean and the mood that we associate with each color. For example, McDonald's red and yellow brand colors are designed to create a sense of activation in us. As McDonald's shifts toward tan and purple, we are expected to shift into a more casual and relaxed "dining and family mode." Similarly, we may learn to expect certain smells from the colors found on packaging or the color of detergents or bars of soap (e.g., yellow detergent is lemon). Many of these commercial color and action associations infiltrate our everyday lives. We now have a full range of meanings and moods that we can associate with specific colors (see table 2.3 for some examples). In this regard, if you give red roses or receive red roses, what message is conveyed? What colors are appropriate for different kinds of events? While we cannot detail all of the situations you may face, after examining table 2.3 you might be able to make some thoughtful and effective decisions when you make color choices.

Modes of Communication Are Not Static

While each of the verbal and nonverbal modes of communication can be isolated individually, unfortunately, during actual ongoing face-to-face interactions all ten of these forms function at the same time. Sometimes these forms reinforce one major image or understanding of another person or the self. In other cases, the forms may be contradictory, and the modes are the source of ambiguity, if not confusion, within a relationship. Moreover, each of these modes may change and evolve as a relationship evolves and changes, as circumstances change, and as different events and rituals become appropriate. Accordingly, while our listing of the specific forms of verbal and nonverbal communication can be useful, we also need to consider how these forms function as human relationships change and evolve.

Table 2.3 Color Meanings and Moods

Color[a]	Positive	Negative
Red	Hot	Death
	Affectionate	War
	Warmth	Revolution
	Passion	Devil
	Life	Danger
	Liberty	Angry
	Patriotism	Lust
	Happiness	Restlessness
Blue	Cool	Sadness
	Pleasant	Doubt
	Secure	Discouragement
	Dignity	Business-like attitude
	Religious	
	Devotion	
	Truth	
	Justice	
	Tenderness	
Yellow	Intuition	Unpleasant
	Wisdom	Disturbed
	Divinity	Cowardice
	Boldness	Malevolence
	Cheerfulness	Impure love
Green	Security	Envy
	Nature	Jealousy
	Hope	Opposition
	Freshness	Disgrace
	Prosperity	Hate
	Leisurely	Aggressive
Purple	Power	Mourning
	Royalty	Regret
	Dignified	Depressed
	Stately	Pomp
	Control	Tragedy

[a] The association between color and various meanings and moods has been explored by a host of researchers for several years. Consistent associations have been reported. This table is a derived summary of several other tables describing these associations. See: Burgoon, Buller, & Woodall (1989), p. 130; Knapp & Hall (2009), p. 116; Malandro, Barker, & Barker (1989), p. 158; Richmond & McCroskey (2000), p. 185.

Verbal and Nonverbal Communication as a Process: Stages in the Development of an Interpersonal Relationship

While we can detail all of the specific verbal and nonverbal modes of communication that influence ourselves and others, we also need to ask how these diverse modes work and function together. Essentially, at any point in time, it is very conceivable that all ten of the verbal and nonverbal variables we have considered are fully operative, defining, and influencing how people interact. In addition, we need to ask how interactions change and develop over time as relationships change and develop. Again, the answer to such queries will depend on the kind of relationships we are dealing with and the contexts and situations in which we communicate. While we might illustrate how verbal and nonverbal communication functions as a process in several different ways, we find the notion of stages in the communication process particularly useful, for it suggests that people change and evolve as relationships develop, that their verbal and nonverbal behaviors change as relationships change, and ultimately that each of these changes can be perceived as relatively unique and are special kinds of phases and periods that characterize human communication. Likewise, the use of stages or phases allows us to note that a change in a relationship may also have junctures or points at which the recognition of change might have to be explicit and dealt with directly.

We have found Julia Wood's (1982) twelve stages in a relationship a particularly useful point of departure. We have updated and modified these stages to more directly reflect our interest in gender communication. These stages characterize an interpersonal relationship from its inception, through a period of intimacy, to a stage in which a relationship is ultimately terminated. Of course, not every relationship passes through all of these stages. Indeed, the vast majority of our interpersonal relationships are unlikely to even reach stage six. Many encounters begin the process, halt at a particular stage, and may even move backward. In a very few cases, however, do we encounter someone with whom we actually move through all of the stages. Sometimes passing through all of the stages makes us healthier and more positive individuals. Sometimes the process has the opposite effect—we can feel hurt and injured, or for a period of time we may desire to opt out of any encounter that even remotely suggests that an intimate relationship may occur. As a result, these stages can be revealing, suggesting how we are changed by those we encounter and how the way we communicate verbally and nonverbally influences the stage or level of intimacy we have with different individuals.

Before we begin we would like to invite you to participate and characterize each stage in terms of how men and women communicate. You can use these stages as a test of what you know and have experienced during interpersonal communication. We will provide you with some suggestions and clues about what we think are dominant ways in which males and females communicate at each juncture, but we hope you will take the lead in depicting each stage in terms of how men and women communicate.

Stage One: Individuals

The first stage of interpersonal communication is shaped by one's individual and unique experiences before even meeting a significant other. Our prior relationships with others—including acquaintances, friends, and intimates—shape and influence our attitudes and goals about what intimacy can and should be. During this stage, although we are seldom conscious of it, we begin to develop definitions of ourselves, what we think the verbal and nonverbal characteristics of our acquaintances should be like, what relatives and good friends will say and do, and what we think an intimate relationship will be like for us and for the significant other with whom we are involved. Indeed, our expectations may even become idealized. It is our expectations that actually become the standards we use when we consider developing intimate interpersonal relationships.

We do think our existing attitudes about relationships are constantly changing. Our previous experiences, what has happened in our families, what are friends go through, the images of relationships we see in the media and on social networks (as well as the changing conceptions of relationships in a larger sociocultural system), all affect us. Accordingly, we need to be extremely cautious when we suggest that as individuals all men have the same kind of experiences and bring the same expectations to relationships. Likewise, we think there are tremendous differences in the experiences that women as individuals have had before they enter an interpersonal relationship.

Yet, some gender differences that have been identified in research findings are intriguing. For example, Baker (2009) has argued that men are more likely to increase their risk taking with women perceived to be especially physically attractive. In other words, as arousal levels increase, the decision to initiate a relationship also increases. However, as Galvin (2006) has argued, "Men and women with masculine inclinations tend to value independence and distance from others" (p. 42). And therein lies the problem. In one sense, the motivation for such a relationship might be easier to act upon when the attraction is based strictly on appearance or sexual interest, for social or task implications are de-emphasized. While physical attraction may exist at this stage, the stage is also marked by tremendous hesitancy and uncertainty (Welch & Rubin, 2002, p. 29). In short, men are likely to take a risk, initiate an action, and possibly move to the second stage if they find someone attractive and sufficiently arousing. Contrary to the masculine orientation, men and women with a feminine orientation may initially use alternative standards for attractiveness. Rather than emphasizing physical and sexual attraction, they may "place a premium on relationship and interpersonal closeness" (Galvin, 2006, p. 42).

It is particularly apt to note that the first stage of an interpersonal relationship is extremely individualistic. And, indeed, an initial tension may exist between masculine and feminine individuals, because each focuses on and functions from a different frame of reference.

Stage Two: Invitational Communication or Auditioning

Of the diverse forms of nonverbal communication that can influence the onset of an interpersonal relationship, perhaps the most critical is proxemics (or the distance between individuals). For example, to experience "love at first sight," two people must be within a common environment or situation and be sufficiently close to make a host of evaluations and judgments about each other. People often initiate relationships with those they work with, for they may be in contact with them for five days a week and eight hours a day. Indeed, if two people are working in the same company, they may already have a host of common or similar interests, a shared view of the kind of social environments that are valuable, and a commonly shared notion of what kinds of tasks or work are beneficial. The invitational or auditioning stage is a period of hesitations in which one is trying to determine if there are shared interests with another, if the other is pleasant, easy to talk to, and potentially a friend.

Feminine and masculine differences also complicate these early interactions. During this stage, feminine people employ a unique set of communication techniques. Wood (2009) has aptly noted that "For feminine people, talk *is* the essence of relationships. . . . Establishing equality between people is a second important feature" followed by "support for others" and a "conversational" and "responsive" mode that is both "personal" and "tentative" (pp. 128–129). In contrast, Wood has argued, "masculine speech" is frequently an "effort to establish status and control," to accomplish specific ends through the use of "conversational command" that has a "direct and assertive" style, which is achieved through the use of more abstract and less personal responsiveness (p. 131). In these senses, the feminine and the masculine actually operate in different ways, seek extremely different goals, and employ conversational modes that are actually at odds with each other. These communication differences may inhibit the quest to acquire information about the other, if not block the ability to convey unique and personal information about the self to another. In other words, in terms of traditional feminine and masculine roles, it is simply extremely difficult to initiate an interpersonal relationship that leads to satisfactory intimacy for both feminine and masculine individuals.

Stage Three: Explorational Communication

When an individual begins to focus on another person's unique and personal interests, attitudes, and values in an effort to determine areas of similarity and personal ways of communicating with each other, he or she has reached an exploratory stage of interpersonal communication. Essentially, the quest here is to determine whether or not sufficient basic values and goals exist to build a common world.

During this period, feminine individuals are more likely to routinely employ touch (such as hugs) to convey support, affection, and comfort while masculine individuals seek to establish a relationship by controlling and determining the environment in which a relationship is to exist. For masculine people, sexual interactions can be an immediate and extremely useful way of engaging in mutual exchanges of personal information and preferences and at least a form of physical intimacy. Insofar as the relationship is developing in ways that please both people, the couple is very likely to realize that they are no longer acquaintances but are, at least, at the early stage of a friendship.

Stage Four: Intensifying Communication or Euphoria

In the intensifying or euphoria stage, individuals begin to realize that they are joining their worlds, finding common and shared experiences that once were part of their individual and separate worlds. In this regard, conceptions of the self and the other begin to change radically. Traditional categories regarding gender, age, race, nationality, and the like are exchanged for conceptions that reflect extremely personal and unique features. In this regard, trust is extremely high, and personal self-disclosures are mutual and frequent. There is ultimately a celebration in what is held in common and differences are ignored and de-emphasized. Self-disclosures, especially regarding perceived similarities, are positively evaluated, and the relationship is perceived by both to be "secure." Both individuals in the relationship engage in a kind of simultaneous "active participation," shift to the use of "we" as a way of talking about their relationship, may make a "commitment to like one another," use nicknames, and "relish finding a friend" in each other (Welch & Rubin, 2002, p. 29). While this stage is aptly identified as a form of "euphoria," nonetheless, differences between feminine and masculine people within the relationship are evident. Feminine people are more likely to look for, seek out, and to emphasize relational intimacy and to believe that this relational intimacy is a more pervasive and primary feature of the relationship than masculine people do (Pearson, Child, Carmon, & Miller, 2009). Specifically, feminine people focus on and emphasize satisfaction, commitment, intimacy, trust, passion, and love more frequently than their masculine counterparts. In contrast, masculine people "decode verbal and nonverbal communication cues differently," focusing more on "socio-sexual constructs" (La France, Henningsen, Oates, & Shaw, 2009). Particularly, masculine individuals tend to rate "flirtatiousness, seductiveness, and promiscuousness" more positively than feminine individuals, and these variables are also used to determine and to measure the degree to which a relationship is viewed as positive. Indeed, in one study, as the perceived degree of socio-sexual interactions increased, the relationship itself was more positively valued by masculine individuals (p. 277).

Stage Five: Revising Communication

Identified as the "integrating" stage by Welch and Rubin (2002, p. 29), this is a transitional period in which a couple moves from their recognition of their relationship as an immediate and ongoing "pair" or "couple" to a couple with an extended future in which revised rules and roles become appropriate and necessary. In this stage of the relationship, each person recognizes the flaws in the other and seeks to provide ways to make changes to eliminate those flaws. On a broader level, the partners also reach agreement on the roles that each will play. Welch and Rubin have specifically argued that this is a time when a couple has a sense of "oneness," they recognize that a "fusion of personalities" is occurring, that they are "best friends," and when they make a "private commitment to the relationship."

During this stage, masculine people are very likely to seek out and negotiate a relationship that allows them opportunities—even a formal confirmation, or perhaps a set of rituals—that confirm their status and identity in terms of position and control as well as the right to initiate direct and assertive commands. Shifting from a framework of hierarchies and control, during this stage, feminine individuals are more likely to negotiate for roles that allow them to have periods—if not formal rituals—of equality, opportunities to render and offer support for each other, and occasions to respond to each other in personal, verbal, and supportive ways.

Stage Six: Bonding Communication

Within an evolving interpersonal relationship, bonding involves making a voluntary commitment to an extended future as an intimate pair at either a public or institutionally sanctioned event. This commitment may involve a wedding ceremony or other public ceremony in which the relationship is defined as enduring and is announced to others. Likewise, this public proclamation involves a similar private event or personal commitment.

Within this context, some specific characteristics emerge. First, the solely here-and-now relationship is transformed into and now possesses a future in which subsequent actions are defined by and enacted by two people working together rather than separately. Second, beyond the individuals involved, the relationship itself becomes an "object" or experience that is cast and held to be stable and enduring. Third, the relationship itself is elevated, and it becomes a standard by which each individual defines and evaluates his or her motives, emotions, values, and understandings.

Ideally, bonding creates a shared or equal identity for the individuals in the relationship and for the relationship or partnership itself. For example, in some cases, the female member of the relationship may adopt the surname of the male member, subtly implying that the name of the male will and should endure. Also, in some cases, the bonding may restrict one member to a primary environment (e.g., the "housewife") while allowing the other partner a wider range of options and possibilities (e.g., the "breadwinner"). However, as we note in chapters 4 and 6, there are signs that the income of some wives exceed the income of their husbands (from 7% in 1970 to 22% in 2007) and some wives have more education than their husbands (from 20% in 1970 to 28% in 2008) (Pew Research Center, 2010a).

Stage Seven: Navigating Communication

Typically viewed and expected to be the longest stage in a long-term relationship, navigating typically involves maintaining a standard level of performance as a couple faces problems and deals with these problems through interrelated cycles of involvement and detachment. In this regard, the partners in a relationship will confirm and revitalize the value of their bond and of the individuals within the relationship (e.g., anniversary celebrations, birthday remembrances, sharing of past events in the relationship, the building of future images of the relationship, etc.). Likewise, while navigating new circumstances and the growth and development of each individual within a relationship, the relationship itself will periodically be redefined, as well as the roles of the individuals within the relationship, as circumstances and goals change (e.g., new rules for public and private conduct, new roles for employment changes, etc.). A redefinition usually occurs with a particularly strong emphasis upon recognizing and identifying new changes, negotiating them, and weaving them into the bond's assumptive framework.

In our view, depending on how masculinity and femininity is handled within a relationship for extended periods of time, types of relationships within the navigating stage are likely to have certain outcomes. Indeed, we would posit the following three predictions about different kinds of masculinity-femininity patterns in long-term relationships:[1]

1. **In a long-term interpersonal relationship, when each individual has only a masculine or a feminine role, the relationship produces boredom.** When individuals within a long-term relationship persistently assign the masculine role to one partner and the

feminine role to the other over an extended period of time, individuals will remain in a relationship even though both are literally bored with each other as communication partners. The masculine individual in the relationship will continually initiate topics, provide essential ingredients in communicative interactions, provide transitions from one topic to another, and decide when and how to terminate communication. In this scenario, the feminine individual really does not need to even pay attention to or even substantively contribute to the communicative activities of the masculine partner. Similarly, when the activities of feminine partners are profoundly separated from the ongoing activities of masculine partners after extended periods of time, the masculine partner no longer needs to pay specific attention to the details offered by a feminine partner. For example, during breakfast, a wife is describing in detail her planned household activities for the day but her husband is really not paying attention—he doesn't *have* to pay attention, because nothing he does will influence the nature or direction of his wife's activities. In either role (masculine or feminine), if that role is extended over a period of time, only minimum confirmation or attention is required from the other partner. As Welch and Rubin (2002, p. 30) have argued, such relationships can be marked by silence, less talk, an increasing list of "touchy topics, and a growing set of ground rules for permissible topics." In all, ultimately, not talking at all becomes an increasingly viable option when dealing with the other partner.

2. **In a long-term interpersonal relationship, when both individuals seek to maintain the dominant masculine role, the predicted outcome is constant struggle and conflict, which leads to separation or divorce.** The dominant masculine role easily comes into conflict with another individual employing the strategies of a dominant masculine role. When both individuals seek to express themselves (as dominant and masculine individuals do), each seeks to control the topic of the conversation, how the conversation is to evolve, when the topic should be changed and what transitions are used for these changes, and when and how the conversation will end. In other words, the long-term effects of two masculine individuals struggling for dominance cause separation. No one has the stomach for an unending fight!

3. **In a long-term interpersonal relationship, when both individuals continually alternate between masculine and feminine roles depending upon their expertise, prior experiences, and understandings, the relationship becomes patterned but also intriguing, exciting, and simply enjoyable.** In these relationships, if the

wife possesses more relevant expertise, prior experiences, and understandings of a particular situation, she should appropriately function in the masculine and more dominant role, initiating and suggesting apt approaches to a situation. In such cases, the husband should appropriately opt for a more feminine, supporting, tentative, and conversational personal style. In circumstances where the husband possesses more relevant expertise, prior experiences, and understandings, he should necessarily assume the masculine role while the wife adopts a more feminine role. Of course, part of such a relationship involves discovering which partner possesses the knowledge necessary to fulfill the dominant role, which requires further exploration of each other. Likewise, as a couple invokes and engages in these various roles in different circumstances, the interaction itself is more intriguing, because precise outcomes are less predictable. In this regard, couples in such relationships will often laugh more, enjoy the modest shifts and turns that occur within their relationships, and generally become more open and involved in how each interaction emerges, develops, and concludes. The couple that alternates between masculine and feminine roles ultimately has a more enduring, intriguing, and satisfying relationship.

Stage Eight: Differentiating Communication

Not all relationships remain in the navigating stage—some relationships end; indeed, as a norm, most relationships ultimately come to an end. The process of disengaging or uncoupling from others can be many things: a breath of fresh air, a profound conflict, a simple shift to another framework of reference with little thought or meaning given to the relationship that is ending, or a way of growing and developing as an individual. We consistently hope that this last option dominates most relationships.

Regardless of how the differentiating stage evolves, the separating process has two characteristics. First, at least one individual in the relationship begins to assert his or her individuality over and above the paired-identity. This process may be triggered because the person no longer believes that the relationship is adapting sufficiently to her or his needs, it no longer promotes equity, or it is simply no longer acceptable. Second, the differentiating communication ultimately serves to challenge the paired-identity, highlight differences in partners, and call attention to individuals' activities extrinsic to the bond.

The sources of differentiating communication can also, in part, be traced to some differences in role perceptions. For example, there does seem to be some differences in what men and women perceive as sex and sexual commitment. Table 2.4 provides a foundation for identifying and measuring such differences (Granell, 2009). Likewise, reasons exist

Table 2.4   What Men and Women Call Sex

Behavior Identified as Sex	Men Viewing the Behavior as Sex	Women Viewing the Behavior as Sex
I kissed another person deeply.	12%	5%
My partner kissed another person deeply.	24%	13%
I had oral contact with someone's breasts/nipples.	14%	5%
My partner had oral contact with someone's breasts/nipples.	33%	20%
I fondled someone's genitals.	19%	13%
My partner fondled someone's genitals.	46%	28%
I had oral contact with someone's genitals.	41%	36%
My partner had oral contact with someone's genitals.	65%	62%

From: Granell (2009).

for believing that women are more likely than men to find that attachment and relational satisfaction are created and conveyed by the use of emotional communication (Guerrero, Farinelli, & McEwan, 2009).

During this period, the individual initiating the separation is more likely than not to display more masculine rather than feminine personality traits (Jordan-Jackson, Lin, Rancer, & Infante, 2008, esp. p. 253). The discourse is ultimately self-serving, designed to terminate a bonding, and ultimately seeks to give status and control back to the initiating individual through a direct and assertive style. Even the most effective of feminine styles is probably unable to counter the strategies that the masculine framework invokes at this stage in the relationship.

Stage Nine: Disintegrating Communication

During the disintegrating stage, fewer and fewer references and comments are made related to the original commitments and unifying symbols associated with the paired-identity. The partners themselves experience a decrease in total communication, for communication itself is one of the markers associated with the paired-identity of their relationship. Indeed, at key points, denials and denigrations of the relationship are made. The scope and depth of the relationship is markedly rejected. Prior commitments about when and how to communicate are ignored, and prior agreements about what topics should be avoided are no longer recognized. And, finally, the rituals associated with the relationship are avoided, if not explicitly rejected.

Stage Ten: Stagnating Communication

When a relationship enters the stagnation phase, interactions between the previously partnered individuals simply becomes awkward. At a minimum, there is a standstill in the relationship, during which individuals wait for the moment when they can formally exit the relationship. The individuals are "marking time," "rigid," and both recognize that there is really "no need to say something" because "it won't be pleasant" and both individuals "know it" (Welch & Rubin, 2002, p. 30). Accordingly, by avoiding each other as much as possible, the former partners reduce the amount of total communication they engage in, limit their communication both in terms of its breadth and depth when it does occur, engage in superficialities, formalities, and logistic and task-oriented conversations. In this case, neither the masculine nor feminine approach is likely to be a desired or appropriate communication style.

Stage Eleven: Terminating Communication

Terminating communication can involve a host of more formal rituals, including divorce proceedings, separations of property, dealing with custody of children and pets, and generally reaching agreements on closure of the relationship. Some of these negotiations may involve the use of a confederate, such as a lawyer or a family member both former partners find "neutral" and trustworthy. In all, this stage increases the physical distance between two individuals and redefines each person as an individual with friends, enemies, and professional colleagues. For some, a more masculine role offers the greatest "protection" against personal attacks and personal sorrow. For others, a more feminine role provides a sense of a positive and inviting future.

Stage Twelve: Individuals

When a relationship ends, people ultimately become individuals again. But, it is not the kind of individuality they possessed when they first entered the relationship. Having passed through all eleven of the prior stages involved in the process, every individual has also gone through some profound and intense personal transformations. Each individual has to redefine and reestablish his or her own goals, ideals, values, attitudes, and senses of the self, others, and even what relationships themselves now mean to him or her. Likewise, the immediately dissolved relationship is compared to and contrasted with past relationships—differences or consistencies in patterns can be identified. In all, every individual passing through these stages becomes a new person, possessing a new identity and a new sense of the self. Most ultimately assess such relationships in a way that allows them to consider future relationships and partnerships of various kinds. We do know that masculine individuals, with consistent patterns of independence and self-determination, find this separation process more awkward, difficult, and personally disabling than feminine people, who seek out support and assistance from others.

Conclusion

In this chapter, we have considered how men and women employ various verbal and nonverbal communication strategies in ways that people define as masculine and feminine. Because we know that some women can be very masculine as necessary, and that some men are able to employ feminine strategies when they are needed, we have gradually and consciously shifted from an equation where men = masculine and women = feminine. We have found it just easier to talk about *masculine individuals* and *feminine individuals*, with the issue of gender less and less relevant to the broader question of how the sexual styles of masculine and feminine function as communication strategies. As we examine how individuals invoke and employ masculine and feminine strategies as they pass through the various stages of the interpersonal communication process, we are increasingly convinced that masculinity and femininity should each be viewed as a communication strategy, each with limitations and possibilities. However, we have concluded that an individual is likely to function as a more effective communicator if all of the strategies associated with masculinity and all of the strategies associated with femininity are appraised as needed, thereby any one of which could be employed for its potential effectiveness regardless of whether or not one is a male or a female.

Note

[1] Our analysis at this point is based upon the analysis of "rigid complementary," "escalating systematical," and "mixed" relationships provided by Watzlawick, Beavin, and Jackson (1967).

SUGGESTED ACTIVITIES

1. **The Universality of the Functions of Verbal and Nonverbal Communication**

   The functions of verbal and nonverbal communication vary from one culture to another, and even from one subculture to another subculture, within a larger cultural system. Examine the functions of verbal and nonverbal communication specified in table 2.1. Think about the special cultural, social, and even religious groups in which you participate. Do verbal and nonverbal communication function differently within each group? Do they result in different outcomes as you move from one subculture to another? For example, is body language used to convey information and real ideas within African American churches? Do women use nonverbal language differently than men in terms of courting behaviors? Are there different nonverbal ceremonies (e.g., wedding and football games) that convey special and different meanings for women and men?

2. **Practical Uses of the Forms of Verbal and Nonverbal Communication**

   Table 2.2 identifies ten forms or channels of verbal and nonverbal communication that each conveys unique and specific information to others. During an interaction with another person, it is virtually impossible to track and monitor the information and meanings conveyed at any given time. Monitor yourself as a communicator in your next five interactions. Which of these ten modes or channels do you most frequently use? Why do you use (and probably trust) some of these modes or channels of communication more than others? In terms of your own training or socialization, what institutions—such as your family, culture, or education system—have conditioned you to use one mode or channel of communication? Now that you are aware of which forms of verbal and nonverbal communication you use and are familiar with, experiment and try using different modes of verbal and nonverbal communication in your next five interactions. Describe your experiences in class or in small groups.

3. **Develop an Emotional Profile for Each of the Twelve Interpersonal Communication Stages**

   The class should be divided into twelve groups. Assign one of the twelve stages to each group. The members of each group should brainstorm and attempt to identify the range of emotional responses possible for their stage. For example, with "Stage One: Individuals," the group could suggest that such a form of individuality can create a sense of independence in some situations, but it might also create a sense of loneliness and depression in others. When the teams have completed their analyses, each team should report its findings to the class. Reactions and questions for each team can extend the emotional understandings of each stage.

3

Mediated Communication and Gender Roles

*M*edia systems surround us virtually all of our lives. Sometimes we focus directly upon those messages conveyed by the media. Sometimes the media constitute the background in which we exist. And, for some five years now, we have even known that almost one-third of us interact with two or more media systems at a time (Center for Media Design, 2005, p. 17). Indeed, media constitute one dimension of our reality. Our communication is frequently, if not predominantly, transmitted through media systems that affect and alter how we perceive, comprehend, and understand the message. Especially since the advent of television in the 1930s, we are slowly learning that far too frequently these media systems can even determine what we know and how we know it.

In this chapter, we want to explore the ways in which the media—particularly electronic media systems—constitute a context for masculine and feminine images. But, far more significantly, we want to suggest that these systems are ultimately the mechanism that can mediate and regulate the symbols that shape, define, and even regulate masculine and feminine images. In this context, media systems themselves are used as our organizing scheme for analyzing masculine and feminine images, their frequency, and even the way they influence our thinking about sexuality. Accordingly, this chapter is divided into five parts.

1. We examine the scope and significance of media systems in our lives. We specifically highlight the growing dominance of these systems in our lives during the last ten years.

2. We provide an extended example of how the masculine and feminine images conveyed through the media can be examined from a research perspective. We want to demonstrate that the media can, in fact, shape our sense of what sexuality is and should be.

3. We draw some powerful illustrations of the kind of masculine and feminine images that can be identified and extracted from contemporary films and music since the 1970s. These images are conveyed and reflected in famous celebrities such as Sylvester Stallone, Arnold Schwarzenegger, Tom Hanks, and the Jonas Brothers for men, and Madonna, Taylor Swift, and Lady Gaga for women.

4. We examine television as a mediating communication system that has conveyed highly selective images about what are appropriate and inappropriate roles for men and women.

5. We examine the Internet, and especially social networks, as mediating communication systems fostering specific masculine and feminine images.

With all of these objectives in mind, our most appropriate point of departure is simply to argue that media systems themselves now dominate our world.

The Pervasiveness of Media Systems in Our Daily Lives

Media systems surround us, and in the most real sense, they actually constitute our environment for significant portions of our daily lives. These media portray and represent a host of diverse individuals, groups, cultures, and even modes of sexuality.

The dramatic increase in media use has been nothing less than astounding. Consider the results released by the Henry J. Kaiser Family Foundation in their January 2010 report *Generation M²: Media in the Lives of 8- to 18-Year Olds* (Rideout, Foehr, & Roberts, 2010). Based upon a "nationally representative sample of 2,002 3rd–12th grade students, ages 8–18 . . . who were interviewed between October 20, 2008 through May 7, 2009" (p. 2), the authors found that total media use was 7 hours and 38 minutes a day. If multiple media exposures or concurrent media experiences (some 29%) are measured separately, then they found that the average amount of time spent with media increased to 10 hours and 45 minutes a day. Table 3.1 provides a convenient overview of these results as well as specific changes in particular media systems over a ten year period.

Specifically, in 2009 media experiences were predominantly with electronic systems, accounting for 92% of all time spent with media while print accounted for only 38 minutes a day, or 8% of all media experiences. When they compared their current results to the findings they reported in 1999 and 2004, media use by 8- to 18-year-olds had increased. They had anticipated that media use had reached its peak in 2004, for the average media use from 1999 to 2004 increased by only 2 minutes, or less than one-half of 1%. However, when the change in

Table 3.1   Average Amount of Time Spent with Each Medium in a Typical Day by 8- to 18-Year-Olds

Medium	2009	2004	1999
TV Content	4 hrs., 29 min.	3 hrs., 51 min.	3 hrs., 47 min.
Music/Audio	2 hrs., 31 min.	1 hr., 44 min.	1 hr., 48 min.
Computer	1 hr., 29 min.	1 hr., 02 min.	27 min.
Video Games	1 hr., 13 min.	49 min.	26 min.
Print	38 min.	43 min.	43 min.
Movies	25 min.	25 min.	18 min.
Total Media Exposure	10 hrs., 45 min.	8 hrs., 33 min.	7 hrs., 29 min.
Multitasking Proportion	29%	26%	16%
Total Media Use	7 hrs., 38 min.	6 hrs., 21 min.	6 hrs., 19 min.

From: Rideout, Foehr, & Roberts (2010), p. 2.

media use from 2004 to 2009 was quantified, average media use per day from 2004 to 2009 increased by 1 hour and 17 minutes, or 20%. The changes from 2004 to 2009 for the following media systems were particularly dramatic due to significant increases in so short a time period: music and audio (+47 minutes per day), television content (+38 minutes per day), computers (+27 minutes per day), and video games (+24 minutes per day). Movies saw no change, and print saw a decrease by 5 minutes per day.

A particularly vivid—yet representative—example of these media experiences and transformations is provided by Lewin (2010), who sought to identify the meanings behind these data. Francisco Sepulveda, a 14-year-old participant in the Kaiser Family Foundation survey, literally has his cell phone with him 24 hours a day. He even sleeps with his cell phone so that he can receive text messages any time they are sent to him during the night. Francisco reported:

> I use it as my alarm clock, because it has an annoying ringtone that doesn't stop until you turn it off. At night, I can text or watch something on YouTube until I fall asleep. It lets me talk on the phone and watch a video at the same time, or listen to music while I send text messages. (p. A3)

And, as we consider those who are 8- to 18-years-old, especially someone like 14-year-old Francisco, it is also important to note that for those who are younger, there appears to be an *increasing* use and dependence on electronic media. The percentage of children 6- to 11-years-old with cell phones has increased from 11.9% in 2005 to 20% in 2009. Additionally, 36% of children aged 10- and 11–years-old had cell phones in 2009 (Mindlin, 2010, p. B2). Finally, as a special note, we would observe that the shift toward using more and more electronic media is not just a feature of the American culture. For example, Magni and Atsmon (2010) have reported by the end of 2009, the number of Internet users in China had

> touched 384 million—more than the entire population of the United States. That's an increase of around 50% over 2008. More-over, 233 million Chinese—twice as many as in the previous year—accessed the Net on handheld devices, partly because China's cellu-lar providers started offering 3G services widely last year. The Chi-nese are obsessed with the internet. People in the 60 largest cities in China spend around 70% of their leisure time on the internet, according to a survey we conducted in 2009.

We would draw several interim conclusions from these findings:

- These electronic media systems constitute powerful environments for young people.

- These electronic media systems are increasingly defining the attention, perceptions, and cognitive processes that young people encounter and acquire.

- Electronic media have, in fact, created the global village described and predicted in the 1960s (see, e.g., McLuhan, 1964; McLuhan & Fiore, 1968).

- Within the confines of this text, as we consider the growing scope and involvement with electronic media systems, we think it is essential to consider the possibility that young people seek out and appear to prefer mediated rather than face-to-face communication.

Determining and Measuring Media Effects: Minority Masculine and Feminine Images as a Case Study

There are a rich variety of ways in which to conduct media effects research. Yet, it is not intuitive or obvious how we know that media systems are affecting how and why we think about masculinity and femininity in the fashion that we do. In this chapter, we have chosen to present one example that will begin to reveal many of the issues that minorities frequently encounter when discussing masculine and femi-nine stereotypes. The following is a summary of the 2010 study, "Asian Americans Beyond the Model Minority Stereotype: The Nerdy and the Left Out," by Qin Zhang.[1]

Zhang begins her analysis by reporting that Asian Americans repre-sent the fastest growing ethnic group in the United States. Their num-bers are projected to increase 213% from 10.7 million in 2000 to 33.4 million in 2050, constituting 8% of the American population. While Zhang explicitly noted that Asian Americans are "traditionally under-represented in the mainstream media," when they do appear, "they are often misrepresented with stereotypical roles" (p. 20). Emphasizing gender and sexuality roles, Zhang reported that "Asian women are frequently depicted in contradictory stereotypes, either as silent, humble, obedient, exotic, and hypersexualized dolls, or as evil, deceitful, seductive, and ruthless dragon ladies" (p. 20). Asian men, on the other hand, "are often portrayed as culturally ignorant, effeminate, asexual, isolated, and subservient martial artists or cunning villains" (p. 21).

Maintaining that "Most racial-ethnic stereotypes about Asian Americans are constructed, activated, and perpetuated by the media," Zhang sought to determine if "people's perceptions of Asian Americans are consistent with the media's racial-ethnic stereotypes" (p. 21). While noting that stereotypes "can be positive and negative," Zhang additionally maintained that "the media stereotypes about Asian Americans are mostly negative, unfavorable, and unflattering," which would "unavoidably result in harmful effects," especially in terms of the "psychological, emotional, and mental well-being of Asian Americans."

To test her claims, Zhang employed a research design provided by cultivation theory, specifically an assumption that "links media content with the acquisition of stereotypes," suggesting that "repeated exposure to media stereotypes might lead to the acceptance of the stereotype as a social reality" (p. 22). In other words, the heavy consumption of minority stereotypes portrayed by the media "contributes" to the belief that the stereotypes are an ideological and centralized part of the American culture. This type of exposure can activate stereotypes about social groups and ultimately affect their acceptance and development, as well as the perceptions of these stereotypes by others as apt depictions of these social groupings.

Zhang first compiled over 50 studies that identified the various images that American media have constructed of Asian Americans and the resulting conceptions and stereotypes. Examples of these studies include: (1) content analyses of media portrayals of Asian Americans on prime-time TV series aired in fall 2004 on six national networks, (2) links made between racial power and the political representations of images of Asians Americans on TV over five decades, and (3) conceptions on TV in the 1960s of Asian Americans as "hordes of depraved, uncivilized heathens who threatened to undermine the American way of life." From these studies, Zhang extracted four major stereotypes: Asian Americans are viewed as more likely to achieve academic success, they are more likely to be viewed as nerds, they are more likely to be viewed as left out of other racial-ethnic groups, and they are more likely to be viewed as the group that initiates fewer friendships with non-Asian Americans.

To determine at what level American undergraduate students (a sample that included both sexes, a wide array of races and ethnic groups, and diverse student groups) held these stereotypes, Zhang constructed four scenarios for each stereotype (i.e., academically successful, nerds, rejected, and unfriendly). Students were asked to read each scenario and then make a determination from 5 (mostly likely) to 1 (least likely) if the central character was Asian, black, Hispanic, or white. As Zhang anticipated, in every case, Asian Americans were stereotyped in a manner that earlier media presentations had provided. Specifically, "Asians were rated the highest in academic achievement," "the highest in the lack of communication and social skills," "more likely to be left out by peers than other racial-ethnic groups," and "less likely to initiate friendship with non-Asian Americans" (pp. 29–31). Zhang concluded that,

> Most racial-ethnic stereotypes about Asian Americans are constructed and perpetuated by the media. . . . Results demonstrate that people's perceptions and judgments about Asian Americans are aligned with the media representations and these stereotypes affect people's intent to interact with Asians. (pp. 31–32)

Zhang was very careful to note that a larger and more diverse sample would be appropriate; that the study did not "test directly the influence of the media on people's racial-ethnic perceptions" (p. 34); and that the experimental design itself, involving the use of four scenarios, might have been more realistic. Overall, we know that stereotyping is caused by multiple factors, not just media systems. But, we do have reason to at least explore the possibility, perhaps even the probability, that media systems influence how we see other social groupings. Ultimately, the purpose of this study was a "preliminary attempt to empirically test whether people's perceptions of Asian Americans are consistent with media stereotypes," and based on its results, Zhang concludes that "these stereotypes impact people's interaction with Asians" (p. 35).

From our perspective, we wished Zhang had continued to focus on the initial masculine and feminine images of Asian Americans that she had detected in American media. In this context, we would note that the images of the nerd and the asocial have both been identified by Turkle (1984, p. 219) as "antisensuality." In this sense, Zhang's (2010) findings do provide direct evidence for the media's portrayal of Asian American males as somehow less masculine than other racial-ethnic groups. Indeed, studies such as Zhang's provide a foundation for exploring the ways in which media effects studies can be completed. At this juncture, we would only note that a much broader range of media effects can and should also be anticipated and examined. Not only can the effect of media systems on social interactions be examined (as Zhang has suggested), but media systems can also be examined to determine if they are influencing what people believe is real (*reality exploration*), if media systems are providing people with a way to avoid reality (forms of *escapism*), or if they constitute specific masculine and feminine models for others (*character reference*) (for a more extended treatment of uses-gratifications theory, its history, and its major categorical features, see Chesebro, 1987). In the balance of this chapter, we examine the ways in which media systems are influencing all of these processes and outcomes.

Masculine and Feminine Individuals and Images in Films and Music

The American film industry, as well as the American music industry, have provided some explicit and powerful images of masculinity and femininity. As you will notice, many of these images have been persistently reinforced over a 20–30 year period in a series of film sequels. And, these images have often been transmitted to millions of people in larger-than-life sizes in dark theatres where the audience's attention is fixed and focused on only the action and portrayals of masculine and feminine images on the movie screen.

For our purposes, we want to divide our treatment of masculinity from femininity in this discussion. For the last thirty years, we do think that masculinity has predominantly been treated far more traditionally and conservatively in films, while feminine images during this same period have been treated as far more flexible and dynamic. Accordingly, we first focus on masculine images in films and music, then we turn our attention to feminine images in films and music.

The Traditional Masculine Image in Films and Music

For almost 30 years, the most traditional of masculine images have dominated the most successful major box office releases. In a series of films from 1982 through 2009, these exceptionally visual and dramatic images cast men as possessing extreme, if not excessive, physiological energy and a tall, broad shouldered, and muscular physique equivalent to what the world's most developed body builders achieve. In addition, they perform the roles of protector and survivor, enhancing their perceived strength and traditional roles.

The Rambo Image of Masculinity.   The first of these images was conveyed by Sylvester Stallone in his role as John James Rambo, who initially appeared in the 1982 film *First Blood*. Cast as what one critic has called the "icon of machismo," Rambo is a courageous but troubled soldier who specializes in violent rescue and revenge missions. In the moral code of the professional soldier, Stallone does not release his fury of bullets and violence until the enemy draws first blood. Once that act occurs, Rambo's justification for virtually unending violence is cast as warranted. Throughout the 1980s and even again in 2008—in *Rambo: First Blood Part II* (1985), *Rambo III* (1988), and *Rambo* (2008)— Rambo constituted a powerful definition and visual and action-oriented image of what masculinity is. The Rambo movies also provided the stimulus for 65 child-oriented animated episodes of *Rambo and the Forces of Freedom*, which was aired on television from April 14, 1986, through December 1986, as well as the video games *Rambo* (1987–1988) and *Rambo III* (1988–1989) for older children.

Similar to the masculine image that dominates the Rambo series, the Rocky series began in 1976 with the film *Rocky*, and continued through five additional sequels spanning 27 years in *Rocky II* (1979), *Rocky III* (1982), *Rocky IV* (1985), *Rocky V* (1990), and *Rocky Balboa* (2006). Grossing more than $1 billion worldwide, Sylvester Stallone portrays Rocky Balboa, who initially seems to be going nowhere in life, but then makes a bid for boxing's heavyweight champion of the world title. The conception of masculinity highlighted in these films emphasized not only physical strength and the importance of rigorous training, but also personal self-determination against overwhelming odds and circumstances. Physical strength and individuality, rather than dependence on a particular community, dominates the conception of masculinity displayed in the Rocky series.

The Terminator Films.   Mimicking the image of masculinity found in the Rambo series, the Terminator series provides a host of traditional conceptions of masculinity as control and power oriented, with physical strength and determination functioning as the means to achieve social status and prestige. The Terminator series featured Austrian born Arnold Schwarzenegger, who literally entered the entertainment industry through bodybuilding. As Schwarzenegger grew up, bodybuilding movie stars such as Steve Reeves and Johnny Weissmuller dominated the cinema. At the age of 18, he won the Junior Mr. Europe bodybuilding contest, and at the age of 20, he became Mr. Universe in 1967 and then again in 1968. In the 1970s, he won the Mr. Olympia bodybuilding contest seven times. Indeed, at 6 foot 2 inches and 250 pounds, Schwarzenegger is a physically imposing male, and for many (as we noted in chapter 1), massive physical size alone constitutes an important marker of masculinity.

In 1970, Schwarzenegger began an acting career in the film *Hercules in New York*. Three years later, Schwarzenegger played a deaf mute hit man for the mob in the film *The Long Goodbye* (1973). In 1976, he was awarded a Golden Globe for his role in the film *Stay Hungry*, but he drew the most attention for his 1977 bodybuilding film *Pumping Iron*. Indeed, by 1982, Schwarzenegger seemed a natural in the film *Conan the Barbarian*. In 1984, Schwarzenegger appeared in the title role in *The Terminator*. He continued to portray masculinity with a cluster of power, physical strength, control, and determination images in virtually all of his later films, such as *Commando* (1985), *Raw Deal* (1986), *The Running Man* (1987), *Red Heat* (1988), *Predator* (1987),

Total Recall (1990), *Terminator 2: Judgment Day* (1991), and *Terminator 3: Rise of the Machines* (2003). Additionally, the Terminator series also fostered *Terminator Salvation* (2009), the television series *Terminator: The Sarah Connor Chronicles,* and it also gave rise to various story line incarnations for several comic series.

Some Indications of Shifts in the Images of Masculinity.   For some thirty years, an extremely traditional conception of masculinity has been predominantly conveyed in the Rambo, Rocky, and Terminator films. Indeed, we find the consistency of these images amazing. Nevertheless, some alternative conceptions of masculinity did emerge during this same time period. Take the roles of Tom Hanks, for example, whose performances include a gay lawyer with AIDS in *Philadelphia* (1993), as Forrest Gump in the film *Forrest Gump* (1994), Commander James A. Lovell in *Apollo 13* (1995), Captain John H. Miller in *Saving Private Ryan* (1998), Chuck Noland in *Cast Away* (2000), and Sheriff Woody in the animated films *Toy Story* (1996), *Toy Story 2* (1999), and *Toy Story 3* (2010). In this cluster of films, the masculine male can and does serve others and the community, reveals the limitations of the male as an active and controlling agent, suggests that there is humor and enjoyment in simply living with others, and in general suggests that the life of the everyday American male can be viewed and understood as a decent, respectable, and even noble form of masculinity.

The Jonas Brothers.   In a similar vein, we find the image of masculinity portrayed by the American pop/rock boy band the Jonas Brothers to offer alternative conceptions of masculinity. The three brothers— Paul Kevin Jonas II (Kevin), Joseph Adam Jonas (Joe), and Nicholas Jerry Jonas (Nick)—first gained popularity in the 2008 Disney film *Camp Rock*. Coming into public notice by way of Nick Jonas (who began his career as a Broadway child star at the age of seven in 1999), the band began releasing a series of four albums. The band was nominated for the best new artist award at the fifty-first Grammy Awards and won the award for breakthrough artist at the American Music Awards.

The image and music of the band offers a rather dramatic alternative to the traditional conception of masculinity portrayed in the Rambo, Rocky, and Terminator series. Indeed, the submissive—if not pleading—tone of "Please Be Mine" provides an alternative to the domination traditionally associated with masculinity. Indeed, an entire series of singles, such as "Mandy," reflect and reveal that males have dramatic, if not desperate, needs for an interpersonal relationship and love. Finally, the Jonas Brothers' publicly articulated commitment to sexual abstinence until after marriage has conveyed an image of a kind of wholesomeness, if not innocence, that stands in direct contrast to the more traditional commitment to lustfulness that characterizes a traditional conception of masculinity.

Justin Bieber.   Yet, the Jonas Brothers are not alone in suggesting that an alternative conception of masculinity may exist. In our view, the image of Justin Bieber contributes to this alternative conception of masculinity. Sixteen-year-old Justin Bieber emerged in the music world through YouTube. In 2007, when he was 12-years-old and living in Stratford, Ontario, his mother began posting videos of his musical performances on YouTube so that his relatives could see him in action. The YouTube performances became popular, and soon the number of watchers reached the thousands. Bieber continued his use of YouTube, and he personally addressed his fans by name and talked to them as if they were friends. Indeed, Suddath (2010) has argued that:

> He seems at first like nothing more than the latest in a line of manufactured teen idols—the Britneys, Justins, Mileys and Jonases that have dominated teenage hearts for the past decade. But beyond his looks and talent, Bieber is something else entirely: The first real teen idol of the digital age, a star whose fame can be attributed entirely to the Internet. (p. 49)

And, his style seems to captivate. "His album *My World 2.0* debuted at No. 1 on *Billboard* and he sold nearly 850,000 copies in just five weeks" (p. 49).

In terms of our discussion about the changing nature of masculinity, we think Bieber is yet another representative of the type of sexuality fostered and promoted by the Jonas Brothers. Rather than conveying strength and domination, Bieber has a "warm smile," "overgrown hair that he brushes forward into his face," "goes straight for the full embrace" rather than a handshake, and is "so small" in height that you have to "bend down to greet him" (Suddath, 2010, p. 49). His lyrics suggest a departure from the efforts to control associated with traditional modes of masculinity. Bieber's first album featured tender ballads about his parents' divorce and a kind of "desperate puppy love to which anyone who has ever been a teenager can relate" (p. 50). Hence, with total sincerity and commitment, Bieber can sing: "You're my one love, my one heart, my one life for sure." As Suddath (2010) concluded after viewing him in a skit with Tina Fey on *Saturday Night Live*: "He was cute. He was funny" (p. 50). In all, then, in the shadow of the Jonas Brothers, Bieber offers an alternative mode of masculinity from those associated with the Rambo–Terminator films. Certainly, we need to watch and observe how this mode of masculinity evolves. We are certain that this mode of masculinity will evolve, but, we are less certain that it will evolve into the mode of masculinity found in many of the popular films of the late twentieth century.

We certainly recognize that some alternative conceptions of masculinity have appeared in films and music, especially during the last 15 years. At the same time, we conclude that the predominant image of masculinity portrayed in films and music during the last quarter of the twentieth century has celebrated in the most traditional of images about masculinity. In the media discussed here, masculinity has predominantly featured, if not promoted, social control and domination by force, a power orientation, and physical strength and determination as the means to achieve social status and prestige.

The Image of Femininity in Films and Music

In sharp contrast to the rather consistent and enduring image of masculinity that has dominated the most successful films of the last 30 years, images of femininity in films and music during this period have been far more dynamic, exploratory, and particularly unique to the individuals associated with dramatic forms of femininity. We make no pretense, at this point, of providing a "representative and random sample" of the women who have conveyed the diverse images now associated with femininity. We are not convinced that such a "random sample" of these feminine images is conceivable, or even possible. We are convinced, however, that three film and music performers do stand out during the last 25 years and especially during the last 10 years. They are Madonna, Taylor Swift, and Lady Gaga. We deal with each here separately, because each offers—in our view—an extremely unique view of what femininity is and how it should be conveyed.

Madonna.   Born in Bay City, Michigan, as Madonna Louise Ciccone, Madonna moved to New York City in 1977, and she released her first album, *Like a Virgin*, in 1984. In 1985, she appeared in the film *Desperately Seeking Susan*, and shortly thereafter, in 1986, the album *True Blue* was released which, unlike other albums at the time, topped the charts in over 28 countries worldwide. By the end of the 1980s, Madonna had become the second most successful music artist of the decade with three number one albums and seven number one singles, surpassed only by Michael Jackson (Rock and Roll Hall of Fame, 2009).

Initially, among a host of images conveyed by her productions in the 1980s, Madonna received condemnation from religious conservatives. The video of her 1989 single "Like a Prayer" featured several Catholic symbols such as stigmata and burning crosses. Beyond these religious images, her albums, videos, films, and books have included sexually explicit materials. For example, in 1990, Madonna's video of the single "Justify My Love" featured scenes of sadomasochism, bondage, same-sex kissing, and brief nudity. Additional explicit sexual materials were also part of her first documentary film *Truth or Dare* (1991), the album *Erotica* (1992), the publication of the coffee-table book *Sex* (1993), and in the erotic thriller *Body of Evidence* (1993). At the same time, and perhaps paradoxically, playing the role of Eva Perón, Madonna was one of the stars of the film *Evita* in 1996, for which she won the Golden Globe award for best actress in a musical or comedy. Moreover, the sound track album from this film included Madonna's singles "You Must Love Me" and "Don't Cry for Me Argentina."

Since the mid-1990s, Madonna has consistently and continually exerted a powerful influence in the music and film industries in a rich and diverse set of musical productions, films, and Broadway performances. Indeed, the Recording Industry Association of America (1999, 2010) ranked her the best-selling female rock artist of the twentieth century and the second top-selling female artist in the United States with 64 certified albums. Likewise, in 2008, the Guinness World Records listed her as the world's most successful female recording artist of all time.

The diverse choices, roles, and images conveyed by Madonna during the last 35 years perfectly illustrate our point about the ever-changing and dynamic role of femininity in popular film and music media. Indeed, in our view, the most consistent characteristic of Madonna's career has been her ability to change and draw attention to change itself as part of the human condition, human emotions, and human experiences. For example, in one video, Madonna perfectly portrayed the traditional femininity of Marilyn Monroe, only to offer yet another conception of her sexual nature in black lace bustier, black nylons, and black high heels. While a "proper lady" might avoid political and religious issues, she has directly challenged images she has found critically important to her background as an Italian and Roman Catholic. And, she has demonstrated competencies in a variety of media requiring visual, vocal, narrative, political, and aesthetic capabilities. Among a host of traditional issues associated with femininity, Madonna has also contributed a rich array of androgynous and masculine images and an ever-changing and constantly evolving set of images. In this view, then, femininity is not just comprised of roles viewed as proper and ideal for a woman, it is also made up of feminine images that include concepts and actions relevant to an active and ever-evolving human being.

Taylor Swift. Taylor Swift is an American country music artist, singer-songwriter, and actress. In 2006, she released her debut single "Tim McGraw," then her self-titled debut album, which was subsequently certified platinum several times by the Recording Industry Association of America. In November 2008, Swift released her second album, *Fearless,* which finished number three in the top-ranking albums for that year, with sales of 2.1 million. At the 2010 Grammy Awards, Swift won four Grammys, including album of the year. She is the youngest artist to ever win album of the year as well as solo female country singer.

Swift is young (born on December 13, 1989), and for Caramanica (2010), she appears to be "pop's leading naïf," "precocious," whose "innocence is threatened by acclaim." Yet, Caramanica has also concluded: "Ms. Swift is the most important new pop star of the past few years."

In terms of our discussion of femininity, we find Swift particularly intriguing. There is no question that the image of femininity she conveys includes innocence, if not a touch of the precocious. In this sense, Swift represents some of the most traditional attributes that femininity is thought to reflect.

Two features of Swift as a performer and lyricist strike us as particularly critical regarding the image of femininity she conveys. First, she has sought to establish a unique relationship with her audience, dissolving the performer-fan relationship for what can only be viewed as a more interpersonal relationship.

> She has aggressively used online social networks such as MySpace to stay connected with her young audience in a way that, while typical for rock and hip-hop artists, is proving to be revolutionary in country music. As she vigilantly narrates her own story and erases barriers between her and her fans, she is helping country reach a new audience. (Associated Press, 2009)

Second, Swift herself has used her music, the lyrical content of her songs, to portray and to reflect other girls and women her age. She is, in this sense, a political and mobilizing force creating unity of spirit, if not experience, among her audience and herself. "She has placed the concerns of young women at the center of her songs, subject matter generally that has been anathema in the more mature world of country singers" (Associated Press, 2009).

In these ways, we see Taylor Swift as a model of femininity that is far more complicated than an initial impression would suggest. Certainly, she reflects and conveys the innocence, if not the precociousness, of a woman her age. In this sense, she reflects and reinforces traditional conceptions of femininity. However, paradoxically, she also infuses strength and power into the image of women her age. She is a mobilizing symbol of and force for recognizing the legitimacy of young women's experiences, for creating unity where previously only innocence was thought to exist. In this sense, we believe that a political and coalescing sense of unity is created by Taylor Swift, thereby even the most traditional form of feminism can allow younger women to see their experiences as shared, to be recognized as a social part of the cultural system, and ultimately to guide them from a sense of innocence to an understanding of what power feels like and finally to a sense of political identity.

Lady Gaga.   On the front page of its entertainment section, a full-page photograph of Lady Gaga appeared in the January 29, 2010, issue of *The Wall Street Journal*. In an elaborate script across the picture, the title of the article appears: "The Lessons of Lady Gaga" (Jurgensen, 2010, p. W1). The subhead of this article is perhaps far more revealing and explains why Lady Gaga would be given a full-page photograph in *The Wall Street Journal*: "With digital dominance, business savvy, a niche-busting sound and 1,001 wardrobe changes, she is a new model for success." Indeed, in 2010, Lady Gaga was identified by *Time* magazine as one of the 100 most influential people in the world, she was named by *Forbes* magazine as one of the world's 100 most powerful people, and in the first half of 2010, Lady Gaga passed President Obama to become the most popular Facebook personality when measured by the number of her fans and friends. Within the music industry, Jurgensen maintains that Lady Gaga has had a broad "impact on music culture in the space of a year, which has been seismic" (p. W1). Certainly, at the 2010 Grammy Awards, she opened the television show doing a piano duet with Elton John, and she was nominated for five Grammy awards, including record of the year. Her debut album generated four number one songs. She also topped the digital sales chart in 2009 with 15.3 million tracks sold.

Included in all of these attributes of success, she has garnered further

> attention beyond the music world with outfits that make her look like a refugee from a sci-fi film. In concert, on video and at past awards shows she has sported full facial masks, worn planetary rings around her head, and framed her face in what looked like a bird's nest. (Jurgensen, 2010, p. W1)

Despite such "vaudevillian" theatrics,

> Gaga's antics only work because "she can really sing." Gaga may turn out to be yet another fleeting pop novelty, but many other industry veterans see her as the real deal, and her ambitious nature and skill at navigating the turbulent industry may make her a durable star. (p. W1)

Specifically, Lady Gaga released her debut album, *The Fame*, in August 2008. Two of the singles on this album, "Just Dance" and "Poker Face," became international number one hits. The album earned a total of six Grammy Award nominations, and won awards for best electronic/dance album and best dance recording. Her second album, released at the end of 2009, was aptly entitled *The Fame Monster*, and the single "Bad Romance" initially dominated it. Subsequently, because of the accompanying video, "Telephone" then became a defining feature. In all, she has sold over eight million albums and 35 million singles digitally worldwide (Nielsen SoundScan, 2010).

The feminism of Lady Gaga is particularly difficult to isolate and identify with confidence and precision. For some, Lady Gaga is nothing less than a divisive international symbol, "galvanizing radical anti-American sentiment in the Muslim world" and "personifying" the "American Temptress" (Stephens, 2010). For others, Lady Gaga has been judged to have roughly the same celebrity appeal, likability, and market potential as Angelina Jolie and Miley Cyrus (Bialik, 2010). Offering a dramatically alternative view of Lady Gaga within the domain of music, Kakutani (2010, p. AR23) has sought to dismiss her as a mere duplicate: "Lady Gaga is third-generation Madonna." Yet, in a far more significant sense, Madonna and Lady Gaga are discrete products of two profoundly different industries, styles, and types of music. As Jurgensen (2010) pointed out, she has made "shrewd use of new digital platforms," and in this sense, Lady Gaga has changed the traditional notion of femininity, for she conveys, at least in part, a sense of the technological as well as a dimension of business savvy. In addition, while her visual appearance might be viewed as the antics of a "woman gone mad with makeup," it is also possible to perceive her visual image as part of a set of "visual theatrics, fashion, and global appeal" that compels attention and has gained number one hit ratings in at least four different countries. Indeed, part of her contract specifically "goes beyond just selling records to encompass everything from touring, merchandise—even her makeup deal" (Jurgensen, 2010, p. W1). Certainly, she may appear clown-like and be viewed as a throwback to the vaudeville era, or simply viewed as a composite of strange stage theatrics.

Yet, we have another conception of Lady Gaga. We think that femininity can and is undergoing a dramatic transformation in three ways. First, traditional notions of the elegant and distinguished "lady" no longer encompass all of the ways in which feminism can be understood or can function. Lady Gaga is a vivid symbol of the fact that feminism can be associated with the digital world (her singles have had 321.5 million plays on MySpace compared to 133,000 plays for Susan Boyle, who claimed the second best-selling album in 2009). In this sense, Lady Gaga's feminism is part of a world that is digitally divided.

Second, Lady Gaga is a successful business person, functioning in an industry where more and more people believe that all music should be free and downloadable to anyone. Indeed, on the "Lady Gaga Official Web Site," her second album, *The Fame Monster*, can be downloaded for $7.99. Lady Gaga has a comprehensive sense of the music industry as global and digital, requiring a lyrical presentation that includes a set of personal and unique nonverbal displays.

Third, while Lady Gaga seems to conceal the potential image of a "girl next door," she has also emulated the diversity of Madonna, and because she does not "fit" any known mold, her unpredictability allows her to cross genres, cross cultures, and to continually change. She may have been influenced by David Bowie, Freddie Mercury, Madonna, and Michael Jackson, but this group of four cannot be easily transcended into a single personality, nor is there an easy method in which to link these four musicians in a way that would ultimately create an artist such as Lady Gaga.

Indeed, Lady Gaga has been extremely careful to avoid any traditional niche. Her 9 minute and 32 second video of "Telephone" on her second album *The Fame Monster* opens with Lady Gaga—in a bust-revealing, vividly contrasting black and white dress with "geometric," high fashion lines, along with excessive eye makeup—being taken to prison. In prison, she is featured in a series of lesbian, violent, sado-masochistic, and partial nude scenes that culminate in a celebratory dance number with Lady Gaga singing and dancing in an all-American red, white, and blue stars and stripes bikini. Ultimately, Lady Gaga is released from prison and joins Beyonce, who is also featured on this album. On their way out of town, Beyonce deliberately poisons her domineering and hostile boyfriend. Both Lady Gaga and Beyonce are hunted by the police for "mass homicide," and as the video ends, they flee in a monster yellow truck with red flames and the words "Pussy Wagon" in foot high letters on the tailgate of the truck (invoking the Uma Thurman exit scene in Quentin Tarantino's 2003 movie *Kill Bill*).

In all, the conception of femininity conveyed by Lady Gaga is para-doxical. Lady Gaga wears the trappings of a traditionally feminine woman (designer hats and dresses, vivid lipstick and overstated mas-cara, nylons, and heels), but her environments and her actions suggest a defiance, if not aggressive reactions, against traditional norms, and in some ways even against men. In these ways, Lady Gaga avoids any kind of convenient classification. For example, while she can avoid the traditional niche, Lady Gaga has also participated in interviews with Oprah Winfrey and Barbara Walters with grace and ease. At the same time, Lady Gaga has functioned as a spokesperson with Cyndi Lauper for MAC Cosmetics' AIDS awareness and treatment fund campaign called Viva Glam (see Silva, 2010). Fully recognizing the contradictions in our final description of her here (for details regarding her views on these matters, see Strauss' 2010 *Rolling Stone* interview with Lady Gaga), Lady Gaga employs the trappings of traditional femininity while at the same time portraying a woman who is solely unique, a woman who provokes with an unpredictable array of outlandish antics and thereby paradoxically functions as a model for uniqueness.

In sum, as we consider the evolution of masculinity and femininity in the film and music industries from the 1970s up to the present, two major conclusions stand out to us. First, the image of masculinity has remained amazingly static, emphasizing some of the most traditional con-ceptions associated with masculinity. Second, the image of femininity has undergone dramatic alterations. The most significant of these changes is that femininity appears to be open to continual change and evolution. We are not maintaining that all women do, in fact, perceive femininity as an open-ended construct that fosters personal and social change, but we do believe that the film and music industries have provided a host of per-formers who are implicitly, if not unconsciously, exploring the different ways in which femininity can be displayed and performed. However, we cannot help but wonder if, by the year 2050, masculinity will *still* be associated with that which endures and femininity will *still* be associated and viewed as a change element in our sociocultural and political systems.

Gender Roles in the World of Television

Even during the same cultural era, media systems can offer extremely different conceptions about what it means to be a man or a woman. Therefore, it becomes real to say that the conception of masculinity and femininity offered in films and music may differ dramatically from the conceptions offered on television. Certainly, the audiences for these media can differ dramatically, especially in terms of age and a generation's specific experiences and understandings of events that comprise its history. Hence, those raised with the radio as a primary medium of mass communication have lived extremely different lives and understand events from very different experiences than those who have always been connected to the Internet and always had text messaging capabilities for as long as they can remember. In all, different audiences interact with and understand the same media in extremely different ways. These claims were repeatedly, if not conclusively, demonstrated in the late 1970s and mid-1980s (Gumpert & Cathcart, 1979, 1982, 1986). Similarly, as the Millennial generation began to emerge and exert an influence upon our culture, Howe and Strauss (2000) detected a series of media access and media content preferences for this generation that distinguished it from other generations. Perhaps the most unique media experience of this generation is its exposure to and use of interactive and collaborative technologies that produced media systems such as Facebook, MySpace, and Second Life. These "new" technologies have created media encounters that are far more personal and individual than any other previous media system (p. 49).

We want to focus here on the ways in which television has treated gender as a social concept. As we trace these historical developments within the world of television, we simultaneously reveal how the American culture has changed and how television has sought to reflect the American culture. While it is not always clear if the results were intentional or not, the historical perspective also reveals how television has functioned as a persuasive device that has shaped the nature and direction of gender role transformations (see, e.g., Dow & Wood, 2006, esp. pp. 263–369; Eveland, 2002, esp. p. 718). We begin our exploration here by examining the portrayals of gender roles in the mid-1970s during prime-time broadcast television series.

Gender Roles in Television in the 1970s

In the mid-1970s, males predominantly constituted the central characters portrayed in prime-time television. During the 1974–1975 season (Chesebro, 1979), for example, some central characters were portrayed by women in television series such as *The Mary Tyler Moore*

Show, *Rhoda*, *That's My Mama*, *Police Woman*, *Maude*, and *Get Christie Love*. At the same time, males were overwhelmingly the central characters in most television series, such as *The Bob Newhart Show*, *The Odd Couple*, *Chico and the Man*, *Lucas Tanner*, *The Rockford Files*, *Barnaby Jones*, *Kung Fu*, *Kojak*, *Medical Center*, *Marcus Welby, M.D.*, *Mannix*, *Gunsmoke*, *Cannon*, *Hawaii Five-O*, *Harry O*, *Ironside*, and the *Six Million Dollar Man*. Moreover, while women were undoubtedly beginning to be portrayed as central characters who could function as leaders, if a comparison is made for this type of role for the 1974–1975 season, males outnumbered women by a ratio of 4 to 1. In terms of television series that portrayed romantic heroes, of the ten that were broadcast during the 1974–1975 season none of the roles were portrayed by women. Certainly, some of the conceptions of males were less than flattering during this period, such as Archie Bunker in *All in the Family* and Fred Sanford in *Sanford and Son*. However, ironically, even these images of men repeatedly placed the male in the leadership and power position. At the same time, we are also convinced that these ironic conceptions of male leadership were clearly overpowered by the role of men in leader, romantic, and even mythical roles in series such as *Mannix*, *Gunsmoke*, *Cannon*, *Streets of San Francisco*, *Barnaby Jones*, *Kung Fu*, *Kojak*, *Marcus Welby, M.D.*, *Hawaii Five-O*, *Ironside*, and *Six Million Dollar Man*.

When the 1974–1975 television season is compared to the 1977–1978 television season, men continue to be portrayed as the controlling and dominant force resolving social conflicts. Indeed, during the 1977–1978 television season, males were cast as the central character 61% of the time, women were portrayed in such roles only 20% of the time, and men and women were both portrayed as central characters in 20% of television series (Chesebro, 1979, p. 47).

> As the data show, the typical central character of current television series is an urban white male professional. Consequently, the typical central television character does not reflect the American culture as it is. In particular, when the decision is made to feature a male or a female as the central character of a television series, males are selected three times more frequently than females. In this sense, popular television series may be considered de facto sexist. (p. 46)

In sum, for women in the 1970s, on television the issue was one of recognition, the recognition that women can exist and function in leadership, romantic, and even mythical roles. At the same time, men were literally overrepresented in human relationships and dramas portrayed on television and they were also disproportionally likely to be cast as urban, white, and professional. For television viewers in the 1970s, urban, white, professional males were ultimately cast as the controlling and determining forces determining the processes and outcomes in life.

Gender Roles Portrayed on Prime-Time Television Series in the Mid-1980s and Early 1990s

By the mid-1980s, television series increasingly began to portray women as central characters in leader, romantic, and mythical roles. Certainly "everyday" conceptions of women were provided in series such as *Alice* and *Kate & Allie*, but even these characters encountered real-life issues that "make a difference" in the lives of others. However, the transformation is far more evident in other series such as *Cagney & Lacey*, *Scarecrow and Mrs. King*, *Jessie*, and *Murder, She Wrote*.

At the same time, when a television series was dominated by a single central character, especially when the central character was cast as a romantic hero, the ratio of men to women is overwhelming. We find the romantic television series to be critical at this point. Admittedly, romantic tales may lack realism, but during this period the central character was portrayed as possessing "prodigious courage and endurance," as being able to "account for more environmental variables in more incisive ways than others, and able to create more effective programs for acting on those environmental factors" (Chesebro, 1986, p. 492). Within this context, in the 1984–1985 season, males were 15 times more likely than women to be cast as romantic heroes (p. 498), a ratio that even continued into the early 1990s (Chesebro, 1991, p. 209).

In all, while women were making major strides as central characters, especially as partners with males, in certain types or kinds of television series, especially those featuring extraordinary abilities, women were simply not cast in relevant and meaningful roles on television prime-time series throughout the mid-1980s and into the early 1990s. Bluntly put, television viewers in the mid-1980s simply did not have an opportunity to visualize or to consider the ways in which feminism might be considered in dramatic and power positions.

Gender Roles at the Inception of the Twenty-First Century

By the end of the 1990s, the roles of men and women in prime-time television series reached a state of equality in terms of representation in virtually every type or kind of drama, especially in portrayals where men and women functioned as partners. Certainly, during the 1998–1999 prime-time television season (Chesebro, 2003), men were vividly featured as central characters in some outstanding television programs such as *Frasier*, *Cosby*, *The King of Queens*, *Everybody Loves Raymond*, and *Walker, Texas Ranger*. At the same time, women were featured in an equal number of dramatic television programs of all types and kinds including *Suddenly Susan*, *Caroline in the City*, *Veronica's Closet*, *The Nanny*, *Touched by an Angel*, and *Sabrina, the Teenage Witch*.

Perhaps far more significantly, ensembles and pairings of males and females began to dominate the way in which central characters were structured. Such series included *Third Rock from the Sun*, *Dharma and Greg*, and, perhaps most vividly, *Friends*.

However, these generalizations must necessarily be qualified. Lauzen, Dozier, and Horan (2008) examined the specific roles male and female characters played in 124 prime-time television programs aired on six broadcast networks during the 2005–2006 season. In their analysis, women were persistently cast in interpersonal roles involving romance, family, and friends. In contrast, male characters were more likely to enact work-related roles. In this regard, Lauzen, Dozier, and Horan also examined why such gender characterizations might occur. One consideration was the gender of program writers. They found that "programs employing one or more women writers or creators are more likely to feature both female and male characters in interpersonal roles whereas programs employing all-male writers and creators are more likely to feature both female and male characters in work roles" (p. 200).

In terms of gender roles, we would like to conclude that at the beginning of the twenty-first century television began to portray gender roles as a function of diverse interactions and the unique personalities of their participants. Unfortunately, we do not think we can render such a conclusion at this time, as some extremely traditional conceptions of masculinity and femininity still exist. In an ideal world, individual contributions might reflect a blending of the best of both masculine and feminine roles (see, e.g., Lindgren & Lelievre, 2009, esp. p. 409). While prime-time television may now equally represent males and females in a rich diversity of dramatic settings, the roles in which males and females are cast remain profoundly discrete and traditional. For example, males are cast in the traditional breadwinner role, while women are cast in "motherly" roles in which they provide interpersonal comfort, support, and engagement.

Moreover, as we have suggested throughout this volume, especially on television, questions of gender continually interact with related questions of racism, homophobia, and classism (see, e.g., Press, 1991). In this regard, television viewers' conceptions of males and females are affected by racial attitudes. For example, Ramasubramanian (2010) has concluded that, "Specifically, in White viewers' minds, the typical African-Americans and Latino-Americans on television are mainly associated with two prominent themes—criminality and laziness" (p. 115). In a related fashion, Signorielli (2009) concluded that while African Americans' participation in television programs in the mid-2000s "reached a level of parity with their numbers in the U.S. population," they were viewed as segregated and isolated from the white population, fostering "a continued sense that minorities and Whites have little in common." And, perhaps more ironically, although at this time these series also predominantly featured black women, Signorielli reported that at the end of the first decade of the twenty-first century, "prime time network broadcast programs" were "less racially representative of the U.S. population than they were at the beginning of the decade" (p. 323). Similarly, when women's bodies were visually depicted in sexual objectification forms (e.g., high skin exposures), women were described with more negative words (Aubrey, Henson, Hopper, & Smith, 2009). In this regard, even in television programs that appear to feature the struggles of women, such as *Sex & the City*, "television's tendency" is "to credit all feminine appearance and behavior as being feminist" (Southard, 2008, p. 163).

Masculinity and Femininity on the Internet

As a communication system, computer-mediated communication emerged in the mid-1980s. In 1989, Chesebro and Bonsall reported that:

> Computers now pervade the typical American home. Dedicated computers are now embedded in dishwashers, clothes washers and dryers, refrigerators, televisions, radios, freezers, ranges, telephones, heating and cooling systems, stereos, microwaves, security systems, and automobiles. As Broad (1984, March) has so aptly noted, the "biggest change" in the American home has been the "introduction of digital electronics, which made its debut in the late 1970s" (p. C8). Yet, these computers were predominantly "concealed," for the computers built into home appliances can be used by a consumer without his or her conscious recognition that an entire set of computers may be repeatedly employed during an average day. (p. 1)

The introduction of the small desktop computer into the American home and workplace has forced people to respond to the computer as a new technology affecting their everyday lives. Small desktop computers made their most decisive impact on the American home during the first half of the 1980s.

Now that the computer had infiltrated itself into everyday business practices and personal use, Tim Berners-Lees decided to take the next step, which was to give computers and computer users the ability to interact with other computers and computer users throughout the world. Seeking to develop real-time and text-processing communication, Tim Berners-Lees created the first protocols (HTML, HTTP, and URLs) central to the operation of the "World Wide Web" (or www in web page addresses). In short, he created what we now call the Internet.

The Internet captured the imagination of a host of different peoples throughout the world. Indeed, nine years after the Internet came into existence, Chesebro (2000) enthusiastically but aptly proclaimed: "The Internet is the single most pervasive, involving and global communication system ever created by human beings, with a host of untapped and unknown political, economic, and sociocultural implications" (p. 8).

Indeed, by the end of 2009, the number of Internet users throughout the world had reached almost two billion people, or 26.6% of the world population. "The numbers prove what we said one year ago. The economic crisis had no effect on Internet growth. On the contrary, we see growth in all parts of the world during year 2009" (Internet World Stats News, 2009). Table 3.2 provides an overview of this massive international growth of the Internet.

While a wide range of analyses of the Internet are possible,[2] we are particularly interested here in examining how questions of gender have been incorporated into this system. However, given the size and scope of the Internet, even our gender analysis of the Internet must necessarily be incomplete. Accordingly, we will only be examining three issues here. First, we examine the degree to which men and women have adopted the Internet, an analysis that denies the myth that women have ignored and avoid technology. Second, while we focus more generally upon the question of gender and the workplace in chapter six, here—because of the overwhelming growth potential of this industry compared to others (Potter, 2008, pp. 386–388)—we do want to examine the role of women in high technology industries, focusing on the degree to which this industry may be discouraging, if not discriminating against, female participation. Third, we suggest how gender issues are emerging on social network sites such as Facebook and MySpace.

Women and Technology

Traditionally, we are told that when compared to the preferences of boys, girls will avoid mathematics, science, and technology. The implication is that math, science, and technology are somehow not "feminine," but rather fall within the "man's world" (Miller, C. C., 2010, p. BU8).

As we examine the Internet, such a claim is not directly or easily sustained. For example, in its November 30–December 27, 2009 survey, the Pew Internet & American Life Project (2010) found that 74% of men

Table 3.2   Internet Users in 2009 by World Region

Region	Population	Internet Users	Penetration Rate	Percent Users
Asia	3,808,070,503	764,435,900	20.1%	42.4%
Europe	803,850,858	425,773,571	53.3%	23.6%
North America	304,831,831	259,561,000	76.2%	14.4%
Latin/Caribbean	586,662,468	186,922,050	31.9%	10.4%
Africa	991,002,342	86,217,900	8.7%	4.8%
Middle East	202,687,005	58,309,546	28.8%	3.2%
Oceania, Australia	34,700,201	21,110,490	60.8%	1.2%
Total World	6,767,805,208	1,802,330,108	26.6%	100.0%

From: Internet World Stats News (2009).

in the United States use the Internet, and that 74% of women in the United States also use the Internet. Additionally, if we consider the gender breakdown in terms of social network use, some 35% of men have a profile on a social network website and some 35% of women have a profile on a social network website (Lenhart, Purcell, Smith, & Zickuhr, 2010). Gender differences simply do not exist in these measures.

At the same time, in terms of use or function with digital communication technologies, some gender-based differences have been detected, especially among children 10- and 11-years-old. Mediamark Research (in Mindlin, 2010) has reported that more girls have cell phones than boys (21.8% of girls have them compared to 18.3% of boys), but that boys were more likely than girls to perform data-intensive activities with their phones, like downloading games and browsing the web.

It is unclear to us, however, whether data-intensive activities will continue to remain a predominantly male activity. As we suggest in chapter 5, the percentage of women attending college is outpacing male attendance at college, and we fully expect that as college students, a higher percentage of women will shortly find data-intensive activities both essential in terms of their long-term careers goals as well as satisfying and fulfilling. In this context, we are reminded of early research regarding video games and participation where men dramatically outnumbered women as participants in multiplayer online video games, until it was discovered that many women found it useful to adopt male names when playing video games (for a more extensive treatment of such issues, see Williams, Consalvo, Caplan, & Yee, 2009).

In all, as far as we can determine, there is nothing inherently male or masculine about digital technologies. The propensity to use such technologies appears to be solely a function of cultural conditioning. As we track different cultural transformations, especially in the area of technology, we believe that women will find it increasingly necessary as well as satisfying to use digital technologies at school, in their workplace environments, and as a source of entertainment.

Women and the High Tech Industry

While women have persistently functioned as users of digital technologies, it is unclear whether they have yet to exert a powerful influence over the industry that develops and controls the distribution of digital technologies. Given the potential growth and development of this industry, as well as its influence on the U.S. and the global economies, exclusion from this industry would constitute a severe omission. As far as we can determine, such an exclusion has already occurred, but we now see signs that this exclusion will be corrected in the immediate future. Consider the following three factors:

First, a set of findings reported by several research firms suggests that major disparities exist between males and females in venture capital options in the high tech industry. Some of these findings are extremely vivid. We think this list of ten findings (in Miller, C. C., 2010) speaks for itself:

- Women own 40% of the private businesses in the United States, but they create only 8% of the venture-backed tech start-ups.
- Women account for 6% of the chief executives of the top 100 tech companies.
- Women account for 22% of the software engineers at tech companies.
- Women account for 14% of the financiers controlling tech start-ups.
- During the creation of a tech start-up, women use, on average, 40% less capital than men and are increasingly involved in successful initial public offerings of stock.
- Women now outnumber men at elite colleges, law schools, medical schools, and in the overall work force. Yet a stark imbalance of the sexes persists in the high tech world, where change typically happens at breakneck speed.
- Only 18% of college students graduating with computer science degrees in 2008 were women, down from 37% in 1985.
- Of the women holding technical jobs, 56% leave their position midway through their career, which is double the turnover rate for men. Twenty percent of them leave the workforce entirely, and an additional 31% take nontechnical jobs—suggesting that child-rearing isn't necessarily the primary reason women move on.
- The latest web start-ups—for socializing, gaming, and shopping—often attract more women than men as users.
- Some of the latest web start-ups initiated by males seem to misjudge the associations of female consumers. For example, "when Apple unveiled its new mobile computing device, it called it the iPad—a name that made many women wince with visions of feminine hygiene products" (p. BU8).

Second, rather than ignore such findings, some initial actions can be taken. As Poornima Vijayashanker (a female engineer who left a technology company to begin her own business) has argued, "If we want more women to be in tech, then we have to have a set of role models" (cited in Miller, C. C., 2010, p. BU8).

Third, gender-mixed high tech ventures are the most successful. "Studies have found that teams with both women and men are more profitable and innovative. Mixed-gender teams have produced information technology patents that are cited 26 percent to 42 percent more often than the norm" (p. BU8).

We are left with the conclusion that much more needs to be done in terms of creating full participation by women in the high tech industry. We are immediately convinced that gender issues cannot be ignored. Indeed, we are convinced that paying attention to gender issues will be one way in which the American high tech industry can become more successful and innovative in the long run.

Gender and Social Networking Sites

Social networks are now some of the most popular media systems in the world. Just one of these systems, Facebook, has over 470 million unique monthly visitors who spend some 2–3 hours per day on the site. While the site is self-identified as interpersonal ("an online version of the relationships we have in real life"), it is also a profoundly commercial enterprise. Indeed, comScore.com (Lipsman, 2010) reported that Facebook was the top display ad publisher during the first quarter of 2010, and that it had 176 billion display ad impressions, representing 16.2% of the market share, which alone generated over $16 million during the first quarter of 2010. Moreover, with the emergence of its relatively recent free service Facebook Connect, Facebook now provides links to virtually all other social networking sites, leading many users to perceive Facebook as the "central hub of the social networking world" (Wortham, 2010). See table 3.3 for a brief summary of some of these major social networking sites.

While some 75% of all American adults use the Internet, social network sites are predominantly and disproportionately a domain of younger Internet users. Certainly, it is true that some 45% of online American adults age 18 and over use social networking sites, up from 8% in February 2005. At the same time, some 65% of teens (ages 12–17) use online social networks as of February 2008, up from 58% in 2007 and 55% in 2006 (Pew Internet & American Life Project Infographics, 2009b). And, particularly, while "18–24 year olds made up 28% of the social networking population," they made up "only 16% of the Internet using population, a difference of 12%." Likewise, those 25–34 and those 35–44 (compared to their representation on the Internet) were also overrepresented on social network sites by 9% and 1%, respectively. However, those 45–54, 55–65, and 65+ were underrepresented on social networks by −7%, −8%, and −6%, respectively (Pew Internet & American Life Project Infographics, 2009b). In sum, social network sites remain systems that are unusually attractive to younger Internet users. Specifically, in terms of using social networking sites and creating a social networking site profile, younger Internet users are also by far the most extensive users (see table 3.4).

Gender differences do seem to exist in terms of media preferences, especially when the frequency of online and face-to-face interactions are compared. For example, compared to women, men report three to

Table 3.3   Social Networks: Size, Origin, Ownership, and Focus

MySpace

Launch August 2003.

Size[a] 125 million unique monthly visitors ("nearly half of them in the United States") and 45.4 billion page views worldwide, with 214.9 minutes on site per user per month.[b]

Owner News Corporation purchased for $580 million in 2005.

Focus "A place for friends."

Peak In June 2005, it was the "most popular social network site in the United States."

Facebook

Launch February 4, 2004.

Size 462 million unique visitors globally in February 2010,[c] and 252 million unique visitors in the United States[b]; 50.6 billion page views worldwide; and 175.3 minutes on site per user per month.

Owner Founded by Mark Zuckerberg. Microsoft Corporation made a $240 million investment in 2007 (5% of the ownership).

Focus "Build an online version of the relationships we have in real life" and "Giving people the power to share and make the world more open and connected."[c]

Peak In June of 2006, Facebook exceeded MySpace in terms of number of unique visitors per month and pages viewed.[d] Its popularity continues to grow around the world.

Bebo

Launch January 2005 with a "major relaunch" in July 2005.[e]

Size 22 million unique monthly visitors (5 million or 23% are in the United States) and 11 billion page views worldwide, with 91.1 minutes on site per user per month.[f] In February 2010, comScore reported that Bebo had a 45% dip in monthly visitors compared to a year earlier.[g]

Owner Criterion Capital Partners

Focus "Bebo is a popular social networking site which connects you to everyone and everything you care about."

Peak Third largest in the United States, but traditionally recognized for its presence in the United Kingdom and western Europe.

---

[a] These numbers constantly change. These numbers reflect June 2008 com.Score reports. For an interpretation of these com.Score reports, see: David Carr, "Hey, Friend, Do I Know You?" *The New York Times*, July 21, 2008, pp. C1 and C6. Average minutes spent on site, per user, per month statistics are provided by com.Score in: Brad Stone, "At Social Site, Only the Businesslike Need Apply," *The New York Times*, June 18, 2008, pp. C1 and C2. Finally, it should be noted that these worldwide numbers differ dramatically for those in the United States. For example, Brad Stone and Higuel Helft report that "29 million people actively use Facebook in the United States," which constitutes approximately 25% of regular unique monthly visitors; see: "Microsoft Seeks an Ad Friend in Facebook," *The New York Times*, July 25, 2008, p. C5.

[b] Jessica E. Vascellaro, "Facebook CEO in No Rush to 'Friend' Wall Street," *The Wall Street Journal*, March 4, 2010, pp. A1 and A8; and Eric Pfanner, "MySpace to Cut Two-Thirds of Staff Outside U.S.," *The New York Times*, June 24, 2009, p. B7. Also, see: Facebook CEO Mark Zuckerberg quoted in Jessi Hampel, "How Facebook Is Taking Over Our Lives," retrieved February 18, 2009, from http://money.cnn.com.

[c] Randall Stross, "World's Largest Social Network: The Open Web," *The New York Times*, May 16, 2010, p. BU3.

[d] David Carr, "Hey, Friend, Do I Know You?" *The New York Times*, July 21, 2008, pp. C1 and C6. Carr has also reported that the number of subscribers under 35 doubled in 2009 while the number of subscribers between 35 and 54 tripled.

[e] As measured by size, Bebo is the third largest social network in the United States, but it is traditionally perceived as having a "strong presence in the United Kingdom, but a distant rival in the U.S. to heavyweights such as MySpace and Facebook"; see: Mirissa Marr and Emily Steel, "AOL Buys Into Social Networking," *The Wall Street Journal*, March 14, 2008, p. A3.

[f] Erick Schonfeld in "Bebo Embraces the Lifestream," *Social Media Influence*, February 24, 2009, http://socialmediainfluence.com.

[g] Jenna Wortham, "AOL Plans to Sell or Shut Bebo Social Networking Site," *The New York Times*, April 6, 2010, p. B7.

one that the time they spend online cuts back the time they spend with flesh-and-blood friends. According to the Annenberg Center for the Digital Future, men are more likely to be strongly attached to their online connections than women, and "women seem to more value their real-world and off-line relationships" (cited in Mindlin, 2008). In terms of types of media preferred, during the course of a week men are more likely than women to spend their leisure time reading media online, while women spend two more nonwork hours reading ink-and-paper books than men. Overall, men spend two more nonwork hours a week online than women do (Mindlin, 2008).

These preliminary observations provide a context for considering how masculinity and femininity function within social networking sites. While social networking sites are less than 10 years old, a wide range of findings now exist and can shape what we know about gender roles in social networking sites. In order to streamline all of these results, we have found it convenient to summarize these findings under several subheadings. However, we have also tried to be as concise as we can in offering these findings. Most of these findings are "first time studies." They lack confirmation or reliability. We strongly encourage you to examine each finding with a critical eye, asking if

Table. 3.4   Generational Differences on Selective Online Social Networking Site Activities

Online Social Networking Site Activity	Online Teens (12–17)	Gen Y (18–32)	Gen X (33–44)	Younger Baby Boomers (45–54)	Older Baby Boomers (55–63)
Use social networking sites	65%	67%	36%	20%	9%
Create a social networking site profile	55%	60%	29%	16%	9%

From: Pew Internet & American Life Project Infographics (2009a).

your experience in social networking sites and in chat rooms confirm what is reported here. In other words, do you agree with each finding? Why or why not?

Masculinity as Quantification.   In many respects, masculinity has traditionally emphasized sheer quantification as an esteemed feature of masculinity. For example, "the larger the penis, the better" is a phrase that typifies traditional conceptions of masculinity. Likewise, traditionally a man is more masculine if he is taller, stronger, or simply has developed more muscles than other men. In all of these ways, masculinity is measured merely by size or volume. Geidner, Flook, and Bell (2007) used this perspective as a way of measuring masculinity on social networking sites. They reasoned that a man was more likely to perceive himself as masculine if he had a large number of friends, and/or that males with more friends would also use more traditional masculine attributes to describe themselves. In other words, they reasoned that a correlation existed between the use of traditional masculine attributes and the number of friends a male had. Needless to say, the correlation might work either way: (1) people are more attracted to men who employ traditional masculine attributes in their profiles, which results in a larger number of people declaring themselves to be friends of males adopting traditional masculine attributes or (2) as males become more popular, they are more likely to enhance their self-conception by employing traditional masculine attributes. To test their hypothesis, they compared the descriptions of men with 150 or more friends on Facebook to the description of males on Facebook with less than 50 friends. Each description was examined to determine if it contained one or more of Chafetz's (1978) seven traditional attributes of masculinity (e.g., physical strength, functional provider/moneymaker, sexually experienced and active, emotionally stoic, impressive intellectually, successful and aggressive in interpersonal relationships, or a combination of these characteristics). While profiles were randomly ordered and examined separately by three different evaluators, nonetheless, Geidner, Flook, and Bell (2007) found that:

> a strong correlation exists between the number of friends on Facebook and perceived masculinity on display in Facebook profiles. The five profiles that listed the highest number of Facebook friends, ranging from 171 to 631 friends, were also the profiles which registered the highest average masculinity score. All of the profiles whose members had less than 50 friends displayed the less traditional masculine traits. This confirms the hypothesis addressed earlier. We found that men with more than 150 Facebook friends tailor their profile to highlight traits that are perceived to be masculine, while men with less than 50 Facebook friends have profiles that are perceived as less masculine. (p. 11)

Racial Preferences and Gender. As we have suggested repeatedly throughout this volume, gender roles are also influenced by and shaped by other social factors such as race, religion, sexual orientation, and social class. In the journal *Social Science Research*, Feliciano, Robnett, and Komaie (2009) sought to determine if a consistent pattern of racial exclusions existed when users stated a racial preference in their dating website profiles. The results of this examination are provided in table 3.5.

As the results obtained by Feliciano and her colleagues suggest, a very strong and significant correlation existed between white females and white males for same-race dates. The powerful question remains: Should racial preferences be perceived as a racial preference, racial bias, cultural bias, or as a form of racial segregation and racism? In our view, racial issues are very likely to emerge whenever questions regarding masculinity and femininity exist.

Table 3.5   Racial Preferences for Dates by White Women and White Men[a]

Racial Preference	White Women[b]	White Men[c]
White Only	64.3%	28.9%
Exclude East Indians	96.2%	93.8%
Exclude Middle Easterners	94.7%	82.2%
Exclude Asians	93.4%	78.6%
Exclude Blacks	90.5%	71.3%
Exclude Native Americans	86.7%	53.3%
Exclude Latinos	76.5%	48.2%
Exclude Whites[d]	4.0%	6.8%

[a] Profiles were randomly selected from people between the ages of 18–50 who self-identified as black, white, Latino, or Asian living within 50 miles of four major cities (New York, Los Angeles, Chicago, and Atlanta). These cities "allow for regional diversity . . . and include cities thought to be the most diverse and tolerant . . . as well as . . . more conservative" (p. 46). Feliciano and her colleagues (2009) additionally noted: (1) "Since we view racial preferences as inputs into eventual marriage outcomes, we also limited the sample to those who were only seeking heterosexual dates" and (2) "We randomly selected 200 profiles for each race/gender combination in each city, for a total sample size of 6,070. This paper is concerned with the dominant group's acceptance of minorities, so we focus exclusively on the sample of white respondents in all four regions (N = 1,558)."

[b] Of the women surveyed, 717 (or 72.6%) stated a racial preference. Out of this number, 519 further specified their preferences. The resulting percentages are given here.

[c] Of the men surveyed, 776 (or 58.7%) stated a racial preference. Out of this number, 459 further specified their preferences. The resulting percentages are given here.

[d] It should be noted that this study does not compare and contrast face-to-face dating racial exclusions to online dating racial exclusions. Indeed, in commenting on this study, Jenee Desmond-Harris (2010) noted: "Racial preferences—or, as some call them, biases—are easier to observe on these sites than in offline settings. Behind computer screens and cutely coded user names, people clearly communicate things about race that few would ever say aloud in a bar" (p. 100).

From: Feliciano, Robnett, & Komaie (2009), pp. 39–54.

Infidelity and Deception. While sexual and emotional acts of betrayal are significant, the most severe acts of infidelity online concern false statements on the Internet about how involved or important the relationship is as well as the goals for the relationship (Docan-Morgan & Docan, 2007). Gender differences do exist here, as (1) women view infidelity as more important than men and (2) women and men are frequently "not on the same page when it comes to infidelity."

In this context, George and Robb (2008) have maintained that "deception is common in everyday communication, accounting for 22% to 25% of social interactions." They concluded that while "there are differences in media use for everyday communication, the differences in lying behavior across media seem to be diminishing" (p. 102). Toma and Hancock (2010) suggest that it is the medium itself—the online environment—that provides a unique opportunity for such deception compared to face-to-face communication. They specifically argue that "communication contexts" can

> influence deception by providing or restricting access to certain social cues, facilitating or inhibiting immediacy, or altering conversational demands. In online dating environments, self-presentations are static (i.e., the equivalent of a monologue rather than a dialogue) and rely solely on visual and linguistic cues (Walther, 2007). These affordances alter the nature of deception primarily by enabling less attractive daters to be deceptive about their physical appearance in ways that would not have been possible in face-to-face meetings. (p. 346)

For example, Toma and Hancock (2010) note that face-to-face daters have only a limited range of options for enhancing their physical appearance (such as wearing flattering clothes and using makeup), whereas online daters have "many options for constructing more attractive personae" including selecting flattering photographs, retouching photographs, or simply stating verbally that they're more attractive than they really are. As a result, other researchers—such as Ramirez and Zhang (2007)—have underscored the importance of using more than one medium of communication ("modality switching") early in a romantic relationship.

Verbal and Nonverbal Intimacy. When same- and opposite-sex relationships are compared, opposite-gender support and self-disclosure "far outweigh same-sex verbal intimacy." Likewise, nonverbal measures of intimacy in opposite-sex gender relationships also "far outweighed those in same-sex interactions." These findings were derived in face-to-face real world environments. However, Ferris and Roper (2002) have found that in virtual realties, "a substantial number of intimacies were initiated by female characters," perhaps because "female characters may feel more comfortable engaging in intimacies as potential dangers are minimized." As Ferris and Roper have concluded, "Some aspects of gendered relationships may be mitigated and democratized in some virtual environments" (p. 53).

Standards Used to Select a Partner.   In his analysis, Rabby (2007) maintained that men will ask out more women using a minimum definition of attractiveness, while women focus on fewer prospects, paying more attention to a partner's education, profession, and income (Lee, 2006). Women will dismiss height as important if income is sufficient (i.e., $146,000 a year or more) (Hitsch, Hortacsu, & Ariely, 2004). At the same time, "indiscriminate" or "desperate" behavior is negatively valued by both sexes.

Relatively Low Selection Rate.   The Pew Research Center (2006) concluded that, "Most young singles in America do not describe themselves as actively looking for romance partners." Parks and Roberts (1998) found that only 26.3% of Internet relationships were "romantic in nature." In this context, Wildermuth and Vogl-Bauer (2007) reported that people—both males and females—actually go out with less than 1% of the profiles they study online.

Sexual Aggressiveness.   In chat rooms, women will initiate as many contact behaviors as men. These behaviors are far higher in number than the initiating behaviors observed in face-to-face gender interactions. As Ramirez and Zhang (2007) have concluded, "Women are more interpersonally aggressive online than in face-to-face interactions."

Differences between Those on Social Networks and Those in Face-to-Face Relationships.   Heavy online users initiate more and longer social contacts with others than infrequent online users. Those more consistently on social networks initiate more social contacts with others than those predominantly in face-to-face relationships and are also more likely to help others with tasks. However, the number of hours spent with family drops significantly for every 30 minutes spent online. In this regard, especially for adolescents, online activities isolate users from face-to-face contacts (Rainie, Horrigan, Wellman, & Boase, 2006).

Impression Management Remains a Central Objective in Internet Chat Rooms.   Based on a survey of 382 undergraduate students enrolled at a medium-sized university in the Midwest, as well as open-ended interviews with 10 of these students, "participants expressed three motivations for impression management in their chat room interactions: the desire for social acceptance, the desire to develop and maintain relationships, and the desire to experiment with identities" (Becker & Stamp, 2005, p. 247). However, the medium of the Internet chat room is a "lean medium" and can be a "barrier to impression management."

While an Internet chat room does allow a participant increased control over how a message is encoded, it also reduces the transmission of social cues, especially nonverbal and sociological information (p. 248).

Modality Switching.   In general, relationships are healthier and endure longer if a variety of media are employed during the early stages of a relationship. Ramirez and Zhang (2007) have found that relationships that are initiated and then maintained online for longer periods of time yield greater intimacy and social attraction than other conditions in which face-to-face contact occurred. The most successful relationships were those in which people employed modality switching (e.g., text only to face-to-face) early in the relationship, but not later. In all, people in a relationship achieve greater intimacy and social attraction if they maintain communication through a rich diversity of contact systems such as social networking, the telephone, instant messaging, and face-to-face communication.

Romance on the Internet.   Parks and Roberts (1998) have argued that some 26.3% of online relationships were romantic. These relationships involved: (1) intense emotional arousal; (2) high levels of caution; (3) strong linguistic connections; (4) a high number of extramarital affairs; and (5) a lack of social support from offline family and friends.

Strongest Predictor of Romantic Success.   While Anderson and Emmers-Sommer (2006) found that similarity—rather than immediacy, receptivity, formality-informality, equality, dominance-subordinate, and common tasks—was the "only relational communication antecedent to be associated with positive interpersonal relationship outcomes," they also concluded that "Intimacy, trust, and communication satisfaction were found to be the strongest predictors of relationship satisfaction for individuals involved in online romances."

Anticipated Future Reduces Uncertainly in a Relationship.   As found by Anderson and Emmers-Sommer (2006), "A very strong, positive correlation emerged between anticipation of future interaction and levels of uncertainty reduction in the relationship." Therefore, the likelihood of future interactions is predicated upon the reduction of uncertainty more than the channel selected for communication. In short, the type of medium used for communication does not seem as important as the parties in the relationship reducing uncertainty by being as clear as possible about their intentions regarding the future of the relationship. Additionally, and perhaps making online communication more responsible and exciting, "in an online environment, the focus of communication is geared toward the exclusive use of interactive strategies" rather than passive and active strategies (see Anderson & Emmers-Sommer, 2006).

The Internet Will Become More Important in Communication. "As the Internet continues to become more commonplace and technologies continue to become simpler, it is likely that individuals will utilize even greater numbers of different Internet-based communication media in the future" (Pauley & Emmers-Sommer, 2007, p. 424).

Friends' Comments Are More Trustworthy Than Self Comments on Facebook Profiles. In terms of the perceived credibility of self profiles, viewers rely more heavily on information and judgments about profiles if the self descriptions cannot be unduly manipulated by the author. Hence, on certain questions—especially about extraversion and physical attractiveness—regarding a self profile, viewers are more likely to value and trust comments by a profiler's friends than the profiler him- or herself (see Walther, Van Der Heide, Hamel, & Shulman, 2009).

In summary, we are left with two contradictory observations about social networking sites. First, social networking sites are outrageously popular media systems. Indeed, if measured by the millions of people participating in these systems every day, they can aptly be said to be the most significant mode of communication in the world today. But, our second observation—and herein emerges our contradiction—is that social networking systems are relatively new, coming into existence in the first decade of the twenty-first century, and accordingly, we lack the kind of rich set of research findings we might expect and may actually need if we are to understand this massive social phenomenon. In all, we know relatively little about the most important mode of global communication today. As a result, each of us needs to thoughtfully and critically examine all that we do when we function as members of social networking sites. In this context, we are only beginning to explore how and when gender comes into play on social networking sites. We believe that research explorations must continue with a far more intensive, coordinated, and vigorous academic effort.

Some have suggested that we can and will bypass the role of gender, and that during the second half of the twenty-first century, "gender will be a meaningless concept. By then, the societal changes we have embraced over the last forty and fifty years will have developed into a wider negation of gender or need to specify what is essentially a socially constructed concept" (Whittaker, 2010). And it would seem that some limitations are being addressed. For example, on Facebook, you can opt out of being addressed as "he" or "she."

We suspect that during the next 40 years, a host of gender issues in the "gender grey area"—such as androgyny, same-sex relationships, and mixed race relationships—will continue to exist within social networking sites and as societal issues. Indeed, using physically strong and competent female athletes as an extended example, Sean Miller (2010) has identified one of the ways in which issues regarding the "gender grey area" has emerged. Helsper (2010) sought to explain why "gender inequalities in Internet use are smaller among younger people" (p. 352). By conducting a descriptive analysis of a representative sample of 1,578 British Internet users, she concluded that "there continues to be small but significant gender differences for most users of the Internet. The findings . . . suggest that gender differences vary for different life stages related to occupation and marital status." Helsper specifically found that these gender differences were "true especially for typical male users." Helsper has reported that "other factors related to life stage will continue to influence gender differences in Internet use in the future."

While we recognize that it is a controversial issue, in our view, we fully expect that gender issues will continue to be of significant concern for those on social networking sites into the immediate future.

Conclusion

In this chapter, we have examined how mediated communication has been shaping and influencing the kinds of gender roles and images that so decisively control and determine masculinity and femininity for so many within our society. Our observations and conclusions in this chapter have been media dependent. Each medium seems to uniquely shape and propose different kinds of masculine and feminine images. For decades, the film and music industries have provided relatively few new or alternative conceptions of masculinity. Indeed, they have featured exceedingly traditional conceptions of masculinity. In contrast, the film and music industries seem to provide a set of increasingly diverse images for women. The television industry has tended to overemphasize men as central and controlling characters in life's dramas and correspondingly to diminish the diverse roles that women can assume as central, powerful, and decisive leaders when dealing with crises. Finally, while social networking sites are now overwhelmingly popular, findings regarding masculine and feminine roles are only now emerging in the published literature of the discipline of communication. In the absence of relevant research findings, we would recommend that individuals continually seek out, explore, experiment with, and ultimately determine the specific gender roles, modes, and attributes that allow them to grow and emerge as individuals. While social and societal standards are always relevant considerations, as they have emerged thus far in the media, we do not think an immediate set of viable, functional, and moral masculine and feminine models exist.

Notes

[1] A confirming study focusing on white male and Asian female relations is provided by Balaji and Worawongs (2010).

[2] Among the wide range of possible issues to consider in terms of digital technologies as communication systems is whether or not digital communication technologies possess unique characteristics that are not part of the functions of other communication systems. In 1995, Chesebro argued, "The new technologies can be defined as generically unique. Three features of the new technologies are initially noteworthy" (p. 17). These technologies are: (1) *Interactive,* whereas the one-to-many model that has characterized mass communication is replaced by a two-way communication through the medium itself (p. 17); (2) *Transformational,* in which the medium is intended and designed to alter and transform the message received, impose a new order on incoming messages, and ultimately transmit a message different in kind than the message originally received (p. 18); and (3) *Intertextual,* in the sense that messages are intentionally and directly linked (hyperlinked) to other messages on other Web sites creating a massive network interconnecting all information systems.

SUGGESTED ACTIVITIES

1. **Going Beyond the Traditional Image of Men in Action-Adventure Movies**

   A host of comedy movies feature plots based on male bonding. Many of these movies are set in fraternity houses or on university campuses. Identify two or three of these movies. What forms of masculinity are shown to be positive and desirable for men? Do you agree with these portrayals? Why or why not?

2. **The Image of "Men" as Sexually Aggressive**

   In the world of music, the Jonas Brothers have specifically portrayed themselves as committed to sexual abstinence before marriage. The "purity rings" they wear have been a constant reminder of this commitment. The implications seem to be that sex can and should wait. While perhaps unintended, do you think the "purity rings" have had an opposite effect? Do they continually emphasize sex? Do they suggest that the image offered by the Jonas Brothers is somehow more innocent and pure than those offered by other men in the music industry? Do you think that a similar kind of image is conveyed by Justin Bieber? If so, how?

3. **The Image of "Women" as Virginal**

   One of the classical ideals of femininity emphasizes the desirability for women to remain virgins before they marry. In many of the music videos of Madonna and Lady Gaga, women are featured as explicitly sexually experienced and exploratory. The virginal image has been "traded in" for a more sexually aggressive image for women. Do women gain significant advantages in society if they shift from a virginal to a sexually aggressive image? In what ways do they gain and in what ways do they lose?

4. **Determining How and When the Medium Is the Message: Comparing the World of Music and the World of Television**

   In a classroom discussion or in small groups, review the dramatic and different histories of the images of men and women that dominate the music and television industries that have been provided in this chapter. Each medium seems to attract different kinds of personalities in a systematic and consistent manner that is related to one medium and not the other. What is it about each industry that accounts for these differences? Do the different audiences of each medium influence how gender images are selected and conveyed? What other factors can account for the different gender images found in music compared to television?

5. **Write a Critical Analysis of Gender and the Internet**

   What is the most important gender issue created by the Internet? Is discrimination against women in the high-tech industry the most important factor to examine? Why or why not? Do social networks provide an alternative context for the creation and understanding of social gender roles? Do the research findings provided by communication scholars generate important suggestions about how gender issues can and should be handled in the next ten to twenty years?

4

Early Socialization in the Home
Influencing Gendered Scripts

> . . . identity is not only a story, a narrative which we tell ourselves about ourselves, it is stories which change with historical circumstances. And identity shifts with the way we think and hear and experience them. Far from coming from the still small point of truth inside us, identities actually come from the outside, they are the way in which we are recognized and then come to step into the place of the recognitions which others give us. Without the others there is no self, there is not self-recognition. (Hall, cited in Lea, 2009, p. 59)

*E*xternal messages, Stuart Hall reminds us, play a critical role in how we come to view ourselves and our place in the world. Fundamental to the identities we create are the early "recognitions" that occur in the home. Among the most basic and powerful messages we receive are those connected to developing gender identity. Gender identity plays a critical role in shaping our "story" and influencing the "narrative" we create for ourselves and display in our everyday lives.

The previous chapters examined how gender identity is formed, conveyed, and valued through the communicative behaviors traditionally associated with masculinity and femininity. In this chapter, we explore how expectations in the home contribute to developing and performing gendered scripts.

The Impetus for and Effects of Dichotomizing and Valuing Behavior

Looking at the world and at behavior in bipolar terms reflects a legacy that can be traced at least as far back as the Pythagorean Brotherhood of the fifth century BC, which embodied their dualism in ten sets of opposites (Wilden, 1987). Consider how we think about the terms they identify:

Limited/Unlimited	Light/Dark
One/Many	Motion/Rest
Odd/Even	Square/Oblong
Right/Left	Straight/Curved
Male/Female	Good/Bad

If gender was not central to the Pythagoreans, its centrality was soon to be established by the Christians. According to Michel Foucault (1985), it became "the seismograph of our subjectivity" (p. 368).

History undoubtedly has shaped our tendency to view the world in terms of opposites. Included in this tradition is the tendency to divide and assign behavioral norms and roles according to sex. It is difficult to think about masculine and feminine behaviors without simultaneously conjuring the sex-trait and sex-role stereotypes that accompany these behaviors. In recent years, much has been written identifying other attributes that ought to be equally valued and encouraged in women's and men's communication (e.g., empathy, cooperation, sensitivity, effective listening, and assertiveness). However, a legacy of literature suggests that we persist in using bipolar terms to characterize men as "adventurous," "active," "dominant," "forceful," "independent," "masculine," and "strong-willed" and women as "emotional," "passive," "dependent," "delicate," "sentimental," "submissive," "feminine," and "nurturing" (Aries, 1987, 1996; Bem, 1974, 1993; Borisoff & Merrill, 1998; Broverman, Broverman, Clarkson, Rosenkrantz, & Vogel, 1970; Douglas & Michaels, 2004; Ivy & Backlund, 2008; Rakow & Wackwitz, 2004; Wood, 2009).

We also persist in linking these traits to multiple frameworks so that stereotypical male or female behavior becomes the presumed norm in diverse situations and contexts. For example, traditionally the appropriate forms of communication in many organizational settings and careers have been defined by masculine behaviors. In contrast, in intimate relationships, feminine behaviors and modes of expression are the norm. Thus, the "standards" for communicative behavior in these public and private domains have privileged whichever sex has been culturally assigned primary responsibility for each particular environment.

Implicit in dividing and privileging behavior according to gender lines is that this behavior in turn becomes the "standard" or "norm" against which "other" or "different" behavior is then measured, judged, and, ultimately, valued.

Through such comparisons the normative behavior for a particular context acquires a kind of power, importance, and legitimacy that are hard to challenge. Women, for example, long were denied access to the upper echelons of corporate America because it was presumed they lacked the competitive skills deemed essential to succeed in this domain. Meanwhile, men long were denied custody of their children because it was presumed they could not provide the nurturing environment that would serve their children's best interests.

Fundamental to how normative behavioral power is exerted is how individuals allow themselves to become subject to, or the object of, power in the first place. As Paul Rabinow (1984) notes, Foucault identifies the processes by which humans are made subjects. One of the processes that Foucault connects to objectification is "dividing practices":

> In this process of social objectification and categorization, human beings are given both a social and a personal identity. Essentially, "dividing practices" are modes of manipulation that combine the mediation of a science (or pseudo-science) and the practice of exclusion—usually in a spatial sense, but always in a social one. (p. 8)

In this mode, the "dividing" is done by the actions of the culture, the society, the government, etc., which primarily establish and promote the norms of the group.

Of particular concern to Foucault is the extent to which individuals "subject" themselves to these "dividing practices," which has to do with

> those techniques through which the person initiates an active self-formation. This self-formation has a long and complicated genealogy; it takes place through a variety of "operations on [people's] own bodies, on their own souls, on their own thoughts, on their own conduct." (Rabinow, 1984, p. 11)

In Foucault's view, "objectification" and "subjectification" are related. The objectifications of a culture, as reinforced by accepted sciences, acquire a certain legitimacy and power. They provide the cultural and intellectual bases for subjectification, whereby individuals come to accept, perhaps even rejoice in, the dividing practices that ultimately help create them.

Foucault (1982) does not address directly how to rectify the process of subjectification. However, he does suggest that:

> Maybe the target nowadays is not to discover what we are, *but to refuse what we are*. We have to imagine and to build up what we could be. . . . The conclusion would be that the political, ethical, social, philosophical problem of our days is not to try to liberate the individual from the state, and from the state's institutions, *but to liberate us both from the state and from the type of individualization which is linked to the state. We have to promote new forms of subjectivity through refusal of this kind of individuality which has been imposed on us for several centuries.* (p. 216, emphasis added)

How might we translate Foucault's suggestion into the general question of standards for gendered behavior and the resultant power that flows from these standards? A first step would be to actively alter the power relations by denying the "dividing practices" that divide women from men. Second, when the practices cannot be denied (childbirth is an example), we can challenge the ways in which dividing practices erect power discrepancies. Third, and perhaps even more significantly, we need to examine our use of the binary terms themselves. The male-female binary no longer should be viewed as sufficient to reflect and capture the full range of our identity. Factors such as race, culture, sexual orientation, class, religion, disability, age, and education play critical roles in how we come to view ourselves and our place in the world. As communication scholars Lana Rakow and Laura Wackwitz (2004, p. 6) suggest in their edited volume on feminist communication theory, it is important to bring to the forefront the multiple voices, experiences, and realities that research has often ignored. They, along with feminist scholars from diverse disciplines, suggest that we not only have to eliminate the formal mechanisms by which power is created, but we should also eliminate the self-formation practices of both women and men by which we all turn ourselves into subjects, and eventually into victims.

The dilemma in resisting the processes of objectification and subjectification as articulated by Foucault stems, in part, from the fact that once behaviors become entrenched in our culture, they constitute "the prevailing 'truth' which, in turn, becomes a justification of the dominant group's hegemony" (Lipman-Blumen, 1994, p. 110). These behaviors become, then, the bases for determining standards for action. This "prevailing truth" is the fundamental issue for those who see gender valuation differences as a consequence of Foucault's contention that power flows from division. That is, until there is division there is no need for power. Once division is achieved, power is inevitable, in his view, and becomes legitimized.

This "legitimate power," insofar as it applies to our expectations for and valuation of gendered behavior, has been traditionally fueled by the acceptance of biological sex differences (or "biological essentialism") as justification for dichotomizing gendered behavior and roles (or "gender polarization") (Bem, 1993, pp. 2–5). Once this division is firmly embedded and the roles, along with the presumed "correct" behaviors for these roles, are established, we are apt to uncritically embrace these behaviors. We are apt to perpetuate and reinforce them in the home, in the classroom, and in the workplace. The following sections examine the impact of these factors on the construction and reinforcement of gender. As you read the examples that follow, recall your own upbringing. Think about the activities you pursued as well as those you abandoned. Consider how you came to value your body. Finally, consider how parental messages have influenced your professional and personal aspirations.

Socialization: Reinforcing Attitudes about Sex Traits and Sex Roles

Hall (1981) has called culture a "silent language" and has explained that cultural norms are learned both directly and indirectly. Gendered behavior is one dimension that is often transmitted indirectly, outside of the conscious awareness of the parties involved.

In *The Female World*, Jesse Bernard (1981) observed that the seemingly neutral question asked when a baby is born ("Is it a boy?" or "Is it a girl?") is neither benign nor without consequences. Knowing the child's sex, Bernard suggested, would come to influence every interaction and impact how parents, siblings, friends, and society in general would respond to the newborn. At the time *The Female World* was published, studies typically regarded gender as primarily role bound, whereby socialization would prepare girls and boys to develop "masculine" and "feminine" traits—traits that were intended to direct males and females into separate, yet presumably complementary, spheres as adults. This approach, according to Kathleen Galvin (2006), is limited because it "reifies difference between the sexes and suggests that gender-specific socialization of boys and girls takes place in and reproduces different masculine and feminine speech communities" (p. 42).

A more current approach views gender as socially constructed, learned, and reflective of the meanings we ascribe to masculinity and femininity. However, the gender identities we construct are neither stable nor neutral, nor do they exist in a vacuum. Judith Butler (1990) is widely acknowledged for theorizing gender as a cultural, rather than as a natural, performance—a performance, moreover, that maintains the status quo of a masculine hierarchy and heterosexuality as the norm. She has suggested that the performance of gender is made visible through the repetitive ways in which we display and use our bodies in an attempt to belong, to deflect, or to hide critical aspects of who we are (Butler, 1988). This process, moreover, is ongoing—one we engage in whether for a real or unseen other (Butler, 2004).

Elizabeth Bell and Daniel Blaeuer (2006) suggest three ways in which Butler's notions of performativity can be particularly useful for examining gender in our interactions with others. First, they suggest that the labels "male" and "female" are not sufficient predictors of "gendered communication styles, strategies, or perceptions" without understanding their cultural roots and how the labels have transformed over time (p. 18). Second, they contend that the long-held assumption that "gender is learned" cannot be uncoupled from the ways in which economic forces as well as the multiple institutions to which we are exposed (such as "church, state, education, medicine, or family") contribute to what is learned (p. 18). And third, they propose that performativity can move us beyond traditional modes of inquiry by shifting the way we interrogate gender: "this scrutiny depends on politics to move us beyond the question, 'What is a good relationship?' to ask, 'How are gender boundaries inclusionary and exclusionary?'" (p. 18).

Despite the fact that many parents do not consciously set out to raise their children according to the traditional sex stereotypes embedded in the "male" and "female" labels to which Bell and Blaeuer allude, a legacy of research indicates that communication between adults and children provides the initial backdrop for learning how gender is performed. In many ways, this backdrop still reflects traditional stereotypes associated with masculinity and femininity. Typically, parents use different terms to describe newborns. Often, they situate daughters in the gentle, sweet, and delicate role and cast sons as strong, active, and alert (Macoby & Jacklin, 1974; Rubin, Provensano, & Luria, 1974; Stern & Karraker, 1989). Children's initial clothing (costumes) and bedrooms (sets) often reflect a pastel backdrop for baby girls and strong, primary colors for baby boys (Ivy & Backlund, 2008, p. 80). Many of our students report that they first became aware of their own gender when their baby brother or sister was born. The landscape of the new nursery was visually distinctive from how their own room was adorned. Moreover, these visible markers of difference were remarkably consistent across diverse cultural, economic, ethnic, and racial backgrounds.

The toys (props) children receive and how they are encouraged to interact with them (scripts) reveal tangible markers of appropriate play, establish initial boundaries for the emotional landscape that boys and girls are expected to inhabit, and emphasize the valuation of appearance, especially for girls. By the age of two, children demonstrate clear toy preferences: girls choose dolls and soft toys with which to play, boys opt for blocks and other objects they can manipulate. Beverly Fagot (1978) connects this "preference" to parental responses. Parents responded positively when their children selected and played with the toys viewed as "appropriate" for their sex. Negative feedback occurred when children opted for toys regarded as "inappropriate" for their sex. Fathers, in particular, were more forceful in discouraging young boys when they played with girls' toys. Julia Wood (2009) notes the persistence of parental influence on the landscape of play: "fathers are more insistent on gender-stereotyped toys and activities, especially for sons, than are mothers. It's much more acceptable for girls to play baseball or football than for boys to play house or cuddle dolls" (p. 171).

By age two, male and female children are encouraged differently to express messages of care. In her study of forty-eight male and female two-year-olds who were pretending to take care of their dolls, Phyllis Berman (1986) found that parents reinforced the girls' behavior when they demonstrated care; they did not encourage this kind of behavior in the boys. These responses led Berman to conclude that the affective display of caring is culturally determined and is determined and valued differently for males and females. Recent studies continue to support this finding. By ages three or four girls show higher levels of empathy than boys and are more attuned to others' distress (Zahn-Waxler & Polanichka, 2004). Psychologists Kate Keenan and Alison Hipwell's (2005) meta-analytic review of research on girls and depression reveals that girls are at greater risk when their ability to empathize shades into doing what others want at the expense of their own needs. While the ability to feel with another is an important skill that should be encouraged in all children, "girls are more often rewarded for putting others' needs first, while boys are more often rewarded for asserting themselves" (Hinshaw, 2009, p. 95).

In an increasingly technology-driven landscape, U.S. doll sales have declined by nearly 20% since 2005. To retain the interest of young girls, companies have responded to this shift by re-creating online doll play on websites such as Stardoll.com and Barbie's EverythingGirl.com. For some, the use of avatars online function the same as traditional dolls: girls can dress them, feed them, and buy them clothes or accessories. However, some highlight a specific function of traditional play with dolls: "when little girls play with dolls, they're practicing being a mommy, practicing tending and nurturing." The extent to which online interaction will create the same tendencies and effects in young girls is too early to assess (Kadaba, 2010). Implicit in these observations is that play continues to be a significant arena for preparing females to assume primary responsibility for providing care—such as child and family care—over the course of their lives.

Early socialization also plays a powerful role in how young girls and boys learn to value their bodies and their appearance. The adjectives that adults employ when describing infants suggest there are distinct attributes that are inculcated and encouraged early in a child's life. Research suggests that descriptors focus on "the size, strength, and bodily activity of baby boys and the beauty, sweetness, and facial responsiveness of baby girls" (Lederman, 2001, p. 80). As early as age 4, children are able to discern characteristics of attractiveness in others (Harter, 1992). While appearance matters to both boys and girls, physical appearance plays a more significant role and is valued more profoundly in women's lives (Bernard, 1981; Borisoff & Hahn, 1997; Davis, 1992; Douglas & Michaels, 2004; Freedman, 1986; Hatfield & Sprecher, 1986; Tarvis, 1992; Wolf, 1991). Psychologist Jean Twenge asserts that an emphasis on physical appearance has shaded into cultivating a princess mentality. In an attempt to provide daughters with "the best of everything," many middle-class parents engage in what Twenge calls "princess parenting," which includes bedrooms, parties, clothing, and messages that reflect a royal, yet simultaneously unrealistic, landscape for how they will be treated once they leave the palace they call home (cited in Basham, 2009, p. 13).

The quest for beauty exacts a powerful toll on young girls and on women—a toll, moreover, that resonates globally. In 2009, the now ubiquitous Barbie doll turned 50. The majority of women in our classes indicate that they were gifted at least one Barbie doll early on. Many students admitted to amassing a large collection, to engaging fully with the clothing, hair styling, and accessories in their Barbie kits, and to accepting unquestioningly the doll's image as one they should aspire to emulate. Other students had a more critical assessment. In recent decades, incarnations of Latina, African American, and Asian Barbies have been introduced. Several of our students appreciated receiving a version of the doll that was not available to their own mothers. But they also noted that the skin tone, facial features, and bodily contours of the dolls they received were essentially Western, Caucasian versions of the doll with slight cosmetic modifications that failed to accurately reflect their own race, culture, and ethnicity.

Recent reports indicate that Barbie's influence continues to extend beyond U.S. borders. For example, over the last two decades, Barbie, with her "hourglass" figure, has supplanted the locally produced Susi in Brazil, whose "guitar"-like contours more accurately reflected the local aesthetic of women's bodies (Rohter, 2007). Other cultures have produced dolls that more accurately reflect local norms to counter Barbie's influence. In 2003, NewBoy Design Studio in Syria introduced the Fulla doll in the Middle East. Dressed in the traditional head scarf *(hijab)* and full-length gown *(abaja)*, "Arab children are now choosing Fulla over Barbie" (Al-Jadda, 2004, p. 23).

Playing with dolls is not inherently problematic. Such interaction can provide an opportunity for all children to learn positive ways of communicating care and other nurturing behaviors. We question, however, the extent to which Barbie persists among the many indicators of societal pressures on young girls to embrace, internalize, privilege, and equate outward appearance and a limited vision of how the body ought to appear in conjunction with their own self-esteem. During this process the internal qualities that are true indicators of beauty may be marginalized. We question a legacy that resonates today that regards beauty as "the only undisputed advantage our Sex has over the other" (Bernard, 1981, p. 61), that treats women "like a live doll" (de Beauvoir, 1953, p. 316), and suggests that a young woman "will have to look . . . in the eyes and faces of the boys who dance with her" to know if she is beautiful (Freedman, 1986, p. 138). We question, moreover, the extent to which the media has persisted in depicting young girls' and women's bodies and voices as child-like, thin, young, sexy, and often powerless (Alexander & Morrison, 1995; Fisherkeller, 2002; Goffman, 1979; Han, 2003; Johnson & Young, 2002; Ross, 1972; Sahlstein & Allen, 2002).

Recent reports confirm the pervasiveness and consequences of this pressure. Eating disorders, including anorexia and bulimia, have primarily been associated with young, white, and middle- and upper middle-class women. There is an indication that body dissatisfaction and a rise in these diseases is emerging in African American, Asian American, and Hispanic women (Brodey, 2005) (in part attributed to the increase of high-visibility performers who are members of these groups) and in women over 40 (Newsome, 2005). However, due to the prevailing assumption about who is affected by these diseases, members of the latter groups often remain undiagnosed and untreated by members of the health care community. Access to media representations of hyper-thin models and beauty pageant winners also has impacted body image in other cultures, causing young women to eschew the traditional rounder, curvier body image in favor of a thin ideal (Onishi, 2002; Rohter, 2007). These pressures are evident, finally, in the marked increase in cosmetic surgery both globally as well as within the United States. Recent estimates indicate that $2.4 billion, $18.4 million, and $8.4 billion is spent annually on plastic surgery in China (where it was illegal prior to 2001), Japan, and the United States, respectively (Azam et al., 2007, p. 63). (We note that these figures include surgery on women and men.) Tehran has recently been dubbed "the nose capital of the world" (Navai, 2007, p. 139). In a culture where only a woman's face is allowed to be seen in public, coupled with a rescinding of a ban on cosmetic surgery, the nose job in Iran has become a "phenomenon that transcends age, class, and religion . . ." (p. 140). And a 2006 report by the American Academy of Facial and Plastic Reconstructive Surgery indicates that over a five-year period, there has been a 65% increase in the number of plastic surgeries performed on African Americans, Asians, and Hispanics in the United States (Azam et al., 2007, p. 58). The report connects this increase in part to higher incomes among these groups. A greater number of women now have the economic resources to alter their appearance; to resculpt the terrain of their faces and their bodies in pursuit of markers of beauty that often deny and erase their own ethnicities.

Despite attempts during the first decade of the twenty-first century to redefine and to present construals of beauty that more accurately reflect women's bodies, as well as a growing recognition that men are also impacted by body image issues (see Balz, 2006; Chesebro, 2001; Jackson, 2006; Martínez, 2008; Trebay, 2008), the burden of beauty remains a compelling challenge that women, most particularly, continue to bear.

We recognize, further, that our understanding of how gender identity, traits, and roles develop has derived primarily from studies conducted on nuclear, middle-class, heterosexual families. The landscape of who is raising children has changed in recent years. In her chapter on gender and family communication, Kathleen Galvin (2006) suggests that since a rising number of children are being raised by single parents, nonbiological parents, and by gay and lesbian couples, family life studies need to include these configurations. She further suggests that attention to a wider array of family life may challenge, in the process, the long-standing view of childhood as a "dress rehearsal" for adulthood—instead, "improvisation" may be a more accurate descriptor (p. 41). Galvin refers to these shifts in defining the family as "kaleidoscopic change" (p. 51). Commenting on the image of the kaleidoscope, Borisoff, Cooper Hoel, and McMahan (2010) note,

> Implicit in this powerful metaphor is that each turn of the knob will produce an image that is complex yet complete; each one different, yet beautiful in its own right. The extent to which current and future studies resist examining the family configurations as located in the margins and using extant and primarily heteronormative criteria as the basis for comparison will affect, finally, whether the views through the kaleidoscope are valued equally. (p. 218)

An expanded definition and valuation of the family has the potential, finally, to transform the terrain of how boys and girls are raised in profound ways.

Let's take, for example, the students in our classes. The majority were raised primarily in traditional family constellations—by two parents and/or by one parent due to divorce or the death of a spouse. Yet traditional constellations do not necessarily reflect traditional parenting roles as a growing number of students report being raised in homes where both parents were employed. In several instances, a mother's earnings were equal to and/or exceeded those of the father. However, the vast majority report that their father was the primary wage earner. Additionally, because their own education and career aspirations were largely encouraged and supported by their parents, it is not surprising that when we begin our lectures on perceptions of gender "differences," many of our students at first assert their beliefs that differences do not exist and that, consequently, avenues for professional development are available equally to women and men.

In order to explore these students' assumptions, one of the authors surveyed approximately 1,100 undergraduate and graduate students from the early 1990s through 2010. The students were asked to write about how they envisioned their personal and professional roles in the future. Their responses suggest that there has been little headway made into incorporating changes in traditional sex roles in marriage and family. In 1991, Susan Faludi noted a backlash in attitudes regarding women and work, a "powerful counterassault on women's rights . . . an attempt to retract the handful of small and hard-won victories that the feminist movement did manage to win for women" (p. xviii). In 1995, Gallup Poll conducted a survey in which the majority of respondents in the United States, Chile, Japan, France, and Hungary stated the belief that the "ideal" family structure would be comprised of a father as primary breadwinner and of a mother who stayed home with children (Lewin, 1996; see Borisoff & Merrill, 1998, pp. 74–75). A definitive break from traditional roles has also been hampered due to a growing recognition since the late 1990s that creating a balance between the professional and personal spheres for women with children who work outside of the home often creates a "time bind" (Hochschild, 1997) that is not easily reconciled. Women are not immune to the warning that pursuing a high-powered career may be incompatible with marriage and especially with having a family (Hewlett, 2002). "The opt-out revolution" (Belkin, 2003) has been framed in a way to suggest that women are redefining success by rejecting the workplace and devoting themselves to their families (Douglas & Michaels, 2004; Warner, 2005).

Two themes reverberate in the students' projections that identify potential pressures they expect to encounter as well as their own predictions for how they anticipate dealing with them: age (or the impact of time on creating their lives) and negotiating the dual roles of professional and parent. As we will see, these factors appear to impact women differently and with greater urgency than they do men.

Age as a Marker for Creating a Life

Within our survey age and the effect of time on their future personal and professional aspirations is one theme that resonates powerfully in women's responses. Particularly, 30 (or the early thirties for many of the graduate students) is identified as a demarcation for establishing themselves personally and professionally. Terms such as "settling down," being in a "stable," "committed," "loving" relationship or "marriage" with someone who is a "soul mate" or "best friend" with whom they can "build a future together" is a recurring theme. They envision themselves professionally as being "established," "respected" in their careers, "financially independent," and "passionate" about what they are doing. As the following comments suggest, the women also viewed 30 as the age by which they will have had or hope to have started to bring children into their lives:

"By age 30, I hope to have started my family."

"Hitting the big 3-0—hopefully married with one or two kids."

"I definitely want to be married . . . to be a young mother and have kids by 30—this would be perfect."

"I feel the clock is ticking and I'd like to have children by around 30."

"On the brink of turning 30 which undoubtedly will warrant a small, yet explosive mid-life crisis."

While a few women indicated that they are adamant about wanting to be child free and others indicated ambivalence about when they might want to have a family, it is clear that for most, they are not immune to the pressure of believing that the romantic, professional, and parental dimensions of their lives ought to coalesce by age 30. It appears that they are aware of the youth-as-equated-with-attractiveness connection that, as noted earlier, pervades the landscape of young girls and women. They are aware, as well, of an accepted, prime biological time that affects women's ability to have children. Their comments echo the cautionary tales raised by economist Sylvia Ann Hewlett (2002): for women who envision both a career and a family in their future, creating a successful life is "extremely time-sensitive and deserves special attention in your twenties" (p. 301).

The notion of time also emerges in the men's responses, however, it appears in ways that impact them differently than women. Prominent in their responses are references to their twenties and thirties as the decades devoted to establishing themselves professionally. Prominent as well are precise labels attached to these goals:

> "Partner in a major law firm."

> "Vice president in the organization."

> "President of my own company."

We suspect that one reason why men are less precise vis-à-vis age and their professional aspirations is due to the fact they are not able to pinpoint the exact age at which they will be able to achieve these professional monikers. We also noticed a small but significant linguistic difference in women's and men's professional aspirations. Several women indicated that they hope to be "respected" in their careers. The term "respect" is absent in the men's projections. This slight difference, we think, is important as it suggests that women, more so than men, do not believe that respect will automatically be conferred on their achievements; perhaps they believe they will have to work harder to earn this label. This nuance, finally, suggests that women, more so than men, connect how they are seen by others as an integral aspect of their own view of themselves as professionally successful.

Time also functions differently in men's projections about their personal lives. While men also articulate the hope of being in "committed," "loving" relationships and having a family, time does not exert a similar pressure for them as it does for women. Those who envision a family in their future indicate that this would occur when they are "financially established," suggesting that they anticipate and accept the traditional role of being the primary financial provider in their family. The fact that the age of 30—or any precise age—is conspicuously absent in men's responses further suggests that they may be unaware of the growing recognition that men are not immune to a biological clock (especially after age 35). Although this clock may tick at a different rate for men than for women, it remains largely a "silent epidemic" (Fisch, 2005, p. 1).

Competing Roles as a Marker for Creating a Life

As we have seen, projections related to the professional and personal spheres emerged in both men's and women's responses. However, the anticipated challenges of coping with and reconciling their personal and professional aspirations resonates most powerfully in the women's responses. Their observations suggest that "having it all" is nuanced and may not be achieved easily. Three patterns emerge in their responses.

Viewing the Work Sphere as Optional

The first pattern indicates that many of the young, predominantly middle-class women in our surveys view their future decision to remain in the workforce as an "option." However, there is a range in how they justify their choices. Many are clear in prioritizing their family over their career as typified by the response,

> "Having a family that is happy and full of love is ultimately more important to me than continuing a hopefully successful career. And so, if that is the end of my working days, then so be it."

Others indicate that their decision to opt out of their careers is predicated on the belief that alternative forms of child care are not adequate, as suggested by the following comment:

> "I hope to be a stay-at-home mom with my children while they're young. To me, it's important that I'm a highly involved parent. I would rather take care of my children than have them stay at a day-care center."

Also raised is the possibility of re-calibrating their professional aspirations after taking time off to raise a family, as indicated in the following observation:

> "As far as working, my first priority is my kids, but that doesn't mean that I want to waste my education. After taking some time off, I'd go back to work, but perhaps at a smaller company that allows me the time to take care of my children."

For others, however, this decision is fraught with anxiety as revealed in this graduate student's comment:

> "I'm not sure how I'll manage work and family, especially since I've always firmly believed that a mother should be there for her child during the first three years. At the same time, I don't want to lose three years of my personal life. Perhaps I'll shift to part-time or

work from home. This tug-of-war between what I want to achieve for myself, what I'm supposed to do as a woman and wife, has been my single greatest source of tension since I got married. I hope I will manage to play all these roles well."

Regardless of how willingly or how tentatively they view this decision, implicit in the opting out discourse is the expectation that their future lives will replicate traditional gender roles: women are primarily responsible for nurturance in the private sphere; men are primarily responsible for providing financial support. This expectation ignores the fact that in the United States, most families with young children are not able to opt out of the workforce. They rely on two incomes for their survival (Douglas & Michaels, 2004; Gibbs, 2009; Hochschild, 1990, 1997). This expectation precludes, as well, envisioning families with men as primary caregivers, despite the fact that increasing numbers of fathers are currently raising children while the mothers are the primary wage earners (Douglas & Michaels, 2004; Gibbs, 2009). As scholars from diverse fields have observed, these responses also reflect a legacy of research suggesting how difficult it is to extricate ourselves from the public and private domains associated with the male/female binary identified earlier (Bem, 1993; Bernard, 1981; Blumstein & Schwartz, 1983; Douglas & Michaels, 2004; Fitzpatrick, 1987; Haste, 1994).

Creating a Life of Balance: The Work/Home Divide

The second pattern that emerged in these self-reported responses relates to the manner in which women who plan to remain in the workforce expect to prioritize their professional and personal lives. What is striking in this group of responses is the recognition that maintaining a career while starting a family is precarious. The following comments reveal this awareness as well as their optimism for simultaneously negotiating their personal and professional obligations successfully:

"Although having a husband and a family has been my dream for many years, I also hope to be in a business setting where I can contribute my knowledge and passion. I hope that I can keep a balance between family and career."

"A home with a beautiful family would be ideal as well as maintaining my professional goals of teaching and consulting. I know that balance will be crucial."

"I'll be struggling between my career and my family—torn between long hours at work and family obligations. But I also know that to be fulfilled, I will have to continue working and be intellectually stimulated on a daily basis. The defining word of this period of my life will be 'compromise.'"

"I expect to be anxious about being a 'good' mother and worker, however, I also want to be fully involved in my children's lives."

"It's difficult to really know whether I'll put family ahead of my career. I do believe one can do both—with the help of a willing and understanding husband."

The "hope" of being able to "balance" their home and work lives in light of the "struggle" and "tension" they anticipate in order to be a "good" mother suggests that their future trajectories are unclear. The anxiety that laces their comments reflects as well the larger societal landscape they have experienced and witnessed. Implicit in their responses is the expectation that regardless of their own professional aspirations, they, and they alone, will assume primary responsibility for child care. Conspicuously absent in this group of responses is the involvement they expect from the father of their children in this balancing act. When referred to, fathers are typically positioned in supporting roles—alongside of or assisting mothers—but never situated as equally responsible for child care. Also implied in their responses is a recognition that the careers to which they aspire will require a commitment that will impede their ability to achieve the "balance" they desire (Hewlett, 2002; Hochschild, 1997; Philipson, 2002).

The Implications of Prioritizing Work over Family on Creating a Life

The third pattern of student responses revealed a conscious rejection of the traditional roles for women as wife and mother, albeit the sources for their outlooks vary. Many respondents attributed this rejection to their own experiences. Several responses indicated that female students associated the difficulties in their mothers' lives with financial dependency:

"I don't want to have to plead with my husband for money the way my mother had to do."

"The power in my family was with my father—he was the breadwinner; he was the professional. I know I am breaking from tradition, but I don't want to be helpless and totally dependent on my husband."

For others, the impetus for financial independence emerged from changes in the family that required their mother to become the sole financial provider:

"When my father became ill, my mother had to assume the entire economic burden for raising us. I realize how fragile life is, especially when one's survival depends on one income alone."

"When my dad left, our financial circumstances changed drastically. My mother had abandoned her career when I was born and her life became a series of struggles because she had been out of the workforce for a long time. I never want to be in the same situation."

These comments suggest that for many women, the drive for financial independence is rooted in coping with adverse conditions. For some, adversity stemmed from a power imbalance they saw in their own parents' relationships. For others, the drive for economic independence was fueled by the challenges they observed when their mothers assumed the primary provider role. Regardless of the source of the impetus, these comments echo the findings of journalist Leslie Bennetts (2007), who suggests that many women who abandoned professional aspirations early on in their relationships and/or opted out of their careers to devote themselves full-time to child care may risk finding themselves a divorce, disability, or death away from suffering severe economic consequences.

Other responses suggested that middle-class women's professional aspirations were proactive, motivated by a desire to define themselves in ways that actively resist traditional assumptions about women's roles as well as reflect social conscience:

> "For me, it is more important to achieve professional goals, as opposed to social goals such as finding a spouse, getting married, or having kids. I feel that I need to prove something to society—mainly that not all women are intent on having a family as their major goal in life."

> "I realize that starting a family at a relatively young age plays into a stereotypical gender role, however, I don't feel the need to give up my career in order to achieve personal happiness. I feel that I can achieve happiness in both worlds."

> "I would like to be in a career that is rewarding and that will make a difference in society."

While the women in this last group of responses indicated that they envision marriage and parenting in their future, for them, their careers are of prime importance. They suggest that decisions about their personal lives will be influenced by their own financial stability and success. Moreover, they frame these future decisions as an active "choice" rather than as an "inevitability." Their responses seem to suggest that this "choice" will not be fraught with the "tensions," "struggles," and "balancing" acts that lace the responses of other women who anticipate having both a career and a family, albeit they do not speculate how the responsibilities for work and home life will be met.

Like the women students, the men's responses suggest that they did not escape the powerful social forces that shape dominant concepts of masculine and feminine behavior. Having a family and career are abiding themes in the men's projections. On the surface these goals are similar to the women's projections. However, there are marked differences in what family life and professional success signified for the male students when compared with their female peers. Although several of the men envisioned themselves married without children, the majority included having children as part of their future. Distinct from the women's responses, many men stated, "I do not see my life changing." While many of the women articulated a need to balance professional goals with their personal lives, the men surveyed did not foresee responsibilities for children as interfering with or impeding their professional aspirations. Implicit in these men's and women's differing responses is that they largely accept the dividing practices that have traditionally cast men in provider and women in caretaking roles.

In light of these dichotomous roles, it is not surprising that the men described professional success differently than the women. Professional and financial success for the women students was often stated within the context of a "rewarding career," in terms of achieving financial independence as a means to avoid becoming dependent on another, or in terms of a concerted effort to break from traditional expectations about women's roles. Concern with being dependent on another was virtually absent in the men's responses. For these men, professional success was consistently cast in terms of what money could buy: "I see my wife and I living in a penthouse"; "owning a large home"; "having the freedom to travel"; or "doing what I want." Consistently, professional success was equated with earning power:

> "I see myself as a recognized creative artist."

> "I'll be running the family business."

> "I see myself as independently wealthy."

While several men expressed the "hope" that the women in their lives will be "fulfilled" or "happy" in their careers, only a very few men depicted their future life as a partnership, as expressed in the following comment:

> "Both of us will be working and taking part in organizing a family. I feel that equality is very important in a relationship—to consider your spouse as you would consider yourself."

The students' responses tell us something about the lives these specific women and men hope to forge. Regardless of the future personal and professional paths they envision, undergirding their projections is the acceptance that caring for the home and for children are primarily women's responsibilities. Based on this underlying notion, we recognize and understand the following:

- Many women describe a future that willingly accepts and embraces home and child care as their primary role and thus anticipate scaling back, postponing, and/or abandoning their professional lives in the process.

- Some women anticipate a period of struggle in order to balance, cope with, and manage the competing obligations of their future personal and professional spheres.

- There is a group of women who anticipate actively resisting the traditional position of women's roles in order to pursue their professional aspirations.

- An overwhelming preponderance of men's responses do not include parenting duties as altering or disrupting their professional pursuits in any substantive ways.

These responses are situated and framed within the tradition of role expectations for women and for men, which are connected to binary ways of thinking and to the consequences of dividing practices described earlier. Largely unexplored by the students were the expanded boundaries of family configurations, including single parent families, families headed by gay or lesbian parents, extended families, or families where fathers either alternate as or serve as primary caregivers in the home (Borisoff & Merrill, 1998; Galvin, 2006; McCann & Delmonte, 2005).

Assumptions about socioeconomic status are pervasive in their responses as well. The women who anticipate both a family and a full-time career envision having adequate finances to outsource certain aspects of their home and child care duties. The women who foresee disrupting, postponing, or opting out of the workforce anticipate that their partners will provide adequate financial support for these choices. These aspirations do not necessarily reflect the lives of working- and middle-class families where two full-time incomes are requisite for survival; where a large majority of women who work full-time outside of the home also assume primary responsibility for a "second shift" of house and child care duties (Douglas & Michaels, 2004; Hochschild, 1990, 1997). Nearly three decades ago, Lillian Rubin (1983) observed the largely taken-for-granted assumption that "Fathers work, mothers 'mother' even when they also work" (p. 175). Men generally see their identities tied to their careers—to the world of work. This outlook, as both Keen (1991) and Hofstede (1998) suggest, is an understandable consequence of an upbringing that largely privileges equating one's sense of self with activities over connecting with others. In adulthood, Kahn (2009) cautions, these early lessons may become a "struggle . . . as men may make choices for work, career, or finances over their families and relationships" (p. 126).

In tandem with learned expectations and roles, women are exposed to societal messages about motherhood, particularly from media. In 1984, bell hooks cautioned against the media's "romanticization of motherhood" and acknowledged a need "to make motherhood neither a compulsory experience for women, nor an exploitative or oppressive one" (Borisoff & Merrill, 1998, p. 78). Subsequent observations suggest that a romantic vision is qualified. Many women continue to struggle with what sociologist Arlie Hochschild (1990) calls "competing urgencies," to meet the compelling demands of their professional lives while simultaneously retaining and fulfilling their roles as wives and mothers. Two decades after hooks' warning, Susan Douglas and Meredith Michaels (2004) contended that the media's romantic portrayal of motherhood has been imbued with a host of warnings suggesting that every aspect of a child's educational, nutritional, and psychological well-being requires hyper-vigilance and a 24-hour commitment that only mothers can provide. Implicit in this new momism is a monolithic portrayal of motherhood that both obscures and marginalizes the breadth of women's lives:

> We can, however, replay the dominant media imagery that has surrounded most of us, despite our differences, imagery that serves to divide us by age and race and "lifestyle choices," and seeks to tame us all by reinforcing one narrow, homogenized, upper-middle-class, corporately defined image of motherhood. (p. 22)

As long as women remain the presumed arbiters of nurturing and child care, there is little incentive to alter child-rearing practices in a way that encourages boys and girls to equally value and display ways of connecting and caring. We are apt to obscure or impoverish the ways in which men engage in or are expected to contribute to the process of care. There have been calls advocating greater egalitarianism in parental participation among mothers and fathers (Chodorow, 1978), and for defining parenting practices similarly for men and women in lieu of viewing mothering and fathering as mutually exclusive (hooks, 1984).

There has been a growing recognition that fathers parent in positive ways. In their meta-analysis of studies involving 30,000 parents, University of Calgary psychologists Hugh Lytton and David Romney (1991) found that mothers and fathers behaved similarly in critical parenting areas, including communicating warmth, nurturance, and responsiveness. The positive effects of fathers' active participation in raising children is similarly supported by Kyle Pruett of Yale University. Pruett's longitudinal study of sixteen families from diverse socioeconomic backgrounds where the fathers took primary responsibility for child care while the mothers worked full-time outside the home revealed a greater blurring of traditional gendered boundaries among the children in their care. Pruett found that children of both sexes displayed "masculine" and "feminine" behaviors, they were able to play with each other, and they didn't separate into "boy versus girl play." Significantly, the young boys learned how to care for a baby and regarded this activity as a "human job" rather than as a "girl's job"; young girls evidenced interest in "what their mothers were doing in the workplace" at much earlier ages (4 or 5) than is typical (8 or 10) (cited in Shapiro, 1990, p. 65). These studies suggest that the capacity to parent effectively is neither innate nor necessarily the purview of one sex. The reality, however, indicates that in many cultures, mothers continue to assume primary responsibility for parenting (Chodorow, 1990; Huang & Pouncy, 2005; Pollack, 1998).

President Barack Obama's (2009) call for fathers to "step up," "be involved," and "to realize that we are our children's first and best teachers" suggests the need to narrow the parental responsibility gap that persists. Although women continue to spend more time than men engaged in child care, the amount of time both men and women devote to this task has increased. Prior to 1995, mothers averaged 12 hours a week on child care. By 2007, the number rose to 21.2 hours a week for college-educated women, for those with less education, the estimate was 15.9 hours a week. For college-educated men the number of hours spent on parenting duties increased from 4.5 to 9.6 hours per week; for men with less education, the number of hours grew from 3.7 to 6.8 hours per week (Parker-Pope, 2010, p. D5). Although this upward trend is positive, closing the gender gap in the allocation of care will hopefully enhance further how the landscape of growing up is experienced by young girls and boys.

Conclusion

We have seen how our attitudes toward family and career may originate with the initial messages we receive at home. We have seen, moreover, the extent to which the recognitions others give us, as Stuart Hall (1993) contends, can powerfully shape how we learn initially to see ourselves, and begin to forge our identities as well as our place in the world. One expectation of the educational process is that it will provide the opportunity for males and females to maximize their potential in an environment conducive to equality. In the following chapter, we turn to an examination of the extent to which opportunity is maximized and equality is achieved.

SUGGESTED ACTIVITIES

1. **Focus on Sex-Role Expectations**
   Write briefly about how you envision your personal and professional life in the next five and then in the next ten years. (You may also obtain this information about your peers by interviewing several students or colleagues.) The class should then be divided into groups to discuss the responses. The following may be discussed with the entire class:

   a. Did the group share goals and attitudes about the future?

   b. Were similar goals and attitudes shared by women? By men?

   c. Do the expressed goals reflect stereotyped gender expectations?

2. **Focus on Early Messages in the Home**

   Try to recall when you first learned about your gender. What were some of the early messages you received? Did you receive similar messages from both parents? The responses may be discussed in small groups. The following may be discussed with the entire group:

   a. Are there specific traits and behaviors that resonate particularly in the women's responses? In the men's responses?

   b. Did you feel limited or constrained by the early messages you received? If yes, how so?

   c. Have you challenged or changed these early messages? If so, in what ways have you done so?

3. **Connecting Gendered Messages to the Media Landscape**

   Thinking about your own exposure to early messages from the media (stories, films, television, and/or music) are there particular examples that stand out that served as models for your own development? To what extent did these models reinforce and/or deviate from traditional stereotypes for gendered behavior?

4. **Rewriting the Early Gendered Scripts/Traits**

   If you could alter early lessons or experiences from your own upbringing, what messages or behaviors would you include? Are there certain traits or experiences that you wish your parents might have encouraged and/or exposed you to? To what extent do these "wished-for" messages, behaviors, traits, and experiences conform to or deviate from traditional masculine and feminine stereotypes?

The Educational Landscape
Connecting Gender and Identity

Schools should provide students with a language of criticism and a language of hope. The languages should be used in order to prepare students to conceptualize systematically the relationships among their private dreams and desires and the collective dreams of a larger social order. New generations of students must be capable of analyzing the social and material conditions in which dreams are given birth, and are realized, diminished, or destroyed. More importantly, students need to be able to recognize which dreams and which dreamers are dangerous to the larger society, and why this is the case. (McLaren, 2003, p. 178)

*T*he groundwork for the "dreams and desires" that students develop over the course of their education is largely laid early on in their lives. Students' hopes and aspirations are not untouched by the families into which they are born or raised, by the communities in which they spend a great deal of their formative years, or by the teachers who wield considerable influence on how the educational process is experienced. Peter McLaren (2003) focused on social justice and how schools can play a crucial role in unmasking the ways in which students' "subjectivities have been ideologically formed . . ." (p. 179). The dreams, desires, and subjectivities help determine identity; identity, in turn, plays a critical role in shaping subsequent dreams, desires, and subjectivities.

Dreams are achievable if students are part of a learning environment that provides them with the opportunity to develop the skills, knowledge, values, and attitudes that will help them to find their places in the adult world. Much has been written to suggest, however, that their learning environment is not a uniform landscape, and that gender (as well as intersections with socioeconomic status, race, ethnicity, sexuality, and culture) powerfully shapes the learning process as well as aspirations for the future.

Over the past several decades, we can point to critical "gaps" that have powerfully influenced assumptions related to intelligence and to academic performance: (1) socioeconomic status and learning readiness; (2) sex differences in academic performance and participation; and (3) representation in the educational landscape. Moreover, these gaps have been used to justify encouraging (as well as discouraging) students toward certain subject areas; they also have been used to implement educational initiatives aimed at narrowing the gaps that persist. Importantly, there is increasing recognition that academic interest, performance, and achievement are not the sole responsibilities of the classroom teacher. In large measure how students experience the academic environment is powerfully influenced by the messages, support, and encouragement they receive in the home. Communication both in the home and in the classroom are inextricably connected to how women and men experience, interpret, and ultimately value their student years. As you continue reading this chapter, think about how your own experiences both in the home and in classrooms have influenced your own educational and professional choices and trajectories.

In recent years, there has been a resurgence of studies that have had a powerful impact on perpetuating assumptions connecting biology (as well as race) to academic ability and to performance. Included in these assumptions is the belief that girls are better suited for subjects related to verbal and reading skills while boys are more equipped for math and science. Other published works have alleged that girls are by nature less interested in math (Pinker, 2002), and that the male brain is more suitable for the analytic skills associated with science and math while the female brain is hard-wired for empathy (Brizendine, 2006; Cohen, 2003; Gurian, 2002). Lawrence H. Summers, while serving as president of Harvard, echoed these assumptions when he suggested at a conference on women and science that women are underrepresented in the math and science disciplines because they may be inherently less adept in these areas (cited in Dean, 2005). Similarly, in *The Bell Curve,* Richard Herrnstein and Charles Murray (1994) attribute the difference in the IQ scores of black and white students to genetics and suggest that intelligence is largely unchangeable.

The observations made above reflect a backlash. Undergirding these messages is an essentialist perspective insofar as gender and race (as seen as strictly biological variables, rather than variables that are socially constructed) are used to explain different interests in academic subjects as well as differences in performance on standardized tests that have long been used to measure intelligence. By privileging nature, what is often minimized or ignored are a host of environmental factors (i.e., nutrition, medical care, physical health, home environment, and socioeconomic status) that have been found to play critical roles on student performance and achievement (Kahn, 2009; Nisbett, 2009). In the following sections, we consider three factors that have been particularly influential in sustaining essentialist messages: socioeconomic status, assumptions about gender and academic performance, and representation in the educational landscape. In addition, we indicate important nuances that have ultimately challenged assumptions about the immutability of intelligence as it relates to academic achievement.

The Environmental Gap: Socioeconomic Status and Communication in the Home

In May of 2009, President Barack Obama nominated Sonia Sotomayor to the Supreme Court. The president's remarks included, of course, her stellar record of achievement. But he also commented extensively on her background: growing up in a housing project in the South Bronx in a family with meager financial resources; her father's third-grade education and inability to speak English; her mother having to work two jobs after her father died; and the unswerving value of education that was communicated in the home. In light of her economic and cultural circumstances, her academic record of scholarship at Princeton University and Yale Law School as well as her substantial 17-year career were deemed remarkable. Sotomayor's "story" is an important example as it illustrates that despite a legacy of studies linking socioeconomic status to academic performance, barriers to academic success can be overcome when strong support and encouragement are provided in the home.

In recent decades, several studies suggest a connection between social class and the quantity and quality of support and encouragement reflected in parents' communications with their children. In particular, studies conducted on professional, middle-class, working-class, and lower-income families reveal significant differences in two areas deemed foundational for preparing children for the learning environment. The first area indicates that young children raised in professional and middle-class homes are exposed to more communication than children from working- and lower-income homes. Psychologists Betty Hart and Todd Risley's (1995) study on white professional, white and black working-class, and black welfare families revealed a major disparity in the number of words children are exposed to on a daily basis with estimates ranging from 2,000 to 1,300 to 600 words per day, respectively. Similarly, socioeconomic status was found to connect with children's exposure to reading materials. Anthropologist Shirley Brice Heath (1982) reported that more books on a wider range of topics were found in middle-class homes in comparison to homes of working-class families.

A second, and perhaps more critical, area suggests a disparity in the quality of communication that takes place in the home. Middle-class and professional parents have been found to employ messages that promote, rather than stifle, interaction. They are more apt to include children in their conversations, pose and elicit questions about their activities, and encourage their children to connect experiences in the home with external events and experiences (Hart & Risley, 1995; Heath, 1982; Lareau, 2003; Mikulecky, 1996). Significantly, children in professional and middle-class homes more frequently receive encouraging comments from parents in comparison to the discouraging comments and reprimands that are heard more often in the homes of working- and lower-class families (Hart & Risley, 1995).

Implicit in these studies is that in higher-income homes, parents are more likely to talk *with* rather than to talk *at* their children. They are more apt to *explain* rather than *order*. There is the sense that the child's view of the world is more frequently legitimated in these homes. Implicit as well are potential consequences that connect with preparing young children for school. Engaging with children through conversation and reading results in enhanced vocabulary when the child enters the classroom (Nisbett, 2009). Messages of support and encouragement provide a foundation for building confidence (Brooks-Gunn & Markman, 2005). Finally, raising children in an environment that promotes discussion and the ability to ask questions lays the groundwork for developing the type of critical and analytical thinking skills that are valued in educational settings (Heath, 1982).

Several recently published works speak to the disparities created by historical, political, economic, and social events and practices that have fueled and perpetuated unequal treatment and access to educational opportunities and resources (Kahn, 2009; Nisbett, 2009; Steinberg, 2009). They point to initiatives to alter and transform a legacy of discrimination in the United States, and reveal, moreover, that marginalization is not limited to the *United States* but occurs in other cultures as well. Richard Nisbett (2009), in particular, challenges hereditarians' assumptions about IQ and academic achievement. He points to studies on adoption (Capron & Duyme, 1989; Moore, 1986), on brain size (Ankney, 1992; Rushton & Jensen, 2005; Schoenemann, Budinger, Sarich, & Wang, 1999), and to longitudinal studies on racial differences in IQ tests (Dickens & Flynn, 2006; Flynn, 2007) that reveal the critical role environmental, more than biological, factors play in narrowing the academic potential and achievement gaps.

Although this section reveals several of the challenges lower socioeconomic families confront in providing a foundation for academic success, personal success stories like Sonia Sotomayor's clearly demonstrate that income alone does not automatically preclude academic achievement.

The Academic Gender Gap: The Power of Assumptions, Expectations, and Attributions

Over the past four decades, considerable scholarly attention has focused on how girls and boys experience, negotiate, and perform in the educational setting. In their meta-analytic survey of studies on sex equity in the classroom, communication researchers Suzanne Jones and Kathryn Dindia (2004) indicated that included among the factors that have been examined extensively between 1970 and 2000 are (1) school subject and academic performance (p. 451) and (2) the teacher's expectation of the student's achievement (p. 450). These factors are interrelated and have contributed to fueling actual, as well as sustaining presumed, differences related to gender and the classroom experience.

Gender and the Subject Divide: Parental Influence

Earlier in this chapter, we noted several recent works suggesting innate differences in males' and females' abilities for certain academic subjects. A legacy of research has fueled these assumptions. However, on closer inspection we see important mitigating factors that have contributed to an essentialist view. We see, as well, contradictory findings suggesting that biological gaps in academic ability and performance may be more illusory than real.

Rosalind Barnett and Caryl Rivers (2004, pp. 149–171) indicate that studies published in the early 1980s were among the first to suggest genetics to explain differences in boys' and girls' performance in math. Particularly influential was Camilla Benbow and Julian Stanley's (1980) examination of nearly 10,000 gifted seventh and eighth grade students' math scores, which revealed that boys outperformed girls. Because these students were in the same classes, the researchers assumed that environmental factors did not account for the performance differences. Instead, they attributed the variation in performance to genetics, suggesting that perhaps boys were better suited for math than girls.

Ensuing studies suggested that factors other than genetics contributed to the disparity in performance. They indicated that boys and girls often receive different types of encouragement and support in the home and in the classroom, and that these factors, more than biology, play a significant role in sustaining the view that girls are less suited for math and science. For example, according to Eccles, Barber, and Jozefowicz (1999), mothers who were aware of the Benbow and Stanley findings had lower expectations for their daughters' performance in math than did mothers who were unaware of the reported differences. The attitudes of fathers also play a critical role in how their daughters regard mathematics (see Fennema & Sherman, 1977). Parental attitudes are communicated in multiple ways. As we have discussed in chapter 4, we expect that parental influences will change as familial landscapes shift.

Parental attitudes toward gender and appropriate academic subject areas are also reflected in the different types of support young girls and boys receive. Several studies indicate that girls receive less encouragement from parents to take courses in and to pursue careers related to math and science than boys (Fausto-Sterling, 1985; Montaresky, 2005; Paglin, 1993). Young boys reportedly receive more parental encouragement than girls to engage in activities that involve problem-solving skills as well as more books and materials related to math (Fausto-Sterling, 1985; Paglin, 1993; Yee & Eccles, 1988). Most significantly, parents are more apt to view a boy's success in problem solving as a natural ability whereas a girl's success in this area is attributed to diligence and hard work (Barnett & Rivers, 2004, p. 168).

Parental attitudes about gender and academic subjects do not arise in a vacuum. They are influenced, in part, by their own experiences and awareness of reported findings on gender and academic ability. The Benbow and Stanley report demonstrates the potential problem that can occur when studies connect findings to biology and ignore potential environmental factors that may contribute to the findings. It is also important to scrutinize the participants in studies that examine gender and academic ability. Many of the reports on male and female performance in math stem from studies on white students. The tendency has been to assume that these findings can be generalized to all students regardless of their background. As Barnett and Rivers (2004) wryly observe,

> Among Latinos, no gender difference is discerned; among African Americans and Asian Americans, there is a small difference favoring females. Why wasn't it called a white male math gene? And Asian males consistently outscored Caucasian males. Why didn't anyone propose an Asian math gene? (p. 152)

As the above-mentioned studies indicate, regardless of how these assumptions are created, all too often they are transmitted by parents to their children in ways both subtle and overt. These messages play a powerful role in shaping, reinforcing, and perpetuating gender-based stereotypes. Ultimately, these messages can exact a toll on a child's own interest, attitudes, and confidence in certain academic subjects as well as limiting their professional aspirations in the future.

Gender and the Subject Divide: The Influence of Teachers

Teachers, like parents, are not immune to a host of research findings and to long-held assumptions that have divided disciplines, ability, and interest along gender/racial/cultural lines. They do not enter the classroom unfettered and uninfluenced by the social landscape and the cultural environments in which they, too, have been raised and educated. Teachers' beliefs about "gender-appropriate" subjects and roles similarly influence academic performance. Jones and Dindia (2004) indicate that recent studies on sex equity in the classroom suggest that teachers' expectations about students' ability and competence in certain subject areas are reflective of the larger societal landscape. As explained in chapter 4, to the extent that women and men have been valued differently for engaging in certain behaviors, these differences have purportedly influenced teacher behavior: "In the context of teaching, boys may not be praised for writing or reading skills, whereas girls may not receive praise for excelling in math because it is assumed that they will not use such skills as adults" (p. 456). Jones and Dindia further indicate that teacher expectations supporting the reading/writing versus the math/science divide emerge as early as elementary school (p. 451).

Teachers' expectations are manifested in multiple ways and they have been found to have important consequences on students' own confidence as well as performance. One major area of research that has significantly shaped and sustained attitudes about gender-appropriate subjects and has been used to explain teacher-student interactions and their consequences derives from cognitive processes theory. As Jones and Dindia (2004) explain, this is manifested by the extent to which teachers' expectations about students' capabilities are conveyed to those they teach, resulting in performances by students that "match," thereby confirming, the teachers' expectations. According to this theoretical perspective, if teachers expect women to do less well in math or science, if they expect men not to perform well in reading and writing, if they expect that race and economic status will affect performance, "then the students will indeed perform poorly because teachers will interact less and possibly more harshly with those students" (p. 456). This cycle has been called the Pygmalion effect by Robert Rosenthal and Leonore Jacobson (1968).

Differences in the ways teachers interact with and/or assess students along gender and disciplinary lines has been well-documented. In the areas of math, science, and technology, for example, when girls receive less encouragement from teachers and counselors to enroll in courses in these areas (Paglin, 1993; Pinker, 2008; Simonds & Cooper, 2001), when they receive less encouragement from teachers to participate in class or to engage directly in experiments (American Association of University Women, 1991, 1992; Jones, 1989; Jones & Wheatley, 1990; Paglin, 1993; Sadker & Sadker, 1985, 1994), and when teachers more frequently *show* girls how to utilize technology rather than to *explain* how to do so (whereas it is the opposite scenario for boys) (Stewart, Cooper, & Stewart, 2003), the overall result is a dramatic gender gap in loss of self-esteem and confidence in these areas. In an educational climate that is perceived as unwelcoming or "chilly" (Hall & Sandler, 1982), students may cope by becoming more passive

(Rosenfeld & Jarrard, 1986), or they may cope by dropping out (Sadker & Sadker, 1994). As a 1992 report of the American Association of University Women (AAUW) indicated, by age 15, even girls who liked these subjects reported feeling less competent than their male classmates.

While female students may be subjected to influences beyond their control in regard to the sciences, males find themselves subjected to similar types of influences in regard to reading, writing, and communication skills. Male students' performance in these areas has been consistently lower than their female classmates in secondary school as well as in college (Eliot, 2009; Garden, 2006; Goldin, Katz, & Kuziemko, 2006; Kahn, 2009; Pollack, 1998; Tyre, Murr, Juarez, Underwood, & Wingert, 2006; West, 1999). One explanation for this disparity is rooted in the assumption that women are more adept than men in these subjects. Communication researchers Dana Ivy and Phil Backlund (2008, p. 377) indicate the toll that sex bias in the educational process can exact on men's performance. For example, Jan Haswell and Rich Haswell (1995) reveal in their study on gender and college-level writing that when evaluators read essays attributed to women writers, they give women higher ratings compared to men. This type of behavior, as Ivy and Backlund (2008) suggest, supports and perpetuates the stereotypical assumption that women are more competent than men in writing ability.

A second, and more problematic, explanation for a disparity in performance along gender lines is rooted in how men themselves value certain subjects. In his work on masculinities, psychologist Jack Kahn (2009) suggests that particularly for men from working-class backgrounds, college is viewed as a site for gaining practical knowledge, which math, science, and technology courses presumably provide. Also, "Research is beginning to suggest that higher education and behaviors associated with a traditional college education (reading, writing, analysis classroom learning) are associated for many men with femininity and with 'middle-class' values" (p. 169). The devaluation of certain subjects because they have been traditionally associated with one sex indicates a pressing need to scrutinize the early messages—in the home as well as in the classroom—that may have fueled this outlook.

The tendency of many teachers to characterize those they teach according to gender reflects a larger propensity to characterize students according to other attributes as well. In her work on unmasking whiteness, Virginia Lea (2009) posits that many teachers are unable to extricate themselves from categorizing those they teach according to class and according to achievement level (i.e., high, low, and middle achievers) (p. 68). Often, these teachers are not aware of the consequences these labels have on what they come to expect from those they teach: "In Platonic metaphors, most teachers apparently still see students as belonging to groups made of differently valued metals. . . . They view official classifications of students as unproblematic—English language learners, special education, at-risk, for example—and their pedagogy derives from these classifications" (p. 68).

Studies indicate that the Pygmalion effect—whether stemming from assumptions about gender, race, class, or achievement level—can be altered when teachers examine how their own assumptions and expectations are communicated to those they teach. The work of social psychologists Claude Steele and Joshua Aronson reveals a direct connection between teachers' expectations and students' performance and exposes the adverse consequences of stereotypical assumptions on student achievement (Steele, 1997; Steele & Aronson, 1995). In their examination of race and performance on IQ and achievement tests, for example, Steele and Aronson (1995) found that African American students' performance is impacted adversely when teachers engage in stereotype threat, that is, when they make race salient prior to testing. Under testing conditions where race is not made salient and teachers assure students that they can all do equally well, test performance improves. Steele (1997) found that stereotype threat similarly impacts women's math performance. When told prior to testing that men tend to score better on math tests, women's scores were lower than in testing conditions where this information was withheld from them. Under the latter condition, Steele reports, women's and men's scores were about the same.

The influence of teachers' attitudes, assumptions, expectations, and communication about student performance is significant in several ways. The studies we refer to expose the considerable power teachers wield in shaping women's and men's view of their own academic confidence and competence in particular subject areas; they reveal, moreover, the fragility of this view. The studies also expose the power of labels and of the dividing practices on situating students within the academic environment: membership in a particular group (i.e., gender, race, class, or culture) is often sufficient to characterize the educational journey for students—a journey, we observe, that is frequently tenuous. But these studies, by unmasking the propensity to categorize others, also demonstrate the potential to challenge and alter a legacy of stereotypes that moves us beyond an essentialist view of academic ability and competence.

Academic Climate and Expectations
for Students' Behavior in the Classroom

Beyond communicating expectations related to academic subjects and performance, teachers play a crucial role in conveying expectations for classroom behavior. Studies conducted over the past several decades suggest that these expectations are often different for male and female students. In particular, they suggest that starting in elementary school and continuing throughout the educational process, teachers both tacitly and overtly create distinct learning environments for the male and female students in their charge.

Despite the passage of Title IX of the Education Amendments of 1972, which intended to guarantee equal treatment of male and female students at all educational levels, subsequent studies reveal that the intention of the amendments did not match the reality of female students' experiences. Powerful images have been evoked to characterize the educational climate, especially for girls and women. Teachers have been found to create—often unintentionally and quite subtly—a "hidden curriculum" that perpetuates gender roles and behaviors that undermine and devalue women's contributions (Lee & Gropper, 1974; Orenstein, 1994). Other results of a "chilly" classroom environment are educators' implicit and explicit messages conveyed to women that they are not welcome in certain classes (Good & Slayings, 1988; Hall & Sandler, 1984; Orenstein, 1994; Pearson & West, 1991; Sandler & Hall, 1986). The disparate ways that teachers reward, criticize, and encourage males' and females' participation in classes intimates that "sexism" persists in the classroom (Sadker & Sadker, 1985, 1986), which "shortchanges" girls' aspirations (AAUW, 1991, 1992, 1998) and suggests that, ultimately, we are "failing at fairness" (Sadker & Sadker, 1994).

The above-mentioned descriptors have been connected to two interrelated aspects of teachers' communication in the classroom. First, studies conducted primarily in the 1980s and 1990s reveal that across disciplines and grade levels, male students have been found to dominate classroom communication. Specifically, male students are more often called on and asked more questions by teachers; they are allowed to talk for longer intervals; and, they are not sanctioned as often for calling out answers, or for cutting-off or interrupting female classmates (Hall & Sandler, 1984; Orenstein, 1994; Riddell, 1989; Sadker & Sadker, 1985, 1994; Sandler & Hall, 1986).

In educational settings where students, in part, are evaluated for their in-class contributions, these findings suggest that teachers inadvertently may be communicating that some voices are more valued than others. This example of the hidden curriculum impacts all students. When girls are not called on to participate, or when they find their contributions cut short or interrupted, their willingness to engage may be adversely affected: "They may become reluctant to participate at all in class, unable to withstand the small failures necessary for long-term academic success" (Orenstein, 1994, p. 44). Boys also may learn an unintended message: there are no consequences when they demonstrate a "lack of respect for their female classmates" (p. 44).

The second consequential finding relates to the praise and criticism that teachers provide to their students. In their meta-analysis of 32 empirical studies that examined "whether teacher-initiated interactions with students, such as praising or blaming, vary as a function of student sex," Jones and Dindia (2004) report no statistical differences in positive teacher-initiated interactions (praise, acceptance, encouragement) (pp. 444, 454). In 11 studies, however, negative teacher-initiated interactions indicate that male students are reprimanded and critiqued more than female students (p. 454). However, studies also reveal that what students may be praised or critiqued for may vary according to the student's sex.

Beginning early in their academic careers, girls are rewarded for behaving in ways that conform to stereotypes associated with femininity. In particular, they are praised for being polite, compliant, and neat; they also receive more compliments on their physical appearance (Gold, Crombie, & Noble, 1987; Orenstein, 1994; Riddell, 1989; Sadker & Sadker, 1985, 1994). Conversely, when they deviate from behaviors associated with the feminine stereotype (e.g., calling out, asserting their views, interrupting), their transgressions may be regarded more seriously. However, not all members of society define and embrace the feminine stereotype in the same way. As Adams and Singh (1998) indicate in their study on race and the school environment, behaviors associated with the feminine stereotype do not necessarily resonate for all women. Commenting on their work, Wood (2009) observes the inevitable clash that may occur when African American girls who have been encouraged at home to value and develop "active, ambitious, assertive, and independent" behaviors "encounter European American teachers and peers" who embrace and value contradictory expectations for how young girls ought to deport themselves (p. 93).

Perhaps due, in part, to the expectation that girls are, or ought to be, more cooperative and diligent in the performance of their assignments, "criticism of female students tends to focus on their lack of knowledge or skill" (Stewart et al., 2003, p. 143; see also Brophy, 1985; Dweck, Davidson, Nelson, & Enna, 1978). As Angela Duckworth and Martin Seligman's (2005) recent study of eighth-grade students reveals, girls evidence more self-discipline than do boys at this age level. These researchers suggest that this difference may, in part, account for the higher grades that girls in this age group receive across disciplinary boundaries. We suspect that if teachers expect their female charges to dutifully and diligently perform their assignments, their lack of preparation may be criticized more harshly and may explain, in part, why girls become more "hesitant" to speak out or "to take academic risks" (Orenstein, 1994, p. 43); to do so may diminish their personhood in their teachers' eyes as well as their own.

Studies suggest that both qualitatively and quantitatively, feedback to male students differs in significant ways. Starting at an early age, boys receive from teachers three kinds of feedback that promote problem-solving and critical-thinking skills: praise, remediation, and criticism. Researchers have identified several behaviors that support the assessment that the learning climate is different for boys. In particular, teachers have been found to: pick up on and use male students' ideas more often; allow male students more opportunities and a longer response time to arrive at answers; ask them more probing questions that tap into analytical skills; and praise them for their intellectual performance (Hall & Sandler, 1984; Orenstein, 1994; Riddell, 1989; Sadker & Sadker, 1985, 1994; Simpson & Erickson, 1983). The negative feedback male students receive has been connected primarily to behaviors that disrupt the class and to a lack of neatness (Brophy, 1985; Dweck et al., 1978; Orenstein, 1994; Riddell, 1989; Sadker & Sadker, 1985, 1994; Simpson & Erickson, 1983).

Several reasons have been offered to explain why male students garner more positive as well as negative attention from their teachers. Jones and Dindia (2004) refer to a series of studies that indicate that starting in elementary school, "boys have been found to misbehave more frequently than girls . . ." (p. 449) (see also Brophy & Good, 1974; French, 1984; Simpson & Erickson, 1983; Stake & Katz, 1982). Also, boys are reportedly more often diagnosed with learning disabilities at an early age (Croll, 1985; Eliot, 2009; Kahn, 2009; Nisbett, 2009; Pinker, 2008). Regardless of the source for acting up, boys

> may be more in the "perceptual field" of the teacher than girls and may therefore receive more attention, not only in the form of teacher criticism and reprimands, but also in the form of praise as a pedagogical tool to help boys better integrate into the classroom environment. (Jones & Dindia, 2004, p. 449)

These mitigating factors may, in part, elucidate why teachers have been found to pay more attention to the male students in their classes. However, as indicated in previous sections on expectations for academic performance, these mitigating factors do not explain the lack of encouragement and support female students have traditionally received in the areas of math and science. If helping students "better integrate into the classroom environment" is of paramount importance to the teaching process, we would expect to find that girls would be more in the "perceptual field" of teachers in these classes. Certainly a majority of students are not aware of these research findings or of the likely motivations behind their teachers' behaviors, therefore, if female students are on the margins of teachers' "perceptual field" in the classes they attend, it is understandable why they may interpret a lack of attention as being less important. In such a learning environment, a "pedagogical tool" is apt to shade into feeling undervalued. In this light, the "hidden curriculum," "chilly climate," and feelings of being "shortchanged" also become understandable.

In this section, we have examined how powerfully parents' and teachers' expectations and communication relating to academic ability, interest, and performance can foster a learning environment that may be experienced as either inclusive or as marginalizing. As the next section reveals, what groups are included or excluded in the curriculum also contributes to how the education process is experienced.

The Impact of the Invisibility Gap on the Classroom Climate

In 2004, Brazilian educator Paulo Freire asserted that, "Nobody can be in the world, with the world, and with others in a neutral manner" (p. 60). A legacy of research indicates that across grade levels and disciplines, the corpus of what is taught in the United States is not neutral. Instead, its contributions and representations predominantly reflect "White, heterosexual, able-bodied, middle- and upper-class men . . ." (Wood, 2009, p. 195). In the process, these representations often minimize, marginalize, or ignore the full range of contributions of those who do not fall into these categories.

In the area of gender, considerable attention has focused on exposing the extent to which women's voices and contributions have been minimized and/or absent across disciplines and across all grade levels. Moreover, within the United States, the majority of those who teach are predominantly white. As Banks (2006) cautions, the worldview of a majority may be shaped by their own experiences and they may limit their knowledge of and interest in addressing topics that are peripheral to their educational preparation. Too often, Jerome Bruner (1996), asserts, both what is taught as well as the classroom environment is "a direct reflection of the beliefs and assumptions the teacher holds about the learner" (p. 47). Assumptions, attitudes, and attributions about class, race, culture, gender, and sexual identity all too often color the lenses—even unwittingly at times—through which educators view and interact with those in their charge.

Scholars from multiple disciplines call for ways to challenge and to broaden what gets included in the classroom as well as how to create a classroom climate that makes visible issues and individuals who have long remained on the periphery of the educational arena. As education researcher Elizabeth Meyer (2009) notes:

> Educational structures wield extraordinary ideological power because of their role in teaching what the culture deems important and valuable to future generations. Ministries of Education, textbook publishers, and teachers determine what lessons are passed on to students and whose knowledge or "truth" is valued. . . . (p. 176)

Several researchers suggest that gender, race, and sexual identity play a critical role in defining the "truths" to which students are exposed. Cheri Simonds and Pamela Cooper (2001) indicate the extent to which readers, texts, and anthologies from diverse disciplines (e.g., communication, economics, history, literature, mathematics, psychology, science) and at all educational levels continue to exclude or under-represent women's contributions to society. They suggest, moreover, that all too often the works to which students are exposed perpetuate traditional and often stereotypical roles for women that do not reflect the current reality of the lives they lead. "Sex-role stereotyping in curriculum materials may be very subtle—so subtle, in fact, that we do not notice it at first" (p. 234).

The subtle ways that gender is indirectly reflected is echoed in Ronald L. Jackson II and his colleagues' (2007) chapter on how white privilege is perpetuated in the classroom:

> Students have consistently come to learn via institutions that the only intellectual and cultural discourses and traditions that are meaningful and significant are those of Whites, despite never having been told that directly. . . . Everything from the selection of course texts and in-class discussions to the introduction of key or "classic theorists" and concepts has contributed to the kinds of intellectual arguments and traditions that will be evoked later by those trained students to explain how the world works. (p. 68)

Elizabeth Meyer (2009) similarly speaks to the ways in which heterosexuality-as-the-norm pervades the educational landscape. This norm is evidenced in the heterosexual romantic literature that is studied as well as by defining and presenting the "'nuclear' heterosexual two-parent family" as the norm across disciplines (p. 177). This lens through which students learn to view the world, she argues, maintains "the heterosexism of the curriculum [that] is invisible to many due to its unquestioned dominance in schools and communities" (p. 177). In the process of normalizing heterosexual behavior, Richard Friend contends that schools thereby engage in "systematic exclusion," a "process whereby positive role models, messages, and images about lesbian, gay and bisexual people are publicly silenced in schools" (cited in Meyer, 2009, p. 177).

All students are impacted when the norm is defined in a single way; when who they see as foregrounded does not reflect their lived experiences or identity. We note that whether addressing gender, race, or sexual identity, the above-mentioned researchers stress both the "indirect" and "subtle" ways in which traditional ideologies and values are transmitted.

The challenge for many educators has been to create a learning climate that is inclusive. Despite a growing recognition that it is important to examine issues related to social justice in the classroom, there are several challenges that limit attempts to include materials related to gender, race, culture, and sexual orientation. For some educators, the inclusion of issues related to social justice is viewed as beyond the purview of what they are expected or should be teaching and is regarded as an "extra" duty (Carr & Lund, 2009, p. 53). Some grapple with where to situate social justice issues in the curriculum. Often this material is added on "to the center or end of a text" (Simonds & Cooper, 2001, p. 235), or "tacked" on to the curriculum (Daffin & Anderson, 2009, p. 438). Positionality speaks volumes: material that is located on the periphery is often viewed as just that—peripheral or on the margins, but not central to what is being taught/addressed.

Some educators connect their reluctance to address social justice to their own academic preparation and background. In these instances, often a lack of knowledge or discomfort with the material is used to explain why some topics related to gender, race, culture, and sexuality, for example, are either avoided or are marginally addressed in their classes (Asante, 1998; Crabtree, Sapp, & Licona, 2009; Jackson et al., 2007; Simpson, Causey, & Williams, 2007). If educators resist augmenting what they know or are unwilling to move outside of their comfort zone, they also limit the borders of knowledge to which their students are exposed. As a consequence, what exists beyond those borders remains invisible and inaccessible to those they teach.[1]

Changing Course through Inclusion

In recent decades, educators from diverse disciplines have increasingly focused on ways to teach and to address social justice issues in the classroom. In the process, educators have focused on rethinking their own pedagogy. Edited works by Shirley Steinberg (2009) and by Robbin Crabtree and her colleagues (2009), for example, bring together researchers from multiple disciplines who offer critical insights on transforming the way they teach. Their insights reflect aspects of feminist pedagogy that challenge several traditionally held notions of teaching that have sustained and reproduced the very hierarchies and power differences that are tackled by social justice issues. This scrutiny directly or indirectly addresses many of the above-mentioned concerns. We point to three teaching strategies that can potentially alter how the educational landscape is experienced.

1. Creating Space for Personal Experience and Emotion

In regard to how students ought to engage in the learning process, the educational arena traditionally privileges the intellect (the mind), which values and equates objectivity, neutrality, and reason with the truth. The extent to which taken-for-granted truths contradict, ignore, marginalize, or negate the lived experiences of all groups who comprise the class setting needs to be addressed in the learning process. Judy Helfand (2009) evokes a "pedagogy of discomfort" that allows space for the expression of feelings.

> To engage in critical inquiry often means asking students to radically reevaluate their worldviews. This process can incur feelings of anger, grief, disappointment, and resistance. . . . In short, this pedagogy of discomfort requires not only cognitive but emotional labor. (p. 90)

2. Rethinking Notions of Hierarchy and Care

The traditional classroom structure, including the role of the teacher, has been linked to erecting, conveying, and sustaining power differences. In an effort to alter the learning environment as a site of embedded power, several researchers advocate the importance of creating a classroom environment where there is space for caring, respect, and opportunities for collaborative learning to occur; where students are viewed and valued as individuals (Crabtree et al., 2009; Helfand, 2009; hooks, 1994; Kim, 2009). Lili Kim (2009) suggests that "the teacher becomes an authority *with* the students, not *over* them" (p. 197).

Studies conducted on both secondary- and college-level students, in fact, suggest that students' educational experiences and performance are enhanced when teachers provide both instructional and emotional support (Hamre & Pianta, 2001; Teven & Gorham, 1999; Teven & McCroskey, 1997).

3. Challenging a Legacy of Categorical "Either/Or" Thinking That Sustains and Reifies Binary Thought

In chapter 4, we identified sets of opposites that have fueled Western thinking. There are several problems inherent with dividing practices and with creating categories that can adversely impact the classroom experience. First, the process of engaging in "either/or" thinking (e.g., white/black, male/female, etc.) shades into valuing one side of the divide over the other. Helfand (2009) observes that "the binaries inherent in either/or often come with prejudgments where one side of the binary is seen as better than or superior to the other" (p. 86). Students can hold different points of view without necessarily one being wrong and the other right—a shift, in her view, that moves us away from "either/or" thinking and moves us toward "both/and" thinking (p. 86).

Second, the labels we use to categorize individuals and groups often obscure, marginalize, or ignore those who do not neatly belong to the categories we have constructed. Writing on the need for greater consideration of multiethnic students, Erica Mohan (2009) exposes the challenges created by the process of categorizing and labeling individuals according to race and ethnicity. Mohan contends that terms commonly used to describe individuals from diverse backgrounds (e.g., "multiracial," "mixed race," "biracial," "mixed origin," "mixed ethnicity," "children of mixed parentage") are problematic because they "reinforce the misconception that there exist biologically defined pure races and discrete ethnicities" (p. 132). Often, individuals subsumed by these monikers feel pressured to choose a single identity or to speak for all members of a particular category—via discussions, surveys, forms, etc.—as if they can, or want to, compartmentalize their lived experiences. Mohan suggests that appropriate and meaningful inclusion in discussions about ethnicity and race can occur when educators "deconstruct and challenge divisive identity categories, not construct new ones" (p. 138). In the process, students have the opportunity to learn and to challenge "the complexities of race and ethnicity, the limitations of these concepts, and the ways in which they have been constructed and employed to categorize, segregate, and oppress" (p. 136).

Elizabeth Meyer (2009) and Mary Fonow and Debian Marty (2009) make a similar case for the need to promote conversations about the dividing practices that have been used to categorize sexual identity. A legacy of erroneous myths, negative stereotypes, and discriminatory practices have sustained a lens that regards heterosexuality as "compulsory" (Rich, 1993) and as normal—a view that increasingly has been challenged in recent years. (The current debate on marriage rights for gays and lesbians is one obvious example.) Meyer (2009), in particular, advocates the need to expose instances of embedded heterosexism within educational structures and the toll exacted on students and educators alike by (1) bringing an awareness to the "unquestioned dominance" of heterosexism within the curriculum; (2) revealing the consequences of believing that one has to hide or mask an identity that is "not valued or welcomed" (p. 177); and (3) challenging and dismantling the "narrow boundaries of language" that perpetuate "the hierarchical binaries of male-female and straight-gay . . ." (p. 178).

A third strategy to examine how labels function and expose either/or thinking is to refocus our attention. Diversity work, including attempts to discuss sexual diversity, commonly focuses on "the marginalized 'other' rather than on understanding the perspectives and experiences of those in the dominant group" (Meyer, 2009, p. 178). This lens can be altered by examining the realities and experiences of heterosexual-identified individuals as a way to reveal heterosexual privilege and expose how this privilege serves "to make some people's relationships and experiences more valued than others" (p. 178) (see Fonow & Marty, 2009). Martin Rochlin's (1977) exercise, "The Heterosexual Questionnaire," is one vehicle for exposing and interrogating the impact of "essentialist terms and constructs that have historically marginalized individuals and groups . . ." (Crabtree et al., 2009, p. 6). Questions such as "What do you think caused your heterosexuality?" "When and how did you first decide you were heterosexual?" and "Would you want your children to be heterosexual, knowing the problems they would face, such as heartbreak, disease, and divorce?" can be used as a springboard for conversations that ultimately connect, rather than divide, participants.[2]

As this section reveals, there are multiple ways to transform the pedagogical landscape; to alter how educators connect with students; and to facilitate closing the invisibility gap of representation that has characterized the content of what is taught. Initiatives for change have positive consequences. In the final section, we point to several studies that suggest a narrowing of the gender performance gap in some academic areas, and we indicate other areas that suggest there are emerging gaps that merit attention.

Closing One Gap, Opening Another

The Math/Science Gap Narrows; the Aspiration Gap Emerges

A series of studies indicate that in some academic areas, a narrowing of the academic performance gap has occurred. This has been especially evident in reports on female students' performance in the areas of math and science. Janet Hyde and her colleagues' (1990) meta-analysis of 254 studies of math performance revealed that 43% of the studies reported that females outperform males; 51% found that males outperform females; the remaining studies reported no differences in performance. In 1998, the AAUW's report suggested a substantial change in the science and math achievement gap for girls. Sociologists Erin Leahey and Guang Guo (2000) reported nearly identical test results on the math scores of 20,000 female and male students. And economist Claudia Goldin and her colleagues' (2006) pan-national review of 15-year-old students in 30 European nations indicated a narrowing in the math and science performance gap between males and females.

In part, closing the performance gap in areas previously associated with male ability and interest is attributed to an expansion of professional opportunities for women during the last three decades of the twentieth century. In part, initiatives to support women's training in math, science, and technology programs have contributed to women's enhanced performance in these areas. Since 1993, the National Science Foundation's (NSF) Gender in Sciences and Engineering program has provided $10 million annually to support K–12 training for girls' engineering and science education. Since 2001, the NSF has invested over $130 million to support Increasing the Participation and Advancement of Women in Academic Science and Engineering Careers (ADVANCE) projects at over 100 institutions and organizations (NSF, 2010). There also have been legislative measures taken; one of the most current being considered is the Fulfilling the Potential of Women in Academic Sciences and Engineering Act of 2008.

Efforts to support and encourage female students are reflected in the healthy application, enrollment, and graduation rates from colleges (Baum & Goodstein, 2005; Marcus, 2000; Tyre et al., 2006) and from reports that their overall grade point averages are higher than their male classmates' (Eliot, 2009; Tyre et al., 2006; Weil, 2008; West, 1999).

In spite of these obvious successes and expanded opportunities, there have been accompanying questions regarding the cost these accomplishments exact on young women's lives.

We point to two gaps that have been identified recently. First, young women coming of age around the turn of the new millennium may be experiencing and internalizing pressure in ways distinct from their predecessors. Psychology professor Stephen Hinshaw (2009) argues that young women today are increasingly subjected to what he terms "the triple bind" (pp. xii–xiii): (1) they are expected to retain behavioral traits associated with the traditional feminine stereotype (i.e., relationship building, empathy, helpfulness, nurturing, obedience, other-centered, etc.); (2) they are pressured to conform to standards of appearance that are often unrealistic, unattainable, and unhealthy as well as incompatible with professional aspirations (i.e., hyper-thin, pretty, and sexy while simultaneously athletic and strong); and (3) they are encouraged to be every bit as competitive, assertive, and ambitious as men to achieve entry into top colleges and careers (in sports, activities, and in academic performance).

As a consequence of these prescriptions for success, Hinshaw (2009) contends that young women's choices are both limited and illusory; that young girls "are ultimately presented with a very narrow, unrealistic set of standards that allow for no alternative" (p. 10). Using examples from his own clinical practice as well as studies conducted primarily over the last three decades, he connects the pressures created by the triple bind to increasingly high rates of stress and a susceptibility to and diagnoses of depression and eating disorders in young girls at earlier ages than in the past. He argues for the need for teachers, and for parents in particular, to be cognizant of how they may be contributing to these pressures, to be vigilant to how both the media and an increasing reliance on technology (e.g., MySpace, Facebook) reinforce and exacerbate anxiety (especially related to body image and appearance). Most important, Hinshaw argues convincingly for the need to pay attention to the inner lives of young girls. While the academic achievement gap may be closing, in the process the emotional fragility gap may be widening.[3]

Hinshaw's work focuses on high-school age students. A recent report suggests the emergence of what we see as an aspiration gap among college-age women. While many women coming of age during the last decades of the twentieth century entered college with the expectation of a full-time, long-term career, indications suggest a priority shift for current students. A survey of 138 freshman and senior females at Yale found that nearly 60% of the respondents anticipated a career hiatus: half projected cutting back on or stopping their careers entirely; half anticipated taking a few years off once they had children (Story, 2005).

These expectations were consistent with many of the students' projections we reported in chapter 4 and were viewed in distinct ways by faculty and administrators at multiple ivy league colleges (Story, 2005). Princeton University President Shirley Tilghman suggested that the path to leadership need not necessarily be equated with uninterrupted career trajectories and that full-time parents are not precluded from playing leadership roles and making positive contributions. University of Pennsylvania Dean Rebecca Bushnell saw efforts to achieve balance in one's life by recalibrating one's goals as both realistic and positive.

Voices of concern were also expressed that suggest systemic societal challenges. In Dean Peter Salovey's view, the expectation that women, and women alone, envision and embrace child care as their responsibility suggests to him "that so few students seem to be able to think outside the box; so few students seem to be able to imagine a life for themselves that isn't constructed along traditional gender roles" (Story, 2005, p. A18). And in Yale Professor Laura Wexler's estimation, such aspirations are unsurprising in a culture that simultaneously holds out opportunities and encouragement to women "with no social changes to support it" (p. A18).

The above discussion suggests an array of questions and potential concerns that in our view will undoubtedly be the focus of researchers, parents, and educators. To what extent will these projected goals of parenthood match the lived experiences of these students? It seems that many young women today are heeding Hewlett's (2002) advice to women who envision children in their future: they need to think strategically in their early twenties about what they want their lives to be like in their thirties. Hewlett (2007) is a strong advocate of women pursuing careers that have both "off-ramps" and "on-ramps." The hope, of course, is that their expectations are achieved. However, the variables involved can be elusive: a woman must establish herself in a career that she can opt in and out of, and she must find the right romantic partner who (1) is amenable to her goals and (2) can provide an appropriate lifestyle on one income (see chapter 6). It is obvious that this hope is limited by economic class: for the majority of women with young children who work outside the home, this aspiration is unavailable to them (Douglas & Michaels, 2004; Hochschild, 1997). Intimated as well is a re-articulation of traditional gender roles and traits. That is, it is unproblematic for women to aspire to and to assume the nurturing and child-care responsibilities in the private sphere while men are expected to retain the protector and provider roles associated with the public sphere.

While future studies will undoubtedly focus on how well women fare academically, professionally, and personally, additional studies and media attention on more diverse groups are needed. The majority of works cited that focus on gendered lives and academic performance largely reflect a heteronormative lens and speak to the experiences of white women in particular, which do not necessarily capture the reality of women of color (hooks, 1984, 1996; O'Neal Parker, 2005). Moreover, while considerable coverage of women's projections for their futures exist, projections on men's aspirations for how they envision their personal and professional lives are notably absent.

Table 5.1   Gender Differences and College in the United States[4]

	Men	Women
Application to College (Baum & Goodstein, 2005; Pollack, 1998)	58%	64–67%
Enrollment in Community College	40%	est. 60%
Enrollment in Four-Year College (Baum & Goodstein, 2005; Evelyn, 2002; Marcus, 2000)	45%	est. 60%
Use Academic Support Services at College (Evelyn, 2002; Gowdy & Robertson, 1994; Hudson, 1988)	30-40%	60–70%
Complete Two-Year Degree (Evelyn, 2002)	30–40%	60–70%
Complete Four-Year Degree (Evelyn, 2002; Tyre et al., 2006)	40–46%	est. 60%

Summarized from Kahn (2009), pp. 167–169.

A Performance Gap or a Reflection of Societal Values?

As we have discussed, a dichotomy of traditional gender views has prevailed in the classroom. In order to mitigate these outlooks, throughout the last three decades of the twentieth century educators worked to close the gap for women in the math, science, and technology areas and to encourage women to pursue careers in fields traditionally dominated by men (i.e., law, medicine, engineering, business, etc.). For men, other traditional views were challenged during this same period—some studies reported an expectation and performance gap for men in the areas of reading and writing, while contradictory findings were also reported. For example, in the area of verbal ability, Hyde and Linn's (1988) meta-analysis suggests only small gender differences in the verbal ability of girls and boys, thereby dispelling the taken-for-granted assumption that girls are superior in this area. In contrast, the pan-national review of 15-year-old students in 30 European nations indicates girls continue to outperform boys in the areas of reading and writing (Goldin et al., 2006). Despite the nuances of these findings, moving into the twenty-first century there has been increasing attention on how male students are faring academically. Terms such as "boys adrift" (Eliot, 2009, p. 18) and "boy turn" (Weaver-Hightower, 2003) have emerged in the academic discourse, as well as the observation that some men view college life as a "risky identity"—particularly those from working-class families (Kahn, 2009, p. 171). These accounts suggest the need for refocusing attention on male students.

In part, concern about how well the educational system is serving male students has been fueled by reports on the college application, enrollment, and retention rates of men and women in the United States (see table 5.1).

The seeds for academic success in college are sown during the elementary and secondary-level school years. Concern for establishing a solid educational foundation for boys has resulted in renewed and vigorous interest in single-sex education. We note that single-sex classes and educational opportunities to enhance the academic preparation of girls has existed for many years. However, initiatives for female students largely grew from a call by feminists to provide educational spaces to spark their interest in academic areas that were traditionally regarded as masculine subjects (math, science, technology). The resulting efforts were designed primarily to close an interest and performance gap that was largely attributable to the socialization process.[5]

For many new wave essentialists (Gurian, 2002; Pinker, 2002; Sax, 2005), biology (i.e., brain and hormonal differences) is used to justify the need for single-sex education. Proponents contend that in such an environment, boys can more readily be encouraged to engage in such subject areas as writing, reading, and the arts by removing the threat that they will be outperformed by girls. Similarly, they contend that girls will fare positively in math and science studies and risk-taking without the fear of being dominated by boys (Eliot, 2009, p. 304). Persuaded, in part, by these arguments, restrictions on *sex*-segregated education under Title IX were lifted in 2006. Over 49 single-sex public schools have opened along with more than 360 boys- and girls-only classrooms—and these numbers continue to grow (Weil, 2008, p. 40).

Despite the basic arguments for single-sex education, in education scholarship it has been difficult to support a conclusive verdict that single-sex or coed schooling is superior over the other.[6] Terms such as "equivocal," "tentative," and "little conclusive evidence" and language such as "the need to exercise caution" are repeatedly used to characterize findings (Harker, 2000; Marsh & Rowe, 1996; Salomone, 2003; Smithers & Robinson, 2006; Thompson & Ungerleider, 2004; U.S. Department of Education, 2005). What can make it so difficult to determine a definitive result is the task of isolating the unique and distinctive factors (e.g., quality of teachers and principals, familial involvement, school resources, etc.) that make up a school, and then judge them against another school's unique and distinctive factors. For example, according to Providence College Professor Cornelius Riordan, "disadvantaged students at single-sex schools have higher scores on standardized math, reading, science and civics tests than their counterparts in coed schools," but there are other factors that are contributory besides biology and gender constructs—there is the crucial role that the process of parental involvement in self-selection and single-sex education plays (Weil, 2008, p. 87; see also Eliot, 2009; Nisbett, 2009). Finally, psychologist Cordelia Fine (2010) cautions that we need to examine the impact of neuroscientific explanations of gender. In her view:

this "popular neurosexism" easily finds its way into apparently scientific books and articles for the interested public, including parents and teachers. Already, sexism disguised in neuroscientific finery is changing the way children are taught. (p. xxviii)

Her work unmasks the many "gaps, assumption, inconsistencies, [and] poor methodologies" (p. xxvii) that have perpetuated the centrality of biology to account for male and female interests, behavior, and academic potential.

Whether single-sex classrooms will be a panacea for addressing the current crisis in boys' education remains to be seen. However, we suspect that using biology to explain gender differences in interest and ability in certain subject areas ignores a larger question: what skills, abilities, and careers do we value as a culture? We noted earlier successful initiatives to steer women into subject areas and careers that have traditionally been dominated by men. These efforts have been largely unidirectional. As Susan Pinker (2008) notes,

> There is no corresponding movement to draft men into nursing, comparative literature, or speech pathology, no incentives or special task forces to tutor men in empathy or interpersonal skills. . . . Currently the message is that disciplines that capitalize on strengths and interests more commonly found among men have greater prestige. (p. 262) (see also Noddings, 2002)

As long as marked wage disparities continue in the aforementioned careers, it is likely that this unidirectionality will persist.

There is also a call for schools to expand the emotional landscape of all students. The ethic of care and learning how to become an engaged, responsible family member is not solely a woman's duty. Several scholars advocate that schools should provide this type of training to all students (Eliot, 2009; Kahn, 2009; Noddings, 2002). Of particular concern to those who question single-sex education is the extent to which masculinizing the educational environment will perpetuate and exacerbate the home/work divide for male students. In Jack Kahn's (2009) view, educational institutions need to be aware of the values they promulgate:

> The problems that boys and men face are not viewed here as a function of not being *masculine* enough, but as not being *feminine* enough. Rejecting femininity is at the heart of the crisis of masculinity. The bottom line from this perspective is not to find lost masculinity, as suggested by the essentialists, but to reject dominant masculinity and discover characteristics associated with femininity. (p. 220)

Kahn calls for activism in schools that includes "teaching men how to create spaces that support more fluid roles for them" (p. 222). The extent to which single-sex education challenges and alters construals of masculinity, in particular, has the potential to influence, and ultimately change, what we embrace as human values.

Conclusion

As this chapter has demonstrated, the environments in which women and men are raised and educated are inextricably connected. The impact of socioeconomic class, parents, and teachers is profound. Students, we have noted, are sojourners in an academic terrain that is not of their own creation. The extent to which the dreams and desires of students are encouraged, nurtured, valued, and supported will influence the extent to which these dreams and desires are ultimately realized.

Notes

[1] We noted several concerns from teachers who want to be more inclusive regarding what and how they teach but may have doubts about their own ability to do so. It is also important to indicate that the reluctance of teachers to address social justice issues may also be political. In many communities, school boards and parents play a powerful role in determining expectations regarding the parameters of what teachers can and cannot teach (i.e., topics related to sexuality, to religion, to race, etc.). Under such circumstances, teachers' reluctance to engage with students about certain issues may connect to their own concern that their careers may be jeopardized. A wide range of pedagogical examples (including panels, scripted dialogues, community outreach, use of media reports, etc.) are included in the edited works by Crabtree et al. (2009) and Steinberg (2009) and are recommended for further reference.

[2] Martin Rochlin's questionnaire on heterosexuality was developed to bring awareness to the subtle and not-so-subtle ways heterosexual privilege functions. Peggy McIntosh (1988) developed a list of items that expose the extent to which white privilege remains a ubiquitous and unchallenged aspect of everyday life. This widely circulated inventory includes observations about how privilege functions (i.e., "I can turn on the television or open the front page of the newspaper and see people of my race widely represented"; "I can if I wish arrange to be in the company of people of my race most of the time"; "I am never asked to speak for all of the people of my race"). Importantly, McIntosh, like Rochlin, shifts the critical lens.

[3] While Hinshaw's (2009) work does make reference to sexual identity, race, and class, the examples he draws on from his clinical practice come primarily from girls who come from white middle- and upper-middle class families and communities.

[4] In his assessment of the findings on gender differences in college, Jack Kahn indicates that one explanation for the discrepancy stems from how men from working-class and low-income homes, in particular, may experience the college landscape. He refers to several studies that suggest that "complex issues of identity and discrimination" may adversely affect men of color more "than their White counterparts (Archer, Pratt, & Phillips, 2001; Burd, 2006; DiMaria, 2006; Ozden, 1996; Zamani, 2000)" (p. 171). Due, in part, to their own view of masculinity, they are less likely to avail themselves of support mechanisms designed to facilitate student progress. To do so may be construed as less manly; as a sign of weakness.

[5] Ann Rubenstein Tisch was instrumental in launching The Young Women's Leadership School in Harlem in 1996 to establish single-sex classes in math and science to help close the academic performance gap in these areas that was "particularly notable among African American and Hispanic females" (Weil, 2008, p. 85). Under her leadership, this program has expanded to other cities nationwide.

[6] In the U.S. Department of Education's (2005) meta-analysis comparing academic achievement in single-sex and coed schools, their review of 40 studies revealed that 8% favored coed schooling, 6% indicated mixed results (reporting positive results for one gender only), 41% favored single-sex schools, and 45% found no positive or negative effects for either type of education (Weil, 2008, p. 87; see also Eliot, 2009, p. 306).

SUGGESTED ACTIVITIES

1. **Children's Literature: Sustaining Difference or Breaking Down Barriers?**
   In their chapter on gender in the classroom, Cheri Simonds and Pamela Cooper (2001) articulate the extent to which children's literature is a powerful source of communicating gendered identity. They write: "A plethora of research demonstrates that children's literature reflects and reinforces sex-role stereotypes. Numerical disparities and stereotyped behavior patterns and characteristics reflected in children's literature teach girls to undervalue themselves and teach boys to believe that they must always be stereotypically masculine" (p. 236). Either in groups or individually, examine three current children's books and assess the extent to which gender, ethnicity, and class stereotypes persist and how such stereotypes are interconnected.

2. **The Impact of Teacher Behaviors on the Self**
   Students will divide into groups of five or six. Individuals should recall sessions from their least favorite and most favorite academic subjects. The recollections should include specific teacher behaviors that influenced their preferences. Discus any patterns that emerge and the extent to which they may be attributed to gender, class, sexual identity, race, or ethnicity. Do you think your experiences shaped your current major and career choice?

3. **The Educational Landscape: An Early Source of Gendered Space**
   In her 1993 book *Gender Play,* sociologist Barrie Thorne reveals the extent to which schools are complicit in perpetuating gendered identity. She observes, "At school, no one escapes being declared male or female whether that difference is relevant or not" (p. 108). Either individually or in groups, identify events and/or activities (in the classroom, during recess, etc.) that reinforce the separation of students. To what extent do instances of separation shape forging friendships, developing interests in particular sports, or how areas designated for play-time activities are utilized?

4. **Current Issues on Education and Social Justice: Challenges and Changes**
   Students should bring in a recent article that addresses education. Topics can reflect a wide range of issues (e.g., academic achievement, single-sex education, comparisons of education from diverse cultures, the influence of parents, etc.). Either in groups or in a class discussion, identify the extent to which these issues reinforce or challenge sex-trait and sex-role stereotypes. Are new issues emerging, and if so, how do they articulate with the aspects of the educational landscape identified in this chapter?

Gendered Scripts
Women and Men in the Workplace

Today, the materials and skills from which a life is composed are no longer clear. It is no longer possible to follow the paths of previous generations. This is true for both men and women, but it is especially true for women, whose whole lives no longer need be dominated by the rhythms of procreation and the dependencies that these created, but who still must live with the discontinuities of female biology and still must balance conflicting demands. Our lives not only take new directions; they are subject to repeated redirection. . . . Many of the basic concepts we use to construct a sense of self or the design of a life have changed their meanings: Work. Home. Love. Commitment. (Bateson, 1989, p. 2)

*I*n her book *Composing a Life,* Mary Catherine Bateson (1989) suggests that the trajectories of successful women's lives are no longer prescribed by monolithic or linear pathways. Through the narratives of women's sojourns through life, Bateson evokes powerful metaphors suggesting that in the closing decades of the twentieth century, we ought to view life as an "improvisatory art" (p. 3); as a "journey" (p. 5). She suggests, moreover, that women as well as men are "migrants in time" (p. 14) and that *we* can be well-served by acknowledging that the aspirations and goals we set for ourselves are "mutable" and will evolve and change over time (p. 9).

Implicit in Bateson's message is the utility of thinking about the lives we compose as a process that is marked by fluidity rather than as rigidly fixed or prescribed. However, she also acknowledges that the spectre of change is "frightening" (p. 8). The comfort of constancy often becomes a competing lure for adhering to tradition. Expectations for how one develops and negotiates one's place in the world are not immune to the spectre of previous generations and to long-held beliefs of what is viewed as both proper and appropriate.

Although Bateson's work reflects greater agency in how women choose to compose their lives, in the ensuing decades following the publication of her work several challenges and barriers continue to resonate. These challenges suggest that the "improvisatory" aspect of this "journey" and the "mutability" of goals and aspirations are not immune to societal assumptions, pressures, and expectations that qualify how this sojourn is experienced. These challenges also suggest that the extent to which the "fluidity" in women's lives stems from choices is, instead, subject to pressures both subtle and overt.

Drawing on diverse fields that include communication, law, psychology, sociology, and the mass media, we examine five major issues that suggest that societal attitudes, government policies, and values embedded in organizational life sustain disparate and often unequal treatment of women and men in the workplace. We also include the multiple "standpoints" of race, ethnicity, and culture that complicate how professional lives are forged and negotiated (Harding, 1991).

Maintaining the Myth of "Women's Work" and "Men's Work": The Impact of Stereotypes on Job Choice and on the Interview Process

Despite the large percentage of women in the U.S. workforce, reports indicate that within the workplace there exists a disparate treatment of women compared to men. While some studies examine how far women have come, others look at how far we still need to go in order to achieve equality for women in the workplace. Over the last two decades, articles in the popular press have heralded: "Best News Ever for Working Women" (Allen, 1993), that high-achieving women continue to challenge and alter traditional construals of leadership and power (Kantrowitz & Peterson, 2007), and that "Life in the Top Jobs is Worth the Effort" (Hymowitz, 2006b). Other articles address the persistence of the "pay gap" for women (Leaf, 2007; Mahar, 1993), deliver the news that the progress of women making it to the top ranks in their fields is "somber" (Dobrzynski, 1996) and "slow" (Rimer, 2005), and that their ranks remain "thin" (Hymowitz, 2006a). In part, many insist that "invisible barriers" (Lang, 2010), "glass ceilings" (Kilborn, 1995), and the "maternal wall" (Kessler, 2007) erect potent barriers for women and minorities. The divergent views reflected in these articles suggest that how the data is examined and interpreted influences our understanding of gender in the workplace.

In May 2010, women comprised 47% of the labor force (72,148,000) and men comprised 53% (82,245,000) (U.S. Department of Labor, 2010b). Yet in the first quarter of 2010, women's median weekly wages ($665) reflected 78.8% of men's weekly earnings (U.S. Department of Labor, 2010a). Although the doors to employment may be open to women, career aspirations and expectations are shaped in part by what individuals perceive as possible. What individuals regard as possible is influenced by how they see themselves as a member within the larger society; these self-appraisals stem, in part, from the messages to which they are exposed. As communication researcher Fredric Jablin (1987) has noted, these messages derive from multiple sources. Family, educational institutions, media representations, part-time work, peers, and friends play critical roles in influencing young women's and men's aspirations for the lives they hope to forge in the world of work.

Think back to the gender stereotypes identified throughout the previous chapters. Rooted in depictions of "femininity" in both the home and classroom are notions of support, care, domesticity, and being other-centered. These traits continue to be associated with some vocations more than with others. For example, certain jobs such as nursing, elementary teaching, and clerical and support positions are still largely regarded as "women's work." Other, more lucrative jobs continue to be associated with "men's work" (for example, engineering, mathematics, computer science, law, and medicine) despite the fact that the practitioner's sex is irrelevant in fulfilling his or her occupational responsibilities (Barnett & Rivers, 2004; Pinker, 2008; Roberts, 1995).

Dichotomizing work according to biology reflects an evolutionary process rooted in historical and social developments. In fact, according to sociologist Jo Anne Preston (2006), "the transformation of teaching from a male occupation to a female occupation was a process that took more than 200 years and was finally completed in the 19th century . . ." (p. 235). Significantly, women were "permitted" entry into this field because school reformers viewed women as possessing several presumably "innate" qualities deemed "appropriate" for this vocation, such as "high moral character, disregard for material gain (and thus not driven by monetary concerns) as well as a natural love of children" (p. 245). This shift in values suggests that the traits, competencies, and abilities we come to associate with a particular vocation are not immutable. However, we recognize that the process of utilizing masculine and feminine stereotypes to characterize careers is not inconsequential.

> Professions acquire sex-specific ideologies, like all occupations, as they are socially constructed, and these constructions are informed by gender ideology—that is, a set of ideas that consider either men or women better suited to do the work required of an occupation because of their supposed innate qualities. (p. 236)

The entrenchment of presumed "suitability" explains, in part, career choices. Whether intentionally or inadvertently, gender-dichotomous occupational expectations may be supported by families who want their children to fit in with dominant societal expectations. Similarly, educators, aware of typical career paths for men and women, may influence their students to conform with and to accept unquestionably the career opportunities associated with each sex. In 2009, 97.8% of preschool and kindergarten teachers, 97.6% of dental assistants, 91.4% of nurses, and 74.45% of office and administrative support positions were held by women while 7.1% of civil engineering positions, 20.2% of computer programmers, 32.4% of lawyers, and 32.2% of physician and surgical positions were held by women (U.S. Department of Labor, 2010a).

According to management and organization professor Gary Powell (1993), children become aware of these "professional ghettos" at an early age (p. 69). They also learn to value gender-stereotyped work differently. Margaret Mooney Marini and Mary Brinton (1984) reported that while 35% of women in their study ages 14–22 aspired to "male-identified" occupations, only 4% of men aspired to occupations that were identified as "female-intensive." This discrepancy in male aspirations, according to Warren Farrell (2005), is attributed in part to accepting that their value as a person is inexorably connected to their earnings: "When men can earn less and be valued more, we will unlock our sons from being human *doings* and free them to be human *beings*" (p. 233, emphasis added). So long as wage disparities between female-intensive and male-intensive careers persist, it is unlikely that the aspirational landscape for men will be altered substantially.

Perhaps as a result of these cultural messages, since the early 1970s women have increasingly entered fields traditionally defined as "masculine" (Collins, 2009; Pinker, 2008; Roberts, 1995). Over a nearly 35-year period, there has been a significant increase in the percentages of women moving into these fields (e.g., from 5 to 27% in the legal field, from 8 to 26% in medicine, from 8 to 26% in science and engineering, and from 2 to 14% in the military) (Gibbs, 2009; Pinker, 2008). Some researchers have associated the increase of women in traditionally male-dominated fields with influences provided by: (1) changing familial role models, such as mothers working outside the home and/or serving as the primary or sole wage earner; (2) parental attitudes about their daughters' careers; and (3) parents' educational levels (Borisoff & Merrill, 1998; Collins, 2009; Hinshaw, 2009; Powell, 1993; Sandberg, Ehrhardt, Mellins, Ince, & Meyer-Bahlburg, 1987). However, descriptors such as "nontraditional" or "atypical" continue to be evoked when women move outside of "pink collar" jobs (see Bernard, 1981), implying that this foray is still seen as unusual. Moreover, the use of metaphors to describe how women experience the workplace ("scaling" occupational or facing "maternal" "walls"; "breaking the glass ceiling"; contending with the "motherhood penalty") provide vivid images that suggest that despite their academic achievements, stereotypical attitudes that impact women's entry, assimilation, and retention in workplace settings have not been eradicated.

The Impact of Stereotypes and Discrimination on Hiring Practices

Gendered stereotypes, as well as stereotypes about groups in general, have been found to exert considerable influence on how individuals are viewed. Studies conducted over the past three decades indicate that from entry to exit, women are typically treated differently than their male colleagues. Often, interview and hiring decisions reflect traditional stereotypes of masculinity and femininity.

Social psychologist Elizabeth Aries (1996) defines stereotype as "a set of beliefs about the characteristics presumed to be typical of members of a group. Stereotypes distinguish one group from another—for example, men from women, or blacks from whites" (p. 163). She goes on to indicate the consequences of stereotyping others:

> Stereotypes can be positive or negative, accurate or inaccurate. To the extent that they are accurate, stereotypes provide information that is useful in forming expectations to help guide behavior. To the extent that they are over-generalizations, exaggerations, or inaccurate depictions of group members, stereotypes can lead to prejudiced perceptions, evaluations, and responses to individuals. (p. 163)

While Title VII of the Civil Rights Act of 1964 specifies that "employers cannot discriminate on the basis of race, color, national origin, age (if 40 or older), disability, or gender," a series of studies reveal that women and other members of underrepresented groups may be subjected to discriminatory practices at different stages of the job application process (Ralston & Kinser, 2001, p. 187). We examine examples of this both prior to receiving an interview and then during the interview.

Discriminatory Practices Prior to Being Interviewed

How applicants learn about potential positions is one area where disparity has been examined. In her work on difference in organizations, communication researcher Brenda Allen (2011) highlights how informal hiring practices disadvantage black job seekers. Referring to Mouw's (2002) study on the propensity for organizations to rely on employee referrals for recruitment (estimated at nearly 50% of all positions), Allen points to how such practices perpetuate racial imbalances: "Recruitment through informal methods such as word-of-mouth reinforces racial homogeneity because employees usually tell people like themselves about job opportunities, and companies often hire applicants who are referred by current employees" (p. 87).

Luo (2009a) notes that this informal networking persists. A recently published study in *Social Problems* revealed that high-level positions are often never advertised and that "white males receive substantially more job leads for high-level supervisory positions than women and members of minorities" (p. A4). Therefore, if an organization seeks to develop a more diverse workforce, intensified efforts to proactively publicize positions are needed.

Who receives a response to an application for employment is a second area that reveals disparate treatment. In their study on responses to unsolicited resumes, for example, McIntyre, Mohberg, and Posner (1980) found that women were less likely than men to receive responses from companies. Nearly two decades later, Russo and Ommeren's (1998) examination of more than 20,000 job vacancies revealed that the same statistical chances of being hired exist for both male and female applicants. Ralston and Kinser (2001) note, however, that who comprises the applicant pool affects one's "chances" of being hired: "if significantly more males make up an applicant pool for a given position, then it is likely that a man will be hired" (p. 189). Implicit in this observation is that unless or until equal numbers of women apply for positions in areas that have been dominated by men, women applicants will continue to be hired less frequently.

The above discussion suggests that as the gender application gap continues to narrow, women's opportunities for securing interviews in traditionally male-dominated fields are likely to improve. As of 2007 women were earning 50% of law, doctoral, and medical degrees as well as 65% of master's and bachelor's degrees (Gibbs, 2009). These figures augur positively for a more equal application pool and ultimately for enhanced opportunities for women.

The stigma of roles is a third example of how initial access to jobs may be denied to women. In her article on work and family conflict, legal researcher Laura Kessler (2007) suggests that the role of parent has more adverse consequences for women applicants than for men. In their examination of how motherhood penalizes women who work, sociologists Correll, Bernard, and Paik (2007) asked participants in their study to evaluate equally credentialed women applicants. Their findings revealed that applicants identified as mothers were viewed as both less competent and less suitable for hiring than women who were not parents (Kessler, 2007, p. 2). However, when male applicants were assessed, fathers were not similarly penalized in hiring decisions.

This study, which is consonant with similar examinations of the "motherhood penalty," reflects deeply entrenched assumptions regarding the presumed incompatibility of parenting and work roles for women. Therefore, the resulting impact on the application and, ultimately, the hiring process is an example of sex-biased discrimination. Kessler (2007) asserts the need not only for vigilance in monitoring attitudes in hiring practices, but argues for employer accountability when instances of violations are revealed.

The stigma of having an ethnic name is a final example of marginalization and discrimination that can occur prior to the interview. A study submitted 5,000 resumes to want ads published in major newspapers in Boston and in Chicago. Findings revealed that "resumes of applicants with 'white-sounding' first names (e.g., Neil, Brett, Greg, Emily, Anne, and Jill) elicited 50 percent more responses than ones with 'black-sounding' names (e.g., Ebony, Tamika, Aisha, Rasheed, Kareem, and Tyrone)" (Allen, 2011, p. 88). In her review, Joan Williams (2010) notes that "white candidates got as many callbacks as blacks with eight additional years of experience" (p. 95).

Interviews with highly credentialed African American applicants indicate that several feel pressure to "downplay" or "dial back" their race by "whitening" their resumes (e.g., changing their names, removing race-based activities) to enhance their chances of receiving a callback or an interview (Luo, 2009b, p. 3). The potential cost of such strategies, however, ought not to be minimized. It is important to be aware of the psychological toll that these steps may have on job seekers. "In some ways, they are denying who and what they are. . . . They almost have to pretend themselves away" (p. 3).

Determinations of "Fit" during the Job Interview

When meeting a job applicant, numerous studies reveal that determinations of "fit" in hiring decisions are based on verbal skills (e.g., demonstrated confidence, competence, assertiveness) and nonverbal factors (e.g., eye contact, dress, attractiveness) (Goleman, 1998; Jablin, 1987; Knapp & Hall, 2009; Ralston & Kinser, 2001; Ralston & Kirkwood, 1995). However, what constitutes effective behaviors and how these behaviors are read by those with the power to make hiring decisions suggest that all too often meeting a job applicant does not diminish the effects of stereotyping associated with gender, race, and culture.

In their review of academic, industry-generated, and popular literature on interviewing, communication researchers Steven Ralston and Amber Kinser (2001) indicate that ideal candidates employ communication tactics that convey appropriate "confidence," "self-assurance," "self-promotion," and "assertiveness" (pp. 197–198). While they acknowledge that neither all women nor all men communicate in ways that conform to the masculine and feminine stereotype, they point out that the verbal and nonverbal languages of the interview "are spoken more proficiently by persons who adopt traditionally masculine communication styles," and as a consequence, "persons who use traditionally feminine communication styles are more likely to be unfairly excluded from job opportunities" (p. 200).

There are several challenges for those women, in particular, who are endeavoring to enter fields traditionally dominated by men. First, they must overcome deeply embedded attitudes stemming from the distinct social roles that situate women in the home (where nurturing, expressiveness, and other-centeredness are valued) and men in the public sphere (where instrumental behavior, assertiveness, and independence are valued) (Eagly, 1987). A review of studies conducted during the last three decades of the twentieth century indicate that men are assessed as more qualified for occupations and positions associated with a male orientation; women, for occupations and positions associated with a female orientation (Ralston & Kinser, 2001, pp. 189–190). A survey of 1,231 U.S. and European senior executives revealed that the association of men with leadership positions still persists (Hinshaw, 2009, p. 15).

A related challenge is that when individuals behave in ways that contradict or violate gender-based expectations, they risk being judged negatively (Berger, Fisck, Norman, & Zelditch, 1977). In their review of gendered practices in the workplace, communication researchers Bren Murphy and Ted Zorn (1996) refer to the fine line women must negotiate to be "read" as simultaneously competent yet not too threatening: "Women seem to be in a 'catch-22,' since communicating in . . . traditionally feminine ways lowers professional credibility, yet not being deferential and sensitive often results in negative labels such as *pushy* and *bitch*" (p. 218).

A recent series of studies reveals the discrepant assessments male and female job applicants receive when they employ similar emotional displays (Brescoll & Uhlmann, 2005). These researchers found that when job applicants (using identical "scripts") described themselves as angry due to a work-related problem stemming from a colleague's incompetence, the subjects assigned the men a higher average salary ($38,000) than the women ($23,550). When the applicants delivered identical scripts displaying sadness about the same situation, both men and women were assigned identical salaries ($30,000). In a second experiment, Brescoll and Uhlmann (2005) found assessments of displays of anger are also linked to job levels. When male and female job candidates were presented as either trainees or senior executives, the angry female executives were judged the most harshly. The subjects evaluated these senior-level women as out of control and as less competent.

These studies suggest that the double bind continues to influence how women's behavior is read. Women are encouraged and expected to succeed like men, yet they are criticized when they use similar behavioral tactics to do so (Buzzanell, 2002; Jamieson, 1995; Putnam, 1983).

Gender is one lens through which applicants are assessed. Recent works suggest that race and culture also influence hiring decisions. Richard Nisbett (2009) contends that stereotypical assumptions about race have negative implications for how black men are assessed, regardless of their credentials. Moss and Tilly (2001), for example, found a connection between employers' attitudes and hiring decisions. To the extent that employers view black men as not possessing equivalent teamwork and communication skills as members of other groups of the same age, they are less apt to hire them. A more glaring example of prejudicial treatment is reported in Pager's (2003) study of hiring decisions. This study reveals that even when prospective employers are provided with evidence that white male applicants may be less qualified than young black males, many employers still privilege white male applicants during the interview. In this instance, white and black appropriately attired and articulate college graduates presented themselves as high school graduates to prospective employers. Despite the fact that only the white applicants divulged having a felony conviction, they were regarded more favorably by prospective employers.

Recent interviews with highly credentialed African American college graduates from around the country suggest recurrent instances where interviewers' reactions to meeting a candidate raise similar questions about fair treatment (Luo, 2009a). References to "surprised looks" upon meeting the candidate, "offhand comments," and "sudden loss of interest from companies after meetings" resonate in their accounts (p. A4). In the words of one of the interviewees who was enthusiastically recruited by a money management firm due, in part, to his business degree from a prestigious institution, the two men from the firm appeared "stunned" upon meeting him: "Their eyes kind of hit the ceiling a bit. . . . It was kind of quiet for about 45 seconds" (p. 4). Significantly, several interviewees attributed these responses to unintentional discrimination, suggesting instead that it may "simply [be] a matter of people gravitating toward similar people, casting about for the right 'cultural fit' . . ." (p. A4).

Our concern is the extent to which "fit" becomes synonymous with race. Communication researcher Mark Knapp and psychologist Judith Hall (2009) posit that "permanent skin colors have been the most potent body stimulus for determining interpersonal responses in our culture" (p. 194). They point out that standards of attractiveness are typically established by the "economically dominant group within a society" (p. 194). In the United States, they contend, this standard has been traditionally associated with "the features of the people whose ancestors immigrated here from northern and western Europe. Among other features, they had 'white' skin" (p. 194). Implicit in their comments are the consequences of those in positions of power to fashion "fit" in one's own image. Several indications of a changing demographic in the United States augers an accompanying reconceptualization and revaluation of traditional construals of attractiveness (Aries, 1996; Hyun, 2005; Knapp & Hall, 2009). For those currently in the job market, however, there is little comfort in future speculation.

The notion of "fit" in the interviewing process is examined through the lens of culture by human resource consultant and career coach Jane Hyun (2005). Her work reflects case studies of Asian professionals (ages 20–40) working in U.S. companies; these professionals include recent immigrants as well as first-, second-, and third-generation Asian Americans. Hyun highlights several key values that researchers have identified as cutting across diverse Asian ethnic groups: "self-effacement," "self-control," "respect for elders," "deference to authority figures," and "maintenance of interpersonal harmony" (p. 8). Hyun's work with both Asian and non-Asian professionals revealed that these values often are reflected in several verbal and nonverbal behaviors during a job interview, which ultimately may undermine success for both Asian women and men (e.g., being soft-spoken, lack of direct eye contact, inability to self-promote and market themselves effectively) (p. 21).

To alter the perception of "fit," Hyun draws on actual and mock interviews to promote verbal and nonverbal behavioral changes in her clients. Numerous scripts are provided and the metaphor of viewing the interview as a "performance" (p. 16) is evoked to facilitate establishing and maintaining eye contact, to facilitate "going out of your comfort zone" in order to "promote oneself" (p. 161), and to "express emotions and enthusiasm" (p. 163). While a brief section suggests that those conducting interviews need to be mindful of how culture influences communication and to resist assumptions of fit that stem from their own background (p. 166), the burden to change is placed on the applicant.

Readers of Hyun's work may be able to perform the interviewing script sufficiently to be hired. Deeply embedded cultural values, however, are not easily undone. We might speculate about the toll exacted on individuals when they try to sustain a performance over time. We also question the appropriateness of prescribing and reifying a narrow range of behaviors that ultimately limit and perhaps impoverish a broader understanding, acceptance, and receptivity to how commitment, competence, and fit may be conveyed and interpreted by those in positions to hire applicants.

A recent survey by the Association of American Colleges and Universities reaffirms the salience of communication as critical for securing jobs (Zernike, 2010, p. 25). Employers were asked to assess what two- and four-year colleges should be emphasizing in order to meet current organizational needs. "The ability to effectively communicate orally and in writing" received the highest rating (89%) while "critical thinking and analytical reasoning skills" and "the ability to innovate and be creative" were emphasized by 81% and 70% of respondents, respectively (p. 25). The extent to which higher education responds to these findings—in particular, the extent to which they perpetuate, disrupt, or expand the range of students' communication competence—may provide one site of change.

Many researchers have already argued that changing demographics (Knapp & Hall, 2009), increased contact of women and men in the workforce (Aries, 1996), and the enhanced caliber of applicants' qualifications (Graves & Powell, 1993) suggest a brighter picture for how women and members of other underrepresented groups are assessed. However, the examples in this section suggest that instances of bias—whether intentional or unintentional—persist. Exposing and challenging instances of negative stereotyping and bias, along with a willingness to examine how our own assumptions and attitudes influence how we read and assess others, have the potential to alter how construals of "fit" are determined. In our view, this process can ultimately lead to a more truly representative workforce.

Box 6.1   Interview-Related Examples from the Field

Below we provide examples from our students and seminar and workshop participants where factors not relevant to the position were raised by the interviewer. There are multiple ways to interpret an event and many decisions to be made regarding how to respond. Consider how their reactions compare to the interviewing processes you (or your friends or colleagues) have experienced as well as alternate approaches/interpretations.

Gender, Age, and Appearance

"I was a finalist for a teaching post. A woman in the department who I knew from conferences contacted me prior to the interview. She suggested that I color my hair (to get the grey out) and wear makeup (to appear younger) because the department was comprised of mostly men 'who seem to respond to women's appearances.' As a feminist, I was shocked that my years of experience, training, and research seemingly would play a secondary role to surface criteria. However, I did want this position and so I followed her advice figuring that if I got hired, I could become myself again." (JoAnne, age 40, who was offered and accepted this college-level position)

Gender and Belonging

"During my interview for an administrative position in a mid-size engineering firm, the head of the company asked me if I had a boyfriend. I was surprised by the question but did answer that yes, I was in a relationship. He then asked if my boyfriend would "mind" my working in a male-dominated company. I told him that my boyfriend is supportive of my professional goals and of any decisions I make to reach them. During the interview I was too nervous to think about the implications of this question. Upon reflection, however, I wondered what his real message was: about women; about belonging; about trust." (Barbara, age 26; she was offered and accepted the position)

Gender and Role Conflict

"I was applying for a first-year associate position with a well-known law firm. During my interview with one of the partners, she suddenly interrupted the interview and made the following comment: 'Listen, I know this is an illegal topic, but I have to tell you that working here is going to be very challenging if you are considering having a family. Although we consider ourselves a family-friendly firm, we've had difficulty retaining women once they've had children. If you're not fully committed to the firm, making partnership is going to be jeopardized.' I was stunned by her words. This was 2006—was this typical of what I would face as a newly minted attorney? My response was visceral. If this was how the firm was trying to sell itself, I felt this would be a toxic environment in which to launch my career. I decided to accept a position with another firm." (Ellen, age 25)

(continued)

Cultural Assumptions

"The interview was going very well until the interviewer [also of Spanish descent] asked me how well I spoke Spanish. When I told him that I didn't speak the language, I noticed a disapproving look. I explained that my parents were born in the U.S. and while I was not raised in a bilingual household, as an adult I appreciated the value of speaking another language. I added that I hoped to eventually learn Spanish. While this response seemed to work, it did cross my mind that being bilingual had nothing to do with an internship in this graphics company." (Carmen, age 20)

Race and Class

"I recently was being interviewed for an internship in a public relations firm. The interviewer was looking at my resume and commented, 'Hmm, NYU is very expensive. I wonder how students afford to go there.' I didn't know how to interpret his comment. Was he saying this because of my race? Did he assume that my family was of a certain socioeconomic class? I replied that my parents were both professionals and supported my decision to go there. When I shared this experience in class, several of the white students thought I was being overly sensitive. When the professor asked if similar comments were made to them during an interview, they responded 'no.'" (Janet, African American, age 20)

The Impact of Difference on Organizational Assimilation and Retention

Individuals entering the workforce hope and expect that they will have the opportunity to make positive contributions, receive appropriate support, and be valued and rewarded for their work. Once hired, however, studies indicate several factors that sustain disparities in how the workplace is experienced, in how one's contributions are read and interpreted, and, ultimately, how they are valued. We examine four interrelated factors that influence the extent to which participation in the workplace is viewed as positive or as problematic, including: (1) wage disparities; (2) mentoring and workplace opportunities; (3) expectations for professional performance; and (4) role conflicts stemming from the clash of personal and professional demands.

The Impact of Expectations and Valuations on Salary Differences

Several studies indicate that, economically, women do not fare as well as men in the workplace. A recent study by the American Association of University Women (AAUW, 2007) reports the emergence of a wage disparity between women and men as early as one year beyond college (with women earning 80% of men's salaries). According to the report, this disparity appears "even when they have the same major and occupation as their male counterparts" (p. 1). The report suggests that this gap widens over time: over the course of 10 years, women's earnings decline to 69% of men's earnings. What is significant are the explanations for these differences: "Even after controlling for hours, occupation, parenthood, and other factors known to affect earnings, the research indicates that one-quarter of the pay gap remains unexplained and is likely due to sex discrimination. Over time, the unexplained portion of the gap grows" (p. 1). We will consider several factors that sustain this gap.

In a series of studies examining women's reactions to earning less than men in comparable positions, Brenda Major (1987) found that women had lower career-entry and career-peak salary *expectations* than men had (p. 139). Moreover, she reported that women dealt with salary disparities by comparing their expectations with those of other women rather than men. Psychologist Morton Deutsch (2000) connects this response to the theory of relative deprivation:

> Members of disadvantaged groups (such as women, low-paid workers, ethnic minorities) often feel less deprived than one might expect, and even less so than those who are more fortunate, because they compare themselves with "similar others"—other women, other low-paid workers. (p. 44)

Diminished expectations have significant consequences on one's earnings and may influence one's willingness to negotiate. In his article on how employer requests for salary history discriminates against women, legal researcher Jeffrey Lax (2007) reported a major disparity in first-time job seekers' willingness to negotiate their salaries: 7% of women as opposed to 57% of men attempted to negotiate their initial earnings. Importantly, when negotiations did take place, candidates "increased their salary by 7.5%, and . . . starting salaries of males averaged 7.6% higher than for females" (p. 50). While this initial discrepancy might not appear significant at first glance, Lax argues that as long as it remains legal for employers to request the salary history of applicants, an initial baseline difference can translate into a sustained and even wider wage disparity over the course of one's career.

Major (1987) argues that only by raising women's awareness about inequities and inequalities in professional compensation and reward systems can women begin to change their notions of entitlement: "For women to recognize the degree to which they are victimized and undervalued in society and by its agents entails psychic costs. So, too, however, does blaming oneself rather than the system for failing to obtain desired rewards" (p. 145). We would add, moreover, that it is not enough for victims of discriminatory practices to become change agents. Employers must also act responsibly to assure fair salaries for employees. Evidence of this responsibility, for example, has emerged on many college campuses where female faculty members receive coaching on negotiating salaries as well as research funds (Rimer, 2005). The type of coaching that women receive is important. Harvard's Hannah Riley Bowles cautions that women are often judged more harshly than men when they negotiate salary and raises. If women are too self-effacing, they risk being offered lower salaries than men and may be viewed as less competent. If they engage in assertive bargaining tactics, they may receive a higher salary, but they risk being viewed as too aggressive, "thereby jeopardizing their futures" (Williams, 2010, p. 141). The studies by Riley Bowles indicate that particularly in industries where salary standards are not clearly delineated, women are advised to tailor their negotiations by explaining "why their request is appropriate, but in terms that also communicate that they care about maintaining good relationships at work" (Bernard, 2010, p. B5). While this advice may be effective, it also underscores the great care women, in particular, need to take in monitoring their messages. A failure to do so can "make it politically risky for women to negotiate" (Williams, 2010, p. 140). Efforts to achieve equal pay are not only important from an ethical standpoint. As illustrated by President Barack Obama's signing of the Lilly Ledbetter Fair Pay Act in 2009, employers risk legal sanctions when they allow wage discrimination to persist (Collins, 2009, p. 357).

It is important to examine the systemic issues that have contributed to sustaining the status and wage disparities that exist in careers where women predominate versus male-dominated careers. These issues leave little doubt that they help to fuel perceptions of relative deprivation, as alluded to above. In their study on compensation differentials, sociologists Jerry Jacobs and Ronnie Steinberg (1995) suggest a possible connection between the perception of "extreme" working conditions (e.g., stress, working in a hazardous environment, completing undesirable tasks) and compensation. Their findings suggest that extreme conditions are *presumed* to be more prevalent in male-dominated jobs, which would contribute to a wage gap. However, because women historically have had neither the economic nor the political power of (self)-definition to establish the parameters for evaluating and valuing jobs, both the attributes of the jobs they held as well as the skills they brought to the workplace have often been rendered invisible (Bem, 1993; Bernard, 1981; Pinker, 2008; Steinberg, 1990). For example, when women were "allowed" to enter the field of teaching, they had no voice in the concommitment reduction in salaries that occurred as male teachers moved into more supervisory roles and/or into teaching special sessions for which they received additional compensation.

Without the power to accurately name one's condition, as Jacobs and Steinberg (1995) contend, "a lack of recognition of the characteristics differentially found in 'historically female' jobs extends to the undesirable working conditions found in these jobs. These working conditions are often not captured in the standard surveys of work attributes" (p. 116) thereby making it more difficult for women to make a case for additional compensation. Thus the nurse, whose job brings her into contact with blood, infectious diseases, and human waste, may have greater difficulty making a case for higher wages than the sanitation worker whose work brings him into contact with potentially disease-producing waste. The "dirt" they deal with, Remick (1984) claims, is perceived differently.

However, the mere absence of extreme conditions associated with male-dominated jobs does not assure similar compensation for men and women. Psychologist Susan Pinker (2008) notes:

> Despite comparable levels of education, teachers and nurses earn less than computer analysts and engineers. Speech pathologists and social workers earn less than most draftsmen and sound technicians. And even within professions, the specialties that attract women—say, family medicine or pediatrics—command lower salaries than those more popular with men, such as surgery, pathology, or radiology. (pp. 261–262)

While she acknowledges the difficulty in determining whether people-oriented jobs are less valued (thus impacting women who gravitate more to positions bearing this label) or whether occupations dominated by women inherit the label of people-centered and thus are compensated less, a society committed to "redressing pay gaps between the sexes" can alter the lens of valuation (p. 262).

The Impact of Disparate Mentoring and Networking Opportunities on Sustaining Workplace Differences

Homer's *Odyssey* introduced the character Mentor, whose role as a wise and faithful counselor has endured over the centuries and whose function has been adopted more recently by organizations. An effective mentor, according to researchers, provides both career and psychosocial guidance. The functions and benefits of such guidance are summarized in table 6.1.

There is consistent evidence that those who have succeeded in their chosen fields have benefitted from a positive mentoring relationship early in their careers (Glater, 2006; Hackman & Johnson, 2009; Johnson & Ridley, 2004; Kessler, 2007; O'Brien, 2006; Rimer, 2005). While formal mentoring initiatives may provide greater overall benefits across race and gender, informal mentoring relationships are typically forged. Moreover, the lack of mentoring carries a risk: "In the absence of such mentoring, you are highly likely to make serious mistakes that will jeopardize your position in the organization" (Richmond, McCroskey, & McCroskey, 2005, p. 7).

Whether mentoring relationships are forged informally or formally, women and members of other underrepresented groups do not receive the same level of guidance as men. In her *Columbia Law Review* article, Susan Sturm (2001) notes: "The glass ceiling remains a barrier for women and people of color largely because of patterns of interaction, informal norms, networking, training, mentoring, and evaluation, as well as the absence of systematic efforts to address bias produced by these patterns" (p. 469).

There are several explanations for the persistence of these "subtle" discriminatory practices (Kessler, 2007, p. 2). One explanation stems from what Richard Zweigenhaft called the "comfort factor" (1984). His study of Harvard Business School graduates revealed that women were often excluded from the mentoring and networking opportunities that occurred in nonstructured ways, such as over a golf game, because men at the top didn't have "the same comfort level with women" (p. 62).

Table 6.1   Mentoring Functions

A. Career Functions	Examples
1. Coach	• orients new employee to workplace climate, values, and norms • provides concrete strategies related to completing tasks • negotiates realistic and concrete deadlines to meet the goals valued
2. Advocate/Protector	• conveys contributions to appropriate colleagues to enhance the new hire's visibility and reputation • serves as "gatekeeper" to help the new hire from becoming overextended
3. Provider of Feedback	• provides constructive critique to enhance contributions and involvement
B. Psychosocial Functions	**Examples**
1. Role Model	• engages in those activities valued by the organization
2. Counselor	• truly listens to and empathizes with issues and/or concerns the new hire may be experiencing • suggests strategies to achieve a balance for engaging in activities valued by the organization • provides realistic goals and time frames for "the next step" in one's career
3. Provider of Confirmation	• offers constructive encouragement that may result in enhanced motivation, feelings of acceptance, and respect
4. Friend	• over time, may serve as an important ally/friend

Adapted from Borisoff (1998), p. 85.

Zweigenhaft's study included graduates from the 1960s and 1970s. However, recent works indicate that women continue to be excluded from the informal networking and mentoring opportunities that continue to "flourish in largely male playgrounds" (e.g., the golf course, at football and baseball games, during after-work drinks) (O'Brien, 2006, p. 4; see also Matias, 2001; Rock, Stainback, & Adams, 2001). As one of our seminar participants noted, being proficient in a particular sport does not guarantee inclusion:

> When our firm publicized an upcoming golf outing, I told my director that I was looking forward to participating. He replied, "We are planning to have the women in charge of the beverage carts." I reaffirmed my interest by telling him that I've been a long-time golfer with a low handicap. He reiterated that they really needed me on cart duty. I was disappointed that I would not be able to participate in a sport I love. However, I was more disturbed by the underlying message conveyed about women's place in the organization. (Sharon, age 28)

While not all traditionally male-dominated organizations engage in activities that exclude some members, to the extent that many continue to do so suggests that the sex-segregated spheres of play that develop in childhood are transposed from the home and school playground into the workplace in adulthood (Sadker & Sadker, 1994; Thorne, 1993; Valentine, 1997). The message conveyed to those excluded from beneficial opportunities is not benign: "To the extent that sex-segregated talk and socializing interfere with receiving effective mentoring, developing advocates, and creating trust, these 'natural patterns' create problems, including gender inequity" (Murphy & Zorn, 1996, p. 221).

Instances of being excluded are not limited to gender. In her work on the effects on women who are part of a minority within an organization, Rosabeth Moss Kanter (1995) reveals that a sense of feeling isolated, of being the outsider, and a lack of mentoring, networking opportunities, and receiving critical feedback are not solely a result of gender phenomena. She notes that these reactions

> echoed the experiences of people of any kind who are rare and scarce: the lone black among whites, the lone man among women, the few foreigners among natives. Any situation where proportions of significant types of people are highly skewed can produce similar themes and processes. It was rarity and scarcity, rather than femaleness per se, that shaped the environment for women in the parts of [the company] mostly populated by men. (p. 298)

We would agree with communication researcher Karen Lee Ashcraft (2006) that being in the minority impacts men differently than it does women. She suggests that when white men enter fields traditionally dominated by women, rather than experiencing isolation and marginalization, they "seem to ride a 'glass escalator' to the top of feminized occupations" (p. 109).

The "comfort factor" is also fueled by caution, in particular, due to men's concern about how engaging with women may be interpreted by others. Specifically, potential allegations of sexual harassment, or being subjected to rumors of romantic relationships or affairs, may be a deterrent to forging cross-sex mentoring relationships. Title VII of the Civil Rights Act in 1964 and a subsequent Supreme Court ruling in 1986 specified illegal workplace behaviors that are indicative of sexual harassment (such as demands for a worker's sexual favors in response to threats or promises termed *quid pro quo*) and defined a hostile work environment as created by either direct or indirect offensive behavior. Many studies have uncovered the pervasiveness of sexual harassment across multiple workplace settings, most notably in male-dominated environments (Bingham, 1996; Clair, 1993; MacKinnon, 1979; Paetzold & O'Leary-Kelly, 1993; Tong, 1984; Wood, 1993).

In response to this recognition, many private and public institutions have developed initiatives to assure a harassment-free work environment. Researchers in the field of communication, for example, have addressed how the use of outside consultants, training materials, simulations, personal narratives, and case studies could effectively be employed to heighten employee awareness and sensitivity (Berryman-Fink, 1993; Booth-Butterfield, 1986; Clair, Chapman, & Kunkel, 1996; Galvin, 1993; Herndon, 1994). We note, however, that this type of training focuses primarily on men's behavior toward women. A recent U.S. Equal Employment Opportunity Commission report indicates that in 2009, 2,094 (or 16.5%) sexual harassment claims were filed by men (Mattioli, 2010). Despite attempts to include information regarding sexual harassment experienced by men in training programs, this advice is often ignored in part because society (as well as juries) seem to be less sympathetic about harassment of men by women as well as about harassment of men by other men (Mattioli, 2010). Additionally, on many college campuses (e.g., MIT, Stanford, Princeton, and the Universities of Michigan, Wisconsin, and Washington), workshops on unconscious bias have been implemented to alter how the academic landscape is experienced by women in academia (Rimer, 2005). In major companies, like the accounting firm Deloitte & Touche, "transparent and dedicated" mentoring procedures are being established (O'Brien, 2006, p. 4).

While legislation as well as organizational initiatives have enhanced employee protection, an unintended consequence is the impact on men's willingness to mentor women. Many men have come to view the workplace as an "'eggshell environment'—a place in which men, especially white men, must constantly monitor what they say and do to avoid misinterpretation and negative judgments" (Murphy & Zorn, 1996, p. 227) (see also Kanter, 1995; Matias, 2001; O'Brien, 2006;

Box 6.2   Salary-Negotiation and Mentoring Examples from the Field

The examples below come from our students and seminar and workshop participants as well as from writings on the topic. Consider the extent to which these examples connect with or deviate from experiences that you, or those you know, have encountered. Consider alternative approaches to assessing and dealing with these situations.

Gender and Salary Negotiation

"I was honored to be offered the position and readily agreed to the terms of the contract. I learned later that a male colleague hired at the same time and with similar credentials negotiated additional research support and a reduced teaching load for some semesters. I now question whether being a woman influenced my reluctance to negotiate and if I would behave differently if I could replay my interaction with the dean." (Anna, age 30)

"When we discussed salary, my boss indicated we would discuss a raise in eight months. I agreed to the lower offer anticipating an adjustment. When the eight months were up, I reminded the boss of our agreement but it seemed that every time I tried to raise the topic it was a 'bad time' or she was 'on deadline.' I know how busy she is and I don't want to upset our good working relationship. Also, as a woman, I'm not comfortable discussing money. However, I'm having difficulty meeting expenses. I was advised to request a meeting at her convenience. More importantly, it was suggested I assess what I would need to meet costs, determine how my expectations coincide with the industry, and be as specific as possible in discussing a time table. I realized that I was so concerned about what my boss would think of me that I put this above what I needed to live on. We have a meeting in two weeks." (Lynne, age 28)

Mentoring/Networking Opportunities: Gender and Culture

"In my experience, when a fellow Asian colleague approaches me to a be mentor, I typically see one of two extremes—the distant, respectful protégé or the dependent . . . sibling. The first protégé is hesitant to call when he's struggling because of his sense of respect for my title and rank, and the second type is completely dependent on me to be his caretaker. . . . Both are ineffective because neither is driving his own career development. . . . I'm not saying that I would never initiate contact with someone my junior, but it goes a long way when a protégé helps maintain the momentum." (Sam, a Chinese American marketing executive, cited in Hyun, 2005, p. 214)

"I'm one of the few women who are engineers in this company. After I was here for a while, I noticed that around lunch time, our unit head would pass by our offices to see if any of my male colleagues wanted to get lunch. At first, it didn't bother me that I wasn't asked because I had work to do and typically ate at my desk. Over time, however, I realized that my colleagues seem to enjoy a more informal, collegial relationship with our boss. I do feel somewhat shut out and wonder if it is too late to do something." (Ellen)

(continued)

"When I was an undergraduate student at a historically black college, I thought of myself as a woman. When I participated in the study abroad program for a semester, I thought of myself as American. When I began my first job in marketing after graduation, I thought of myself as black. There was no one who looked like me in upper management and it was difficult to find a role model—someone to help me with my career. Thinking about these experiences made me realize that how we think about our identities is connected to context and situation." (Rhonda, age 24)

Rock et al., 2001). For some, "The gift of mentorship is becoming . . . the minefield of mentorship" (Farrell, 2005, p. 170). The result, as Allen (2001) observes, is that women in general "are less involved in mentor relationships than men" (p. 224). While withholding or minimizing mentoring opportunities may not be readily redressed through formal channels, the effects of not engaging proactively with new members who are most in need of guidance and mentoring are palpable. Opportunities for contributing in ways that are critical for increasing business, making partner, achieving tenure, or garnering a promotion have a direct impact on one's wages. In instances when these opportunities are foreclosed due to the "comfort factor," wage disparities become harder to redress.

Expectations for Professional Performance

Organizational culture can be defined as a set of expected behaviors that are generally supported within the organization. This set of expectations or norms usually consists of unwritten rules that have an immense impact on behavior as well as on how employees experience the workplace environment (DeWine, 1987; Goleman, Boyatzis, & McKee, 2002; Hackman & Johnson, 2009; Richmond et al., 2005).

Drawing on the work of studies that identify behaviors associated with effective management and leadership, as well as from our own consultancies with organizations, we summarize in table 6.2 the attributes and behaviors of leadership that are viewed as positive. We will discuss the relationship between these communicative acts and stereotypes as related to gender, race, and culture.

The traits in table 6.2 reflect a transformation from an exclusively hierarchical system based on a "dominator" model of effective organizational communication to a "partnership" model that stresses cooperation, collaboration, and connectivity (Eisler, 1987, p. 206). They reflect, moreover, a wide range of behaviors. For many, incorporating a blend of behaviors that on the surface reflect traditional behaviors associated with masculine and feminine stereotypes appears to be the management style of choice. As Borisoff and Merrill (1998) indicate, numerous studies have demonstrated a positive correlation between the increasing number of women in collegial positions with men and an increase in men's use of supportive statements . . . a decrease in argumentativeness . . . and a decline in the likelihood of men ascribing gender-based stereotypes to their female colleagues. . . . (p. 99)

Relatedly, many studies of contemporary professional women and men report minimal differences and greater overlap in their behaviors. Harlan and Weiss' (1982) study of 100 managers (50 males and 50 females) revealed more psychological similarities than differences: "Men and women were found to have very similar psychological profiles of high power and achievement needs, high self-esteem, and high motivation to manage" (p. 91). Similarities have also been found in the ways male and female managers express themselves in such areas as affective behavior, influence tactics, autocratic versus democratic behaviors, and facilitative communication (Wilkins & Anderson, 1991). Carol Watson's (1994) meta-analysis of studies found men and women negotiators similarly competitive. Her study revealed that perceived *power* and *status* rather than *gender* were determined to be more signif-

---

Table 6.2   Behaviors Associated with Effective Management

Personal Characteristics

1. high self-confidence	8. inspires trust
2. high motivation to manage	9. decisive
3. high need for self-actualization	10. sensitive to diversity issues
4. accessible to others	11. shows interest in and concern for others
5. nonjudgmental of others	12. sincere
6. able to manage stress	13. effective networker
7. self-awareness	

Professional Qualities

1. embraces organization's values	8. creates inclusive environment
2. expresses a team orientation	9. highly competent
3. has an open-door policy	10. fosters cooperation
4. delegates responsibility	11. democratic approach
5. maximizes employee potential	12. is consistent
6. facilitates change	13. effective problem solver
7. highly effective	14. creates collegial atmosphere

Communication Behaviors That Reflect Personal and Professional Traits

1. listens willingly and effectively	4. encourages equal communication
2. provides positive feedback	5. conveys empathy
3. offers constructive criticism	6. nonverbal and verbal behaviors are congruent

From: Aries, 1996; Eagly & Johnson, 1990; Goleman, 2006; Goleman et al., 2002; Hackman & Johnson, 2009; Morrison et al., 1992; Powell, 1993; Richmond et al., 2005; Ryback, 1998; Wilkins & Anderson, 1991.

icant in influencing negotiator style. While Watson's work reveals that women are equally adept at conforming to traditional behaviors associated with effective negotiating, Linda Putnam and Deborah Kolb's (2000, p. 83) model of negotiating suggests a rethinking of construals of "effectiveness" from a feminist lens. We note that several of the qualities and behaviors they promote (e.g., equality, collaboration, self-knowledge, interdependence through connectedness, empathy, dialogue, etc.) mirror current qualities associated with positive managerial behaviors and attitudes.

Role Conflicts

While many organizations employ a rhetoric that outwardly values diversity, inclusiveness, collegiality, equality, and maximizing employee potential (as conveyed in table 6.2), in many instances members of the workforce experience a disconnect between the articulated values and how they are treated. Several researchers identify factors undergirding disparate treatment and demonstrate how these disparities contribute to feeling pressured to manage one's interactions strategically, to negotiate the professional landscape from the margins. We consider four examples that illustrate the consequences of this pressure.

Sexual Identity.   Sexual identity is one factor that fuels a sense of marginalization. While Brenda Allen (2011) notes that "A strong and visible gay, lesbian, bisexual, transgendered, and queer (GLBTQ) community and their allies seek to ensure equal opportunity and treatment across many sectors of society" (p. 117), adoption of the "don't ask, don't tell" policy by Congress in 1993 explicitly required GLBTQ members of the military to conceal their identity to avoid being discharged (a consequence reportedly affecting more than 13,000 personnel) (Bumiller, 2010, p. 18). Although most workplace settings do not mandate such dire consequences as losing one's job, the spectre of disapproval, not being accepted, and the potential for reprisals to occur are, for many in the workforce, powerful motivators to mask one's identity, or to perform an inauthentic identity in response to what Judith Butler (1993) contends is "the heterosexual imperative [that] enables certain sexed identification and forecloses and/or disavows other identifications" (p. 3).

On February 2, 2010, Admiral Mike Mullen, Chairman of the Joint Chiefs of Staff, indicated in his comments to the Senate Armed Services Committee that he was "troubled" by the current policy that "forces young men and women to lie about who they are in order to defend their fellow citizens" and indicated his own belief that "allowing gays and lesbians to serve openly would be the right thing to do" (Bumiller, 2010, p. 1). While we recognize that many fields and organizations do not send mixed messages about valuing employees, the December 2010 repeal of the "don't ask, don't tell" policy could close the gap between lip service to and true acceptance, thereby altering a pattern that has led some organizational members to feel compelled to mask their identity.

Visibility.   Being situated as "other" is also influenced by the extent to which members in the workplace feel that they can participate equally and contribute fully. Visibility is a second example that influences one's willingness to participate as well as expectations for contributing. Patricia Parker (2002), for example, examines how senior-level African American women across diverse fields negotiate and manage their interactions and their identity in workplace settings where they have been traditionally underrepresented. One thread of Parker's research suggests that, particularly in meetings with their white male colleagues, women executives frequently confront instances when they are interrupted or ignored and when colleagues co-opt their ideas (p. 258). A recurring theme in her interviews is mindfulness: the women are well aware of their positionality as nonmajority members. However, the strategies they employ to counter being silenced, talked over, ignored, or co-opted reflect a range of communicative behaviors (e.g., overtly reiterating their point if initially ignored, waiting until the end of a meeting to voice their concerns, strategically networking before meetings to garner support).

Although the women in Parker's work share equal roles, titles, and power with their male colleagues, her work sheds light on the extent to which overt markers of status are tempered by representation. For about one-half of the women, "their subjectivity as Black women was an ever-present source for framing the context of interaction and deciding on a course of action, whether it was to resist, subvert, or otherwise transform the interaction context" while others chose to "downplay, ignore, or even deny race" (p. 263).

Research illustrates that gender is not a monolithic construct that is "simply imported by individuals into the workplace" (Ashcraft, 2006, p. 101); rather, the range of behaviors suggests fluidity, as executive women's determinations of their communication strategies are informed by "the discrete contexts, situations and relationships" of the organizations in which they work (p. 100). Taken-for-granted assumptions of what is "normal" emerge. Regardless of the strategies employed, they occurred in response to, or in spite of, the dominant culture values:

> Significantly, their White male colleagues, unaware of how their own discourses might be perceived as contributing to creating the conflict, were positioned to avoid such self reflection and intellectual work. That is, as part of the dominant culture, they were positioned to see their actions as normative, with little reason to challenge the taken-for-granted ways of doing things. (Parker, 2002, p. 264)

Essentially, the female executives were, in Silvia Gherardi's (1995) terms, "travelers in a male world" (p. 109).

Interest, Expertise, and Competence. Expectations of interest, expertise, and competence is a third factor that influences positionality. How organizational members are used to represent their workplace is often connected to identity. While sensitivity to diversity is viewed positively, when dominant group members of an organization presume that interest and competence are linked primarily to one's culture or race, what is viewed as a "normal" affiliation may be experienced instead as pressure, inappropriateness, or as marginalization.

In a series of works using feminist standpoint theory to frame a black woman's socialization within predominantly white institutions, Brenda Allen (1996, 2000, 2011) recounts discrete moments where invitations for service were experienced through a nuanced and often contradictory lens. As a "token," she "often is called upon to represent either women or people of color, or her particular racioethnic group" in multiple formal and informal venues (1996, p. 265). She cautions against assuming that one's gender or race be equated with interest or expertise. Moreover, she exposes the contradiction of being pressured or "expected" to engage in activities above and beyond what is required while simultaneously being aware that "the organization may not recognize, acknowledge, or value these contributions" (p. 265).

Similarly, legal scholar Frank Wu (2002) describes the toll exacted when one's culture is a presumed arbiter of expertise. He indicates that he is continually called upon to provide the Asian perspective on a variety of issues. The problem, in his view, is that it is only in this arena where he is regarded as an expert:

> I'd like to show that I know about more than Asian Americans and care about more than Asian Americans. The problem is that a spokesperson becomes the stereotype. I have been cast in my role: an Asian American placed in a vacuum. Nobody wants to hear me or any other Asian American talk about welfare reform, unless the topic is turned into "welfare reform and Asian Americans." (p. 38)

These examples reflect a power imbalance, for they suggest that calls for engagement, participation, and representation largely reside with whoever determines how and where nondominant organizational members are allowed to contribute. As Wu poignantly notes, the abiding belief in individualism in the United States is, for many who are outside of the white world, merely a fabrication:

> I alternate between being conspicuous and vanishing, being stared at or looked through. . . . In most instances, I am who others perceive me to be rather than how I perceive myself to be. Considered by the strong sense of individualism inherent to American society, the inability to define one's self is the greatest loss of liberty possible. (p. 8)

It is important to challenge the seemingly normal and unexamined assumptions that perpetuate equating identity with interest and expertise.

Unequal Pay.   A fourth example of marginalization occurs when individuals are tracked or paid differently because of their identity. In his book *Why Men Earn More,* Warren Farrell (2005) suggests that the wage disparity between women's and men's salaries can be attributed, in part, to women choosing to specialize (e.g., in medicine, finance, law) in areas that pay less; he alleges that this disparity also stems from the differences in the number of hours spent at work. Implicit in his assessment is the conclusion that an increased willingness by women to make different choices and to put in the time would reduce the salary gap.

Several studies suggest that other forces are at work in maintaining disparate wages. In 2003, economists Michael Shannon and Michael Kidd's examination of wages in the United States projected that despite the closing of the education gap between women and men, the wage gap would narrow by only 25% (approximately a 7 cents per hour improvement) between 1995 and 2040. A survey conducted by the National Association for Female Executives revealed a correlation in women's and men's salaries in high-status positions (Larson, 2006). In lower salaried fields (e.g., teachers' aides, office clerks, receptionists) women earned between 80–100% of men's earnings. In higher-income fields, the gap widened: "female neurosurgeons earned only 69.2 percent of what men earned. Women scientists doing medical research earned just 71.3 percent of their male colleagues' income" (p. 77). In engineering, women earn 82% of their male peers (p. 78). A survey of 4,100 women and men who received their MBA between 1996–2007 reported an average discrepancy in starting salaries: women on average were paid $4,600 less than their male counterparts (Lang, 2010, p. 11A). This comparative study—which included Europe, the United States, Asia, and Canada—reported that men tend to be hired at higher levels and are promoted more quickly than women: "These inequities persist regardless of global region, years of prior experience, industry, aspirations and parenthood status" (p. 11A). In their examination of how Asian women are impacted, Amy Caiazza and her colleagues (2004) found that the women in their study earned approximately 75% of what white men earn in the same field. And a study of equally credentialed accountants by sociologist Louise Mary Roth (2006) revealed that "women earn 39% less than men with the same background and family status characteristics" (p. 211). In light of these discrepancies, it is understandable why Ilene Lang (2010), president and CEO of Catalyst, argues that not only does the glass ceiling persist, in her view, "the glass ceiling is much lower than you think" (p. 11A).

Norms and Informal Practices.   While efforts to redress pay inequities continue, it is also important to address informal and often unintentional discriminatory practices that sustain wage disparities across fields. One example of how presumed norms can adversely affect career opportunities relates to cultural stereotypes. Brenda Allen (2011), for example, suggests that the term "model minority," which is associated with Asian

Americans and with such traits as cooperation, compliance, and passivity, may shade into assumptions that Asian Americans "are not interested in climbing the corporate ladder" (pp. 84–85). In a study that focused on Asian women, despite their increasing presence in the workforce, they are woefully underrepresented in senior-level positions: "they make up less than 0.5% of corporate officers at the 429 Fortune 500 companies that provided these data: Out of 10,092 Fortune 500 corporate officers in 2002, only 30 (0.29%) were Asian women" (Hyun, 2005, p. xviii).

As long as self-promotion is viewed as normal and requisite for rising within the workplace, Asian women may be especially impacted despite their educational achievement because "Asian cultural values, whether learned or reinforced by family, work against their ability to successfully navigate the corporate ladder" (Hyun, 2005, p. xviii). We suggest the need to challenge taken-for-granted criteria for assessing promotability. It is important for those in positions of power to identify talented members of their workforce and perhaps broaden construals for how positive and valued contributions are assessed.

Relatedly, when traditional norms remain unquestioned, instances of discrimination are apt to persist. Roth's (2006) examination of gender equality in securities firms on Wall Street revealed no statistically significant differences in educational background, numbers of hours spent at work, or in academic performance. However, her interviews did indicate disparate treatment in work assignments. "Women are more likely to work in public finance. . . . [S]ex segregation within the securities industry constituted an important source of gender disparity and . . . men and women were shifted in different career paths at various points in their careers" (p. 210). In particular, she found both corporate finance and sales and trading to be male dominated (where earnings were between 173% and 210% more than peers in support functions) (p. 212). Moreover, even in instances when women and men were performing the same financial functions and working similar hours, her study revealed that female respondents earned less, leading her to conclude: "A consistent and statistically negative effect of gender on compensation suggests that some form of residual discrimination shapes earning disparities among comparable individuals on Wall Street" (p. 213). Roth suggests that part of this discrepancy may be connected to how employees are assessed: despite objective markers, assessments are not immune to subjective appraisals. Part of this discrepancy, in her view, may also stem from homophily: high-paying clients were predominantly men and they may have been more comfortable working with men in the firm.

These examples suggest the need to examine arguments such as Farrell's, which allege that bias and discrimination no longer exist. The challenge for workplace settings that strive to become more diverse is to create and support initiatives that alter patterns of assignments and assessments that are identity-based rather than competency-based.

Box 6.3   Perceptions of Interaction: Examples from the Field

The following examples come primarily from workshop and seminar participants in diverse organizational settings. We present recurring issues followed by assessments from senior-level individuals. As you look at these examples, think about how these issues articulate with your own experiences as well as alternate approaches.

Whose Messages Get Heard?

A. Responses from women regarding interaction in small-group settings
- "Men find it easier to talk over women."
- "If given the chance, I'm heard as effectively."
- "I feel I'm constantly overlooked."
- "I'm constantly being interrupted and not allowed to explain."
- "I think people treat you the way you let them treat you. If you present your-self in a confident manner, you are treated as such, regardless of gender."

B. Responses from men regarding interaction in small-group settings
- "In my culture, it's rude to interrupt or to contradict my superiors in an open setting. I don't believe that silence is only gender-related."
- "Because English is my second language, I find that I am unable to compete with native speakers. As a result, I often don't participate or contribute."

C. Assessments from senior-level members
- "Because many of our meetings are geared at brainstorming on issues or projects, I assume that participants will jump in with ideas. Everyone's involvement matters. It is also my responsibility to make sure that all have an opportunity to contribute—I try to allow for time to elicit input from everyone—even if this requires suggestions after the meeting."
- "I've noticed that men in our group tend to cut to the chase. Women often take more time speaking. When we're on a tight deadline, this can create challenges."
- "It's important to be positive and proactive and to get clarification when needed. Messages such as 'Here's where I am on this . . .' or 'I want to make sure I'm on point with the project . . .' lets me know where an employee is and what's needed."
- "Know your supervisor's style. Do they prefer aural or visual interaction? He/she needs input that is on target. Carve out time if needed—we're all in this together."

Perceptions on How Men Monitor Behavior When Interacting with Women

A. Women's observations
- "Men feel they have to be more sensitive if women are around. . . . Sometimes they guard what they say."
- "Men are slightly more polite—perhaps they feel men can handle being yelled at or scolded and women can't."
- "The result of choosing their words more carefully can be both good and bad: if they are constantly watching what they are saying, this can lead to a lack of camaraderie and to not getting appropriate feedback."

B. Assessments from senior-level members
- "Relevant and helpful feedback is critical. If you feel that a supervisor is holding back or is being vague, it's important to request feedback. The bottom line is that you need this information to succeed."

(continued)

- "Men may not even be aware they're treating you differently. If you have questions or concerns, then ask. Don't wait for your regular review."
- "Experience working with women may be a factor. They may not be used to having women as colleagues. Fortunately, the more time you spend working with someone, more trust develops."

Task Assignments

A recurring theme in women's responses is that they would like to become involved in more challenging projects. Often they feel they are overlooked, that requests for these types of engagement are ignored.

A. Assessments from senior-level members
- "It's important to consider—do men feel the same way? What types of assignments are typically given to more junior-level members? It may be an organizational climate issue rather than a gender issue."
- "Be positive. Message tactics matter. 'I'm not being challenged' may be heard as a criticism or complaint. There's no value added by this approach. Instead, be positive. Plant the seed that you're eager to become more involved. For example, 'I'd like more exposure in this...' or 'There's an opportunity to attend a session on....'"
- "Have your 30-second elevator speech ready for when you run into senior members. If asked, 'How's it going?' don't just reply 'Fine.' Be able to mention some talking points on what you're working on. It's also helpful to know your boss's interests (e.g., sending an article or information relevant to current issues and/or projects)."

The Discourse on Work/Life Balance: Impact on Attitudes and Decisions That Maintain Gender Differences

To this point, we have examined subtle and overt forms of discrimination. In this section, we will consider issues that result in one's decision to alter one's engagement in the workplace. In particular, we look at both the causes and effects of these decisions—decisions that are more nuanced than they may appear on the surface.

Parental Views: Time in the Home, Time in the Workplace

A series of recent polls suggest interesting shifts regarding women's and men's roles both in the workplace and in the home. A large majority of women and men reportedly view women in the workplace as "positive for the economy" (80% of women and men) and view "stay-at-home dads" as "more acceptable than in the past" (85% of women and 79% of men). These findings suggest greater receptivity to expanding roles for men in the home and acceptance of sustained participation by women in the workforce (Gibbs, 2009, pp. 30, 33).

Despite this receptivity, surveys also suggest that time at work impacts mothers and fathers differently. Women's responses, in particular, indicate that they continue to see themselves as responsible for the "second shift" of caring for the home and for children (Gibbs, 2009). One disparity is reflected in the reported number of hours fathers and mothers spend with their children on a daily basis (see chapter 4).

In addition, several surveys of working parents suggest a discrepancy between what women and men view as an ideal working situation for achieving balance in one's personal and professional life. A recent Pew Research Center (2007) survey, for example, reveals a sizable shift in working mothers' attitudes toward full-time employment. In 1997, 32% of the working mothers surveyed felt that full-time work was an ideal situation for them, while 48% felt that part-time work would be an ideal situation. A follow-up study conducted 10 years later indicated a trend in the opposite direction: 21% of working mothers considered full-time work ideal while 60% viewed part-time work as preferred. These figures suggest a disparity not only in attitudes toward one's place in the public sphere, they also suggest an aspirational gap in the amount of time women would like to spend in the home.

In light of this reevaluation, it is not surprising that a majority of women and men report that it is "better for the family if the father works outside the home and the mother takes care of the children" (Gibbs, 2009, p. 32). Seventy-two percent of fathers with children under the age of 18 view full-time work as an ideal situation for them (Pew Research Center, 2007, p. 3). Moreover, their willingness to assume responsibility for child care if their "spouse or significant other's income could comfortably support the entire family" declined from 49% in 2005 to 37% in 2008 to 31% in 2009 (Careerbuilder.com, 2009).

The coinciding of men's increasingly positive view of seeing their primary place in the world of work along with an increase in the number of women embracing part-time work as preferable suggests that parents are complicit in the allocation of care to women. Reports indicate that there are 5.2 million stay-at-home mothers whose income derives from their spouse or significant other (Farrell, 2005, p. 85). In contrast, there are reportedly 159,000 stay-at-home fathers whose income derives from their spouse or significant other (Rebeldad.com, 2009).

While it is impossible to determine from the above discussion whether parents' preferences for full-time versus part-time employment reflect an ideal in the best of all possible worlds or an ideal given current societal support systems (e.g., accessible and affordable child care, the ability to take family leave), several works suggest that multiple factors contribute to sustaining a disparity of caregiving for working men and women. The aspirational and professional goals of women appear to be affected in ways that influence the choices that they make.

Attitudes toward Work and toward Care in the Home

Several researchers identify aspects of the contemporary landscape that may affect women's careers. Significantly, these issues suggest that women must make choices that will have considerable consequences if they do not choose wisely. In their examination of how construals of careers have evolved, communication researchers Patrice Buzzanell and Kristen Lucas (2006) evoke the metaphor of a "journey" to describe the traditional trajectory of work. This journey is marked by constancy, hard work, and typically by a linear path leading to retention and promotion over time (see Crittenden, 2001; Douglas, 2010; Farrell, 2005; Hewlett, 2002; Kessler, 2007; Larson, 2006; Pinker, 2008; Williams, 2010). Over the past three decades, as women have increasingly entered fields previously dominated by men, and as the workplace has increasingly become more fragile, unpredictable, and tenuous due to increased global competition and economic downturns, new challenges as well as additional metaphors have emerged that expand and make space for how women prescribe and experience their professional journeys.

In lieu of the linear trajectory associated with men's careers, the image of a kaleidoscope has been evoked to describe women's work lives:

> Like a kaleidoscope that produces changing patterns when the tube is rotated and its chips fall into new arrangements, women shift the pattern of their careers by rotating different aspects of their lives to arrange their roles and relationships in new ways. Women's careers, like kaleidoscopes, are relational. (Mainiero & Sullivan, 2006, p. 329)

These turns in the metaphorical kaleidoscope often are reflected in women's decisions to recalibrate their professional aspirations and goals, to scale back their careers, to opt out of the workforce either temporarily or permanently, to relocate to support their partner's career, and/or to establish their own business (Borisoff, 2005a, 2005b; Buzzanell & Lucas, 2006; de Marneffe, 2004; Douglas, 2010; Douglas & Michaels, 2004; Farrell, 2005; Hewlett, 2007; Kessler, 2007; Stone & Lovejoy, 2006; Vavrus, 2007).

Sylvia Ann Hewlett (2002) has described the potential risks for women who invest too much of themselves and their time in linear career pathways, resulting in trajectories that can have adverse consequences on creating successful personal relationships. Her interviews with high-achieving women (as well as with some men) suggest a consistent undercurrent in the women's stories: while they may have achieved enormous monetary success in their diverse careers, often they look back with deep regret at what their professional success has cost them personally. Implicit in Hewlett's message is that women who are seeking careers in heretofore male-dominated areas need to recalibrate their professional aspirations in order to make space for their personal lives.

Women also are cognizant of messages regarding what qualifies as good parenting. They are not inured to messages that they are putting the welfare of their children at risk if they are unable (or unwilling) to oversee scrupulously every aspect of their child's life. Moreover, messages from the media suggest that when problems occur, mothers are to blame (see chapter 4). From a postfeminist lens, there is a double bind for women: women are equal and free to pursue work outside of the home, "even in jobs previously restricted to men" (Douglas & Michaels, 2004, p. 24), as long as they sustain equal involvement in intensive mothering. Similarly, Judith Warner's (2005) interviews with 150 mothers suggest that adherence to "new momism" is revealed in how mothers view their role as a parent. Many have come to view raising a child as a "job" (p. 6), as their "life's work," assuming in the process a "winner take all parenting" mind-set (p. 215). This mind-set ultimately transforms children, in one mother's view, into a "product that parents can be proud of and that reflects well on them" (p. 224). We note here the metaphoric transformation: in the process of transforming nurturing into a job, the child is also transformed from a human being into an inanimate object. Unexamined in this discourse on mothering is a conspicuous absence of examining fathers' roles in children's lives. As psychiatrist Anna Fels (2004) observes,

> The impact of poor or absent fathering has been largely ignored by both the scientific community and the popular press. We simply do not scrutinize the children of sixty-hour-a-week male professionals the way we scrutinize the children of working mothers. (p. 301)

In 2003, journalist Lisa Belkin presented an alternative view of motherhood in her article "The Opt-Out Revolution." She posits that the rising number of stay-at-home mothers (along with an increase in women who have "scaled down" or "redefined" their employment) stems from a shift in outlooks and priorities (p. 44). In her view, highly credentialed women are "rejecting the workplace" (p. 44) and are infusing their definition of success with such terms as "balance" and the "choice to parent" (p. 45). She notes: "women are redefining success. And in so doing they are redefining work" (p. 45).

Although opting out of the workplace predates Belkin's piece, her work resonates in part because she regards the choice to parent full-time as a "revolution" that reflects women's agency, power, and presumed decision-making as unfettered from external pressures or constraints in the workplace and in the home. "As women look up at the 'top,'" she writes, "they are increasingly deciding that they don't want to do what it takes to get there" (p. 45).

The above discussion suggests discursive shifts in how we talk about women's workplace experiences as well as how we talk about motherhood. It suggests that as we enter the second decade of the twenty-first century, the issues involved remain unresolved, tenuous, and fraught with controversy. The rhetoric that is used is, in part, skewed and is often an incomplete representation of how women view their careers and their decisions regarding their parenting and caretaking roles.

In the following sections, we examine the nuances embedded in the choice discourse. We consider, too, recommendations to alter the workplace in ways that will ultimately extend and expand the meaning of choice in concrete ways for women as well as for men. These changes have the potential to alter how individuals experience their lives at work as well as how they experience their lives in the home.

Nuances of "Choice" in the Opt-Out Revolution Discourse

Several concerns have been identified in response to the media's representation of an ostensibly increasing and decidedly optimistic view of women's choices or projected choices to opt out of their careers or to scale down their aspirations (Belkin, 2003; Story, 2005; Wallis, 2004). We consider the scope and factors (both subtle and overt) that suggest a more nuanced and realistic picture. We will also consider the question of what women are opting into.

The Extent to which "Opting Out" is a Revolution.   Recent national labor force data indicates that in 2009, 71% of women with children under the age of 18 and 64% with children under age six were in the labor force (U.S. Department of Labor, 2010c). Moreover, in instances when women do take time off from work for child care, often they are opting out for brief time periods. Citing studies that indicate that "the average 'off-ramp' for professional women who become mothers is approximately one year or less, and for a significant portion it is just a few months," legal researcher Laura Kessler (2007) suggests we "should be skeptical about claims of a revolution," as Belkin's piece proclaims. In Kessler's view, "there is no 'opt-out revolution,' not even a mini one" (p. 3).

The Participants.   Those lives that are reflected in articles and books about this revolution do not speak to most women's lives. Many feminist scholars observe that media coverage has cast its lens on well-off, well-educated, and well-compensated mothers. Women outside this rarefied coterie are precluded from joining the revolution (Crittenden, 2001; Douglas, 2010; Douglas & Michaels, 2004; Kessler, 2007; Steiner, 2006; Vavrus, 2007). Reporting is also racially skewed as the mothers interviewed are primarily white women. In 2005, a larger percentage of educated black mothers with children under 18 participated in the labor force than their white counterparts (83.7% versus 74%) (Clemetson, 2006, p. 2). This disparity of participation suggests that "black women are opting out of the 'opt-out' debate" (p. 1). As *Washington Post* writer Lonnae O'Neal Parker (2005) observes, conversations about mothers feeling guilty about working or considering work an option was a "foreign" concept to her, "something I had never heard in all the conservations with all the black women I had ever known" (p. 12). Her work suggests that the angst reflected in the debates about working mothers obscures the experiences of black women:

> It seems few of the combatants and cultural arbiters in the mommy wars see me in three full dimensions—to the extent that they see me at all. They seem not to realize that women of color might have different imperatives, a different history, different sets of assumptions. . . . I find myself deeply unmoved by people who are unable to look outside of themselves or pick up lessons from other histories and cultures. (pp. 13–14)

Who is left out of the discourse and media coverage includes white working- and middle-class women and their experiences and challenges, as well as the voices of Latinas (Clemetson, 2006; Douglas & Michaels, 2004; Steiner, 2006; Vavrus, 2007). In Vavrus' (2007) view, a seemingly singular focus on an educationally, economically privileged group ignores the critical systemic issues that merit scrutiny: "By obscuring wage- and family-labor conditions that seem ripe for transformation, opting out stories manage to quell what could be a real mother's revolution by diverting attention away from public solutions" (p. 59).

Subtle and Overt Factors That Influence Women's "Choice."   A third area of concern is exposing the systemic work-related structures to which Vavrus alludes. Several researchers suggest that deploying the choice rhetoric precludes an examination of the workplace policies and practices that impact women and mothers' decisions most profoundly. Vavrus (2007) exposes the illusory nature of "choice":

> Obviously choice in and of itself is not a bad thing, particularly if these mothers are making choices in an environment in which both men and women of all races and class positions possessed equal amounts of power and could exercise it in a similar fashion with good results. But as feminist scholars point out, the notion of choice when applied to the question of who might stay home to take care of the kids is an almost meaningless one in the United States. (p. 53)

There are indications that for many women who decide to leave the workplace (either totally or partially), the opting out discourse suggests a retreat rather than a revolution. We turn to several factors that influence these decisions.

Work Demands.   In light of our discussion thus far, it is not surprising when Stone and Lovejoy (2006) cite "sixty hour" work weeks and 24/7 "accountability," an "all or nothing" commitment, "workplace inflexibility," and the inability to negotiate reduced or part-time work as contributing to 86% of their working mother participants' decisions to leave their jobs (pp. 144–145).

The women interviewed by Judith Warner (2005) similarly indicated the "incompatibility" of work and parenting to time-related "obstacles" in the workplace as the impetus for their departures (p. 51). And Sylvia Ann Hewlett's (2007) surveys and focus group interviews reveal that women (as well as some men) in diverse fields (e.g., finance, media, law) found alternative work arrangements, including flextime, part-time hours, and telecommuting, to be "toxic" or "off limits" where they worked (p. 32).

Mainiero and Sullivan (2006) indicate that these negative appraisals of the workplace do not emerge to the same degree in men's descriptions of their workplace experiences. The men who participated in their studies reportedly could keep "their work and non-work lives separate" in part "because the women in their lives managed the delicate interplay between work and non-work issues" (p. 330).

Effects of Legislation on Workplace Practices.   From a legal standpoint, although passage of the Pregnancy Discrimination Act prohibits discrimination on the basis of pregnancy, "courts have refused to interpret discrimination on the basis of sex 'plus' an employee's need to adjust her work schedule to care for a child as unlawful sex discrimination under Title VII's 'sex-plus' theory" (Kessler, 2007, p. 4). As a result, many workplace policies and practices associated with linear careers that require strict adherence to fixed schedules, long hours, and limited absenteeism "disproportionately and negatively affect women workers . . ." (p. 4).

With passage of the Family Medical Leave Act (FMLA) in 1993, which allowed for up to 12 unpaid work weeks of leave for child and/ or family-related care, women and men would presumably receive much-needed support to meet the demands of both work and family. Studies indicate that in reality, approximately one-fifth of employees covered by FMLA actually avail themselves of this option (Kessler, 2007, p. 4); many are unable to forego wages for 12 weeks. Moreover, due to disparities in men's and women's salaries, as well as societal views of women as the arbiters of care, more women than men actually take a leave (Hoffman & Cowan, 2008; Kessler, 2007).

Beyond salary differences, as Kirby and Krone (2002) and Hochschild (1997) indicate, workplace climate impacts one's willingness to take a leave for child care. These researchers contend that supervisors' and colleagues' attitudes about the appropriateness and fairness of leave-taking to tend to a child can have an enormous impact on one's willingness to apply for a leave. In the view of many organizations, commitment to the job is equated with being there and men (more so than women) are viewed as less dedicated when they take time off for child care. In the view of many colleagues, child care leave results in the remaining employees having to pick up the slack of the absentee worker.

A final limitation of FMLA is affordability. Comparative examinations of support for child care indicate a glaring lack in the FMLA provisions both in monetary support and length of time allowed (Crittenden, 2001; Douglas, 2010; Hochschild, 1997; Larson, 2006; Meisenbach, Remke, Buzzanell, & Liu, 2008). For example, "While 163 countries . . . offer paid maternity leave and 45 provide paid paternity leave, the U.S. does not" (Douglas, 2010, p. 298). This disparity in societal recognition and support of care leads Rebecca Meisenbach and her colleagues (2008) to conclude that "the U.S. has one of the weakest legislative family leave policies out of all the developed nations in the world . . ." (p. 20).

The Influence of One's Partner on the "Choice" of Care. Embedded in the opting out discourse is the push-pull tension between the lure of work and the lure of care. Framed from a lens of "relationism," Mainiero and Sullivan (2006) suggest in their kaleidoscope model that midcareer women seek "balance" in their lives. While child care as well as family care may be included in this pursuit of balance, the consequence is "adjustments to their career ambitions" to meet their caretaking demands (p. 332). It is important to consider the extent to which the role of primary caretaker is freely chosen by women or reflects, in part, internal and external pressures.

Maternal desire, not wanting to miss out on the early stages of a child's development, viewing mothers as the best providers of care, and experiencing guilt while at work reflect recurrent themes in women's accounts for choosing to leave the workplace. As explained earlier, these decisions often are made in conjunction with a company's inability or unwillingness to facilitate adjusted or alternative work schedules (Crittenden, 2001; de Marneffe, 2004; Douglas & Michaels, 2004; Hewlett, 2007; Mainiero & Sullivan, 2006; Stone & Lovejoy, 2006; Warner, 2005). If barriers to the workplace were removed, we might ask if the same choices would occur.

In their accounts, however, we find that for many women a lack of support in the workplace is matched by a lack of support in the home. Differing attitudes about home and child care roles may ultimately fuel a woman's decision to leave the workplace or drastically alter her schedule. Recall the reported responses of male students in chapter 4. In their projections for the future, the majority envisioned being the primary wage earner and they projected that their partner would be responsible for care in the home. This sentiment was echoed in interviews with male students at ivy league colleges in Louise Story's report (2005). Interviews with high-income male professionals in Sylvia Ann Hewlett's (2002) work also sustained a traditional view of family life: included in their vision was a house, children, and a wife who would be there for them.

Sociologists Pamela Stone and Meg Lovejoy's (2006) study on professional women's choices to opt out of the workforce reveals how these expectations are framed as well as the impact they ultimately have on influencing one's decisions. Several accounts linked women's decisions to wage differences: their husband's "high octane careers" required more time and commitment (p. 150). Women's accounts were also connected to ideology: their husbands' mothers were there for them full-time, and they wanted to continue this model in their own lives (p. 151). Even in instances where husbands "professed an egalitarian stance toward women's decisions about whether to cut back on their careers, captured in the frequent refrain, 'It's your choice'" was the tacit message that women could continue to work if they chose to do so (p. 152). However, they would have to cope with child care primarily on their own. The willingness of men to offer to participate or share duties in the home was conspicuously absent in the women's accounts.

Shifting the Focus: What Are Women Opting Into?   The opt-out discourse is framed as a natural extension of a relational orientation that is seemingly embraced freely. Media coverage has largely portrayed a positive picture (Belkin, 2003; Douglas & Michaels, 2004; Kessler, 2007; Vavrus, 2007). According to Vavrus (2007), media stories often avoid what well-off mothers opt into: "copious amounts of uncompensated labor . . ." (p. 54) with impossibly high standards (as Douglas and Michaels [2004] explain) that can exact a toll over time. Themes of self-doubt, inadequacy as a parent, not meeting their own high standards, and feeling overwhelmed undergird the women's stories in Warner's (2005) interviews. This self-questioning is understandable. As Borisoff (2005b) notes,

> There is a fundamental difference between public- and private-sphere "jobs." Work in the public arena provides rewards and rights in the form of paychecks, raises, promotions. . . . Work performed in this domain is highly valued and employees are recognized for doing well. Absent in the home are these visible markers of support, recognition, appreciation, and valuation. (p. 261)

Vavrus (2007) notes further that media stories often ignore the "financial, if not psychological, powerlessness" that is often a consequence when women opt into full-time parenting (p. 54). Many writers and researchers have noted that a decrease in women's participation in the workplace is often accompanied by a simultaneous loss in status and power within the home (Bennetts, 2007; Crittenden, 2001; Fels, 2004; O'Neal Parker, 2006; Warner, 2005). Husbands' comments such as "Here's what I'd like you to do . . ." and "You don't have anything to do today, do you?" are heard as demands that convey a lack of respect (Warner, 2005, pp. 249, 250). For women who prior to their parenting role were wage earners living in what they regarded as egalitarian relationships, this shift is often accompanied by a "perfect madness" toward their husbands. As one mother observed, "What did you do today?" became a loaded question (O'Neal Parker, 2006, p. 69).

A diminution in feeling respected was often matched by an unantici-
pated loss of power in financial decision-making. This disparity can
exact a toll:

> Marriages are more male-dominated when women are not economic
> partners, which tends to decrease the quality of interaction. If your
> partner is also your paycheck, you're in a difficult position to make
> demands. . . . If you earn no money, or less money, you're going to
> be less likely to win when you have disagreements, and this
> decreases the quality of the marriage. (Bennetts, 2007, p. 207)

For many women, time spent resenting one's partner for not being
involved enough, for devaluing one's role, and for exerting one's power
impact feelings of intimacy and closeness. A sense of "living apart
together" powerfully characterizes the consequences of a power imbalance (Warner, 2005, p. 256).

Ann Crittenden (2001) notes that "family financial arrangements are
like snowflakes in their infinite variety," thus making it difficult to ascer-
tain the full range of decision-making among couples surrounding money
(p. 111). However, she acknowledges the received wisdom "that the subtle balance of power in a marriage is tilted in favor of the spouse who
contributes the money" (p. 112). Men, too, are not immune to a shift in
power when they no longer are the primary wage earners (Bennetts,
2007; Jackson, 2004; McNeil, 2004). Rob Jackson (2004) comments:
"In any family the breadwinner has an extra measure of influence, and
ours was no different. I quickly came to understand that I was the man of
the house but not the power" (pp. 139–140). Former corporate lawyer
Robert Michelson echoes this sentiment when he, like Jackson, took on
the role of stay-at-home spouse: "Something clearly happened. . . . I felt
the change in my ability to push certain points of dispute. . . . I wasn't
the strong partner" (Crittenden, 2001, pp. 113–114).

Although it appears that those who control the purse strings are
afforded greater power, we did note a subtle but significant distinction
in the men's accounts. They report that their wives were sensitive to the
wage disparities and were careful to assure financial equality in their
relationships. They attribute this sensitivity to the fact that the women
in their lives had been on the other side of the financial equation and
were keenly aware of the negative consequences of feeling powerless.
As sociologist Julie Brines has observed in her study of labor division in
marriage, women more than men endeavor to establish equality when
they outearn their husbands. Her research revealed that "men tend to
share more housework as their wives' incomes approach theirs. But
when wives make much more, the wives also tend to do much more
housework" (cited in McNeil, 2004, p. 3). Brines found this behavior
"particularly common for black working women" (p. 3). We suspect
that this shift in women's behavior reflects efforts to recalibrate the bal-

ance of power within their own relationships. In a culture that has tended to equate a man's worth with his capacity to earn and to provide for his family, a disruption in the ability to fulfill these expectations may be felt more acutely by the men.

Finally, Vavrus (2007) contends that media coverage of opting out stories ignore potential challenges to "re-entry into the labor force . . ." (p. 54). Several articles suggest "help to get going again" (Rosen, 2006), offer "signs of easier re-entry" (Chura, 2005, p. 1), and propose that the boss will come "calling" after the baby is born (Belkin, 2007). Often, however, many programs designed to facilitate reentry (particularly university-sponsored programs) are highly selective, provide limited enrollment, and are costly (Palmer, 2010; Rochman, 2009; Rosen, 2006). Moreover, recent reports indicate that economic conditions affect prospects for reentry. For example, according to MomCorps (a firm established in 2005 to match women seeking white-collar positions in companies that offer flexible hours), in March 2010 there were 34,000 applications for 54 positions (Rochman, 2009, p. 70). A report by the Center for Work-Life Policy echoes similar barriers for women seeking full-time posts, indicating that only "4 in 10 women who stop working are able to find full-time jobs again" (Palmer, 2010, p. 29).

Although changes in the economy exacerbate challenges in the job search process (more so for white-collar than for blue-collar positions), "on-ramps" are more difficult to negotiate than "off-ramps" (Ehrenreich, 2005; Hewlett, 2007). Moreover, initiatives to foster reentry do not necessarily address what Crittenden (2004) refers to as a "cognitive bias" toward unpaid labor in the home: "Many people associate housewives and mothers at home with menial labor and the lowly chores of cleaning, laundry, changing diapers, babysitting. They see a full-time parent and envision those routine tasks rather than the complex problem-solving, the subtle relationship work, the multitasking and motivational skills" that are included in these roles (pp. 221–222). She notes further that stay-at-home fathers are not immune to these negative ascriptions: "these fathers report that they too suffer a stigma when they attempt to reenter the workforce . . ." (p. 223). While companies such as Deloitte & Touche, Tomatsu, and IBM have been cited as exemplars for creating mechanisms to maintain connections and to shepherd back into the workforce those who have taken extended leaves, these examples are touted as exceptions (Collins, 2009; Hewlett, 2007; Mainiero & Sullivan, 2006). For those who are exploring alternative workplace sites, negative attitudes about unpaid labor in the home may keep them permanently off-ramped. Law professor Joan Williams advocates for combating this pervasive bias. She argues that "discrimination based on bias against parents ought to be as illegal as discrimination on the basis of race or gender. . . . [A] ban on discrimination against people with family responsibilities should be added to state antidiscrimination statutes" (cited in Crittenden, 2004, p. 223).

The rhetoric of choice, coupled with the expectation of care, are not neutral representations of the contemporary landscape for women in the United States. As Fels (2004) notes, having children affects women most acutely and "is all too often the death knell for women's ambitions" (p. 36). In her view, "They are expected to do the vast majority of child care despite the lack of respect, social support systems, financial security, or financial remuneration" (p. 238). As long as parenting and working outside of the home are viewed as individual choices that women make freely, and as long as family-related decisions are regarded as private matters by both employers and the government, the impetus to effect changes that could positively alter the landscape of work and of the home often remain unexamined. Buzzanell and Lucas (2006) posit the need to "rearticulate career as a means of enhancing quality of work (and nonwork) life" (p. 172). In the final section, we identify recommendations for change that can move us toward this rearticulation.

Prospects for Altering the Workplace: Challenges and Recommendations

Construals of workplace structures, values, and expectations have remained remarkably persistent. However, many researchers note a growing recognition of a need for change and identify how many companies have responded in ways that can potentially alter and create broader, fairer, and more inclusive venues to revalue the lives we forge both within and beyond the borders of wage work.

Revisiting Linear Careers as a Primary Trajectory for Success in the Workplace: Shifting Views of Employees

There are indications of aspirational shifts and reenvisioning priorities related to the world of work and of home. Ehrenreich's (2005) and Philipson's (2002) characterizations of twenty-first century workers as "passionate" employees who willingly allow themselves to become "married" or "anchored" to the job and for whom a crushing workload is accepted unquestioningly provides an incomplete picture of how the workplace is regarded by a wider range of constituencies.

Recent reports suggest that more and more Gen X and Gen Y ("millennial") men, for example, are willing to recalibrate their careers. Stone and Lovejoy (2006) contend that "younger generations of men are increasingly interested in working less and devoting more time to life and family" (p. 155). Similarly, recruiting firms report that many "Gen Y men (as well as women) are more interested in social responsibility, high ethical standards, and time for family than they are in salary . . ." (Hewlett, 2007, p. 256). One recent survey indicates that 40% of working fathers "would consider a cut of 10 percent or more" to spend more time with their children (Careerbuilder.com, 2009, p. 1). Yet another suggests that working fathers would take advantage of flexible working arrangements (e.g., telecommuting, flexible schedules, job sharing) if offered by their company (Lorenz, 2007, p. 1).

Signs of recalibrating participation in the workplace is similarly being embraced by members of the baby boomer population. Hewlett (2007) notes that "over the next twenty years, some 78 million baby boomers will grapple with the question of how not to retire—to ramp down without ramping off" (p. 256). She indicates that about 70% of workers in this cohort also will be seeking flexible work arrangements and reduced hours (p. 256). We would speculate that in light of the economic challenges that erupted most dramatically in 2008—impacting in the process one's ability to retire—this percentage may well exceed the 70% that Hewlett reports.

A final underexamined group are those women situated on what Jane Gross labels the "daughter track" (cited in Hewlett, 2007, p. 162). Included in this group are women (and we would argue, many men) who are either child free or who are at an age where child care is no longer an issue. For this group, engaging in care for elderly parents requires more of their attention and time. An estimated 20 million employees are engaged in this type of care. African American women are even more impacted. They also engage in extended family and community caregiving, spending an estimated 12.4 hours per week engaged in this type of care versus 9.5 hours for white women (Hewlett, 2007, p. 36; Hewlett et al., 2005).

To attract and to retain talented employees, companies have a vested interest in offering, encouraging, and supporting alternative ways for prescribing and assessing commitment to and productivity in one's job. We turn to examples of altering the terrain of workplace performance that are ostensibly meeting the needs of employers and employees alike.

Revisiting Face Time as the Arbiter for Productivity: Valuing Flexible Working Arrangements

> Instead of assuming that employees should demonstrate their ambition through long hours, face-time, and travel, firms need to recognize their employees have both work and personal obligations. Work should be redesigned around this "dual agenda." (Mainiero & Sullivan, 2006, p. 335)

There are indications that employers are becoming increasingly responsive to this dual agenda by implementing a variety of alternative opportunities that uncouple commitment from face time. Work arrangements such as compressed and flextime schedules enable workers to alter the number of days or hours they work in the office while retaining full-time status. Remote work, such as telecommuting (either full- or part-time), also allows employees to maintain a full-time schedule. And job sharing and part-time employment enables employees to remain engaged while simultaneously allowing employers to retain talented individuals who contribute positively.

In particular, companies including Ernst & Young, Citigroup, Sun Microsystems, Booz Allen, IBM, and British Telecommunications are cited as exemplars of developing programs that deviate from the traditional linear model of work (Belkin, 2007; Collins, 2009; Hewlett, 2007; Holland, 2006; Mainiero & Sullivan, 2006; Stone & Lovejoy, 2006). Importantly, assessments of these initiatives indicate that proactive, top-down support as well as clearly valuing employees' contributions, regardless of their current status in the workplace, result in higher retention rates, lower instances of absenteeism, and enhanced performance. Moreover, employers' attitudes affect employees' willingness to participate in alternative work programs. Signs of success are indicated by reports that 95% of Sun Microsystems' workforce participate in the company's flexible schedule programs (Mainiero & Sullivan, 2006, p. 335). Ninety-nine percent of women on leave returned to British Telecommunications due, in part, to its Freedom to Work Program (Hewlett, 2007, p. 124). When Ernst & Young launched its Flexible Work Initiative, 34% of the 4,900 employees who applied were men (p. 120). And the number of employees participating in telecommuting has reportedly risen from 6 million to more than 13 million in less than a decade (Holland, 2006, p. 1).

Despite these ostensible successes, there are current challenges that some of these opportunities pose. First, telecommuting does not necessarily solve the financial obligations for child care for employees with young children. Second, physical isolation may be accompanied by feeling emotionally disconnected from workplace colleagues and friends. Metaphors of the workplace include such terms as "professional community," "family," and "home away from home" (Hochschild, 1997; Philipson, 2002; Wallace, 2004). Physical separation can make it harder to secure and to provide the kind of support, assistance, and camaraderie that are more readily forged in person. Third, the absence of regular face-to-face contact has implications for the negotiation of one's performance. Sociologist Richard Sennett (1998) contends that working at home provides illusory freedom from the workplace: "A flextime worker controls the location of labor, but does not gain greater control over the labor process itself . . ." (p. 59). Employers, he suggests, are concerned with losing control over the absent workers; employees are concerned with demonstrating engagement and connection. Workers therefore "exchange one form of submission to power—face-to-face—for another which is electronic," whereby involvement "has shifted from the time clock to the computer screen" (p. 59). Power over the worker has merely shifted to a virtual domain: "In the revolt against routine the appearance of a new freedom is deceptive. Time in institutions and for individuals has been unchained from the iron cage of the past, but subjected to new, top-down controls and surveillance" (p. 59).

The spectre that one's physical presence remains an abiding indicator of commitment and engagement ultimately informs one's willingness to consider working from home. Thirty-nine percent of the female respondents in Hewlett's (2007) study regard telecommuting as a "pipe dream. Although it is theoretically 'on the books,' in reality, one dare not take up this option" for fear of adversely affecting their career (p. 226). Hewlett's respondents held primarily upper-level posts. While many work environments indeed make flexible schedules hard to negotiate, law professor Joan Williams (2010) argues that the work of high-level professionals more readily lends itself to being accomplished beyond the confines of an office. They "can work their sixty hours a week any time and any place they want," thus affording them at least the potential for greater "autonomy and flexibility . . ." (p. 209). For those employed in middle- and low-wage jobs, "rigid, highly supervised schedules," "rotating shifts," "unsocial hours," and the need "to hold two or three jobs at once" erect formidable barriers that are harder to address and to overcome (p. 209).

Alternative work arrangements may also pose a challenge for how employees are evaluated and rewarded. Mainiero and Sullivan (2006) report that flexible opportunities often result in severely impacting one's earnings. In the field of law, they indicate that "90 percent of U.S. legal firms offer part-time career options to employees but only about 4 percent choose this option because 33 percent of legal professionals believe it will hurt their careers and their pay . . ." (p. 337). They advocate using "project work, the outcomes of their performance, and how they balance work/nonwork demands" as alternative criteria for how this cohort is assessed and rewarded (p. 337). "'One size fits all' programs" should be avoided, instead, a range of benefits that speak to employees' divergent needs should be offered (p. 338) (see also Kirby & Krone, 2002).

Advocating for Wider Representation: Moving Diversity Initiatives Beyond Lip Service

Reuters chairperson Niall FitzGerald speaks to the critical need for diversity in the workplace:

> This issue of diversity is newly at the core of business. It's no longer a question of being nice, or being politically correct. Rather, it is an urgent, strategic necessity. Unless you reach out and tap the widest possible pool of talent (more than half of which is women), you simply won't have the wherewithal to drive a strategy. (Hewlett, 2007, p. 106)

Recent studies acknowledge how companies benefit from becoming more inclusive. There is increasing recognition that a diverse workforce fosters the generation of creative perspectives and alternatives that may be otherwise limited in homogeneous groups (Ehrenreich, 2005; Papa, Daniels, & Spiker, 2008; Surowiecki, 2005). As Hewlett (2007) notes, "any kind of difference—race, class, or gender—can have this kind of effect" (p. 101). A more diverse workforce has been linked as well to promoting positive connections in a global landscape that is neither exclusively white nor male (Dexter, 2004; Hewlett, 2007). Perhaps most significant from a business lens are reports connecting diversity to productivity (Crittenden, 2004; Hewlett, 2007; Lang, 2010). Studies indicate that across discrete industries, companies with greater diversity among senior-level employees outperform companies lacking a female and minority presence at the top. This would suggest that companies that value diversity may develop policies and be open to action plans that grow the bottom line: "For example, a leadership team that is 'knowledgeable enough to leverage diversity is likely to be creating effective policies, programs, and systems, as well as a work culture, that maximize a variety of its assets and create new ones.'" (Hewlett, 2007, p. 103).

In spite of this recognition, both unconscious and overt stereotypes and bias continue to be a major barrier to the advancement of women and other underrepresented groups. Lang (2010) recommends that organizations should "build in checks and balances that root out unconscious biases" through reviewing data on salary trajectories and development initiatives for its employees (p. 11A). Mainiero and Sullivan (2006), Hewlett (2007), and Kessler (2007) call for more direct company accountability. They advocate that proactive hiring, mentoring, and opportunities for networking and promotion become benchmarks against which those in positions to move women (and, we would add, other underrepresented groups) along the pipeline are evaluated.

Reevaluating the Meaning of Child Care

In 1973, Young and Willmott predicted that by the twenty-first century, a more symmetrical heterosexual nuclear family would emerge: a family in which both partners would work outside the home and would work within the home. Then there would be "two demanding jobs for the wife and two for the husband. The symmetry will be complete" (p. 278). Sociologists Jean Stockard and Miriam Johnson (1980) and psychologist Sandra Bem (1993) cautioned that this symmetry cannot occur until attitudes toward caring for home and family are regarded more positively. Changing construals of how we define families, as described in chapter 4, undoubtedly will alter our understanding of "symmetrical." And despite reports cited earlier in this chapter of men's desire to become more involved in the home, a gap between more involvement and assuming responsibility for one's child persists.

We are not at a point where we can claim to have achieved the equal commitment to home and work that Young and Willmott predicted.

Gail Collins (2009) ends her book by observing that despite transformations in women's lives since 1960, the issue of child care remains a formidable challenge to women's success:

> The feminist movement of the late twentieth century created a new United States in which women ran for president, fought for the country, argued before the Supreme Court, performed heart surgery, directed movies, and flew into space. But it did not resolve the tensions of trying to raise children and hold down a job at the same time. (p. 393)

Conclusion

Throughout this chapter we have pointed to challenges in family leave policies, accessible and affordable child care provisions, and to escalating hours in the workplace that sustain these "tensions" and require ongoing scrutiny. We noted as well shifts in many workplace settings that suggest employers are becoming increasingly responsive to the changing values and needs of those they hire. These transformations auger positively for how work and productivity are prescribed and evaluated. But we are also cognizant that many of these initiatives are adopted by companies that are regarded as pathbreakers. The impetus for change still resides in how willingly employers alter their view of workplace engagement. As noted by the contemporary researchers we have cited, without systemic policy changes that would render these transformations ubiquitous rather than exceptional, these tensions will continue to be evoked in future works.

We have also noted throughout this chapter the barriers and challenges that influence how we negotiate our place in the world of work. Career decisions, organizational entry, assimilation and success, and the ability to balance our personal and professional lives are not unaffected by stereotypical assumptions about gender, race, culture, sexual identity, and age. These assumptions influence how we are viewed by others and influence how we, in turn, view the professional lives we forge. Exposing these assumptions enables us to resist them and allows us to create spaces for all individuals to compose their lives, as suggested by Bateson's comments at the start of this chapter, in ways that are personally and professionally rewarding.

SUGGESTED ACTIVITIES

1. **Identifying Career Competencies**

   Interview an individual in your field who is responsible for hiring decisions (and/or someone who is aware of how these decisions are made). What are the criteria they use for assessing applicants (e.g., oral and written communication competencies, experience, education, etc.)? What specific communication behaviors do they indicate as positive? As negative? Either in groups or as part of a general discussion, identify any themes or patterns that emerge within or across fields; identify any patterns that conform to and/or deviate from traditional stereotypes related to gender, culture, and/or race.

2. **Intergenerational Survey: Connecting Expectations**
   Interview a family member who has had the experiences of being a partner/spouse and a parent. Ask the following questions:

   a. Prior to living with your significant other, what did you expect your roles to be as a partner/spouse, parent, and professional?

   b. Have your experiences matched your expectations? How so? If not, how so?

   c. If you could have changed anything regarding your role and duties, what would they be?

   d. What advice would you offer to younger generations regarding these roles?

   Either in groups or as part of a larger dialogue, discuss what the responses reveal about expectations, pressures, and tensions related to how couples forge their lives. Are there patterns in the responses that speak to what you should consider in forging your own future? If applicable, to what extent is there consistency across cultures?

3. **Metaphors as Reflective of the Workplace**
   Metaphors offer a powerful way to view how we experience and view the world (e.g., we may view life as a "journey," as a "roller coaster with ups and downs," as an "adventure to be enjoyed," or as a "mystery book"). Interview someone working in the field you plan to pursue. Ask her/him to provide a metaphor for the following items and to explain why this metaphor was chosen:

   a. My workplace environment is like a _____ because

   _____ .

   b. My supervisor is like a _____ because _____

   _____ .

   c. My coworkers are like _____ because _____

   _____ .

   What kinds of descriptors were evoked? What kinds of insights were provided about expectations, interaction, and relationships within and across fields?

4. **Examples from the Field: Extending the Conversation on "Difference" in the Workplace**

    Throughout the chapter, examples from students and seminar participants related to the interview process, salary negotiation and mentoring, and to perceptions about interaction were introduced. Conduct your own interviews and ask individuals to provide examples from their own experiences in either one or all of these areas. What challenges emerge? How might they be addressed? To what extent do their examples reflect, challenge, or augment issues related to one's positionality (gender, class, race, culture, sexual identity, age)?

References

Adams, C., & Singh, K. (1998). Direct and indirect effects of school learning variables on the academic achievement of African-American 10th graders. *Journal of Negro Education, 67,* 48–65.

Alexander, A., & Morrison, M. A. (1995). Electric toyland and the structures of power: An analysis of critical studies on children as consumers. *Critical Studies in Mass Communication, 12,* 344–353.

Al-Jadda, S. (2004, December 14). Move over Barbie. *USA Today,* sect. A, p. 23.

Allen, B. J. (1996). Feminist standpoint theory: A black woman's (re)view of organizational socialization. *Communication Studies, 47,* 257–271.

Allen, B. J. (2000). "Learning the ropes": A black feminist standpoint analysis. In P. Buzzanell (Ed.), *Rethinking organizational and managerial communication from feminist perspectives* (pp. 177–208). Thousand Oaks, CA: Sage.

Allen, B. J. (2001). Gender, race, and communication in professional environments. In L. P. Arliss & D. J. Borisoff (Eds.), *Women and men communicating: Challenges and changes* (2nd ed., pp. 212–231). Long Grove, IL: Waveland Press.

Allen, B. J. (2011). *Difference matters: Communicating social identity* (2nd ed.). Long Grove, IL: Waveland Press.

Allen, E. (1993, February). Best news ever for working women. *Glamour,* 198–201, 225.

Alyn, K., & Phillips, B. (2010). *Men are slobs, women are neat: . . . And other gender lies that damage relationships.* Wheaton, IL: Harvest House.

American Association of University Women. (1991). *Shortchanging girls, shortchanging America.* Washington, DC: Author.

American Association of University Women. (1992). *The AAUW Report: How schools shortchange girls.* Washington, DC: AAUW Educational Foundation and the National Education Association.

American Association of University Women. (1998, October). *Gender gaps: Where schools still fail children.* Washington, DC: AAUW Educational Foundation.

American Association of University Women. (2007). *Behind the pay gap.* Washington, DC: AAUW Educational Foundation.

Anderson, T. L., & Emmers-Sommer, T. M. (2006, June). Predictors of relationship satisfaction in online romantic relationships. *Communication Studies*, *57*, 153–172.

Ankney, C. D. (1992). Sex differences in relative brain size: The mismeasure of women, too. *Intelligence*, *16*, 329–336.

Archer, L., Pratt, S. P., & Phillips, D. (2001). Working-class men's constructions of masculinity and negotiations of (non)participation in higher education. *Gender and Education*, *13*, 431–449.

Aries, E. (1987). Gender and communication. In P. Shaver & C. Hendrick (Eds.), *Sex and gender* (pp. 149–176). Newbury Park, CA: Sage.

Aries, E. (1996). *Men and women in interaction: Reconsidering the differences*. New York: Oxford University Press.

Asante, M. K. (1998). *The Afrocentric idea*. Philadelphia: Temple University Press.

Ashcraft, K. L. (2006). Back to work: Sights/sites of difference in gender and organizational communication studies. In B. J. Dow & J. T. Wood (Eds.), *The Sage handbook of gender and communication* (pp. 97–122). Thousand Oaks, CA: Sage.

Associated Press. (2009, September 15). Taylor Swift. Retrieved March 12, 2010, from http://topics.nytimes.com/top/reference/timesstories/people/s/taylor_swift

Aubrey, J. S., Henson, J. R., Hopper, K. M., & Smith, S. E. (2009, November). A picture worth twenty words (about the self): Testing the priming influence of visual sexual objectification on women's self-objectification. *Communication Research Reports*, *26*, 271–284.

Aufderheide, P. (1992). *Beyond PC: Toward a politics of understanding*. Minneapolis, MN: Graywolf Press.

Azam, S., Chu, Y., Conlan, E., Dunlap, E., Flahive, E., Glyde, C., & Wexler, S. (2007, October). Erasing ethnicity: Has the craze for a more Westernized look sparked a global identity crisis? *Marie Claire*, 57–63.

Baker, M. (2009, April). Is she worth the risk? *Men's Health*, *24*(3), 34.

Balaji, M., & Worawongs, T. (2010, June). The new Suzie Wong: Normative assumptions of white male and Asian female relationships. *Communication, Culture & Critique*, *3*, 224–241.

Balz, C. (2006, September 25). We look marvelous. *Newsweek*, 11.

Banks, J. A. (2006). *Race, culture, and education: The selected works of James A. Banks*. New York: Routledge.

Barnett, R. C., & Rivers, C. (2004). *Same difference: How gender myths are hurting our relationships, our children, and our jobs*. New York: Basic Books.

Basham, M. (2009, June 12). Bringing up princess: Turning girls into narcissists. *The Wall Street Journal*, p. W13.

Bateson, M. C. (1989). *Composing a life*. New York: Plume.

Baum, S., & Goodstein, E. (2005). Gender imbalance in college applications: Does it lead to a preference for me in the admission process? *Economics of Education Review*, *24*, 665–675.

Becker, J. A. H., & Stamp, G. H. (2005, September). Impression management in chat rooms: A grounded theory model. *Communication Studies*, *56*, 243–260.

Belkin, L. (2003, October 26). The opt-out revolution. *The New York Times Magazine*, pp. 44, 45, 58, 85.

Belkin, L. (2007, May 27). After baby, boss comes calling. *The New York Times*, pp. G1, G2.

Belkin, L. (2009, October 4). The new gender gap. *The New York Times Magazine*, pp. 11–12.

Bell, E., & Blaeuer, D. (2006). Performing gender and interpersonal communication research. In B. J. Dow & J. T. Wood (Eds.), *The Sage handbook of gender and communication* (pp. 9–23). Thousand Oaks, CA: Sage.

Bem, S. L. (1974). The measurement of psychological androgyny. *Journal of Consulting and Clinical Psychology, 42*(2), 155–162.

Bem, S. L. (1993). *The lenses of gender: Transforming the debate on sexual inequality*. New Haven, CT: Yale University Press.

Benbow, C. P., & Stanley, J. (1980). Sex differences in mathematical ability: Fact or artifact? *Science, 210,* 1262–1264.

Bennetts, L. (2007). *The feminine mistake: Are we giving up too much?* New York: Hyperion.

Berger, J., Fisck, M. H., Norman, R. Z., & Zelditch, M. (1977). *Status characteristics and social interaction*. New York: Plenum.

Berman, P. (1986). Young children's responses to babies: Do they foreshadow differences between maternal and paternal styles? In A. Fogel & G. M. Melson (Eds.), *Origins of nurturance: Developmental, biological, and cultural perspectives*. Hillsdale, NY: Erlbaum.

Bernard, J. L. (1981). *The female world*. New York: Free Press.

Bernard, T. S. (2010, May 15). A toolkit for women seeking a raise. *The New York Times,* pp. B1, B5.

Bernard, T. S., & Lieber, R. (2009, October 3). The high price of being a gay couple. *The New York Times*, pp. A1, A14.

Berryman-Fink, C. (1993). Preventing sexual harassment through male-female communication training. In G. L. Kreps (Ed.), *Sexual harassment: Communication implications* (pp. 267–280). Cresskill, NJ: Hampton Press.

Bialik, C. (2010, February 27–28). Lights, camera, calculator! The new celebrity math. *The Wall Street Journal*, p. A2.

Bilefsky, D. (2009, November 26). Soul-searching in Turkey after a gay man is killed. *The New York Times*, p. A12.

Biller, H. B. (1968). A multiaspect investigation of masculine development in kindergarten-age boys. *Genetic Psychology Monographs, 78,* 89–139.

Biller, H. B., & Liebman, D. A. (1971). Body build, sex-role preference, and sex-role adoption in junior high school boys. *Journal of Genetic Psychology, 118,* 81–86.

Bingham, S. G. (1996). Sexual harassment: On the job, on the campus. In J. T. Wood (Ed.), *Gendered relationships* (pp. 233–252). Mountain View, CA: Mayfield.

Bizzell, P., & Herzberg, B. (Eds.). (1990). *The rhetorical tradition: Readings from classical times to the present*. Boston: Bedford Books of St. Martin's Press.

Blumstein, P., & Schwartz, P. (1983). *American couples: Money, work, sex*. New York: William Morrow & Co.

Booth-Butterfield, M. (1986). Recognizing and communicating in harassment-prone organizational climates. *Women's Studies in Communication, 9,* 42–51.

Borisoff, D. (1998, May). Strategies for effective mentoring and for being effectively mentored: A focus on research institutions. *Journal of the Association for Communication Administration, 27*, 84–96.

Borisoff, D. (2005a, January). Transforming motherhood: "We've come a long way," maybe. *Review of Communication, 5*(1), 1–11.

Borisoff, D. (2005b, October). Home is not "where the heart is": The millennial motherhood dilemma. *Review of Communication, 5*(4), 259–267.

Borisoff, D., Cooper Hoel, P., & McMahan, D. (2010). Interpersonal communication: Trajectories and challenges. In J. W. Chesebro (Ed.), *A century of transformation: Studies in honor of the 100th anniversary of the Eastern Communication Association* (pp. 205–235). New York: Oxford University Press.

Borisoff, D., & Hahn, D. F. (1997). The mirror in the window: Displaying our gender biases. In S. J. Drucker & G. Gumpert (Eds.), *Voices in the street: Explorations in gender, media, and public space* (pp. 101–117). Cresskill, NJ: Hampton Press.

Borisoff, D., & Merrill, L. (1998). *The power to communicate: Gender differences as barriers* (3rd ed.). Long Grove, IL: Waveland Press.

Bornstein, K. (1994). *Gender outlaw: On men, women, and the rest of us*. New York: Vintage Books.

Brescoll, V., & Uhlmann, E. (2005). Can an angry woman get ahead? Status conferral, gender, and expression of emotion in the workplace. *Psychological Science, 19*, 268–275.

Brizendine, L. (2006). *The female brain*. New York: Morgan Road Books.

Brodey, D. (2005, September 20). Blacks join the eating disorder mainstream. *The New York Times*, pp. F5, F8.

Brooks-Gunn, J., & Markman, L. B. (2005). The contribution of parenting to ethnic and racial gaps in school readiness. *Future of Children, 15*, 139–168.

Brophy, J. (1985). Interactions of male and female students with male and female teachers. In L. C. Wilkinson & C. B. Marrett (Eds.), *Gender influence in classroom interaction* (pp. 115–142). Orlando, FL: Academic Press.

Brophy, J., & Good, T. (1974). *Teacher-student relationships: Causes and consequences*. New York: Holt, Rinehart, & Winston.

Broverman, I. K., Broverman, D. M., Clarkson, F. E., Rosenkrantz, P. S., & Vogel, S. R. (1970). Sex role stereotypes and clinical judgements of mental health. *Journal of Consulting and Clinical Psychology, 34*, 1–7.

Brunell, L. (2008). Feminism reimagined: The third wave. In *Encyclopedia Britannica 2008 Book of the Year*. Chicago, IL: Encyclopedia Britannica.

Bruner, J. (1996). *The culture of education*. Cambridge, MA: Harvard University Press.

Bumiller, E. (2010, February 3). A call to topple policy for gays in armed forces: "The right thing to do." *The New York Times*, pp. A1, A18.

Burd, S. (2006). Working-class students increasingly end up at community colleges, giving up on a 4-year degree. *Chronicle of Higher Education, 52*, A23.

Burgoon, J. K., Buller, D. B., & Woodall, W. G. (1989). *Nonverbal communication: The unspoken dialogue*. New York: Harper & Row.

Butler, J. (1988). Performative acts and gender constitution: An essay in phenomenology and feminist thought. *Theatre Journal, 40*, 519–533.

Butler, J. (1990). *Gender trouble: Feminism and the subversion of identity*. New York: Routledge.

Butler, J. (1993). *Bodies that matter: On the discursive limits of "sex."* New York: Routledge.

Butler, J. (2004). *Undoing gender.* New York: Routledge.

Buzzanell, P. (2002). Employment interviewing research: Ways we can study underrepresented group members' experiences as applicants. *The Journal of Business Communication,* 257–276.

Buzzanell, P. M., & Lucas, K. (2006). Gendered stories of a career: Unfolding discourses of time, space, and identity. In B. J. Dow & J. T. Wood (Eds.), *The Sage handbook of gender and communication* (pp. 161–178). Thousand Oaks, CA: Sage.

Caiazza, A., Shaw, A., & Werschkul, M. (2004). *Women's economic status in the States: Wide disparities by race, ethnicity, and region.* Washington, DC: Institute for Women's Policy Research.

Campbell, K. K. (Ed.). (1989a). *Man cannot speak for her: Volume 1—A critical study of early feminist rhetoric.* New York: Praeger.

Campbell, K. K. (Ed.). (1989b). *Man cannot speak for her: Volume 2—Key texts of the early feminist.* New York: Praeger.

Capron, C., & Duyme, M. (1989). Assessment of the effects of socio-economic status on IQ in full cross-fostering study. *Nature, 340,* 552–554.

Caramanica, J. (2010, February 2). For young superstar Taylor Smith, big wins means innocence lost. *The New York Times,* p. C5.

Careerbuilder.com. (2009, June 17). Fewer working fathers willing to be stay-at-home dads than previous years. Retrieved from http://www.careerbuilder.com/share/aboutus/pressreleasesdetail.aspx

Carr, P. R., & Lund, D. E. (2009). The unspoken color of diversity: Whiteness, privilege, and critical engagement in education. In S. R. Steinberg (Ed.), *Diversity and multiculturalism: A reader* (pp. 45–55). New York: Peter Lang.

Center for Media Design. (2005). *Middletown media studies.* Muncie, IN: Ball State University.

Chafetz, J. S. (1978). *Masculine, feminine, or human? An overview of the sociology of gender roles.* Itasca, IL: F. E. Peacock.

Chesebro, J. W. (1979). Communication, values, and popular television series—a four year assessment. In H. Newcomb (Ed.), *Television: The critical view* (3rd ed., pp. 16–54). New York: Oxford University Press.

Chesebro, J. W. (1986). Communication, values, and popular television series—an eleven-year assessment. In G. Gumpert & R. Cathcart (Eds.), *Inter/media: Interpersonal communication in a media world* (3rd ed., pp. 477–512). New York: Oxford University Press.

Chesebro, J. W. (1987, December 3). Effects of mass media on human communication. Lecture presented at the all-university symposium series at the University of Puerto Rico, Rio Piedras, PR.

Chesebro, J. W. (1991, Summer). Communication, values, and popular television series—a seventeen-year assessment. *Communication Quarterly, 39,* 197–225.

Chesebro, J. W. (1995). Communication technologies as cognitive systems. In J. T. Wood & R. B. Gregg (Eds.), *Toward the twenty-first century: The future of speech communication* (pp. 15–46). Cresskill, NJ: Hampton Press.

Chesebro, J. W. (2000, Winter). Communication technologies as symbolic form: Cognitive transformations generated by the Internet. *Qualitative Research Reports in Communication, 1,* 8–13.

Chesebro, J. W. (2001). Gender, masculinities, identities, and interpersonal relationship systems: Men in general and gay men in particular. In L. P. Arliss & D. J. Borisoff (Eds.), *Women and men communicating: Challenges and changes* (2nd ed., pp. 32–64). Long Grove, IL: Waveland Press.

Chesebro, J. W. (2003, Fall). Communication, values, and popular television series—a twenty-five year assessment and final conclusions. *Communication Quarterly, 51*, 367–418.

Chesebro, J. W., & Bonsall, D. G. (1989). *Computer-mediated communication: Human relationships in a computerized world*. Tuscaloosa: The University of Alabama Press.

Chesebro, J. W., & Fuse, K. (2001, Summer). The development of a perceived masculinity scale. *Communication Quarterly, 49*(3), 203–278.

Chodorow, N. J. (1978). Mothering, object-relations and the female Oedipal configuration. *Feminist Studies, 4*, 137–158.

Chodorow, N. J. (1990). Gender, relation, and difference in psychoanalytic perspective: Essential papers in psychoanalysis. In C. Zanardi (Ed.), *Essential papers on the psychology of women* (pp. 420–436). New York: New York University Press.

Chura, H. (2005, November 20). Some signs of easier re-entry after breaks to rear children. *The New York Times*, sect. 10, pp. 1, 3.

Clair, R. P. (1993, June). The use of framing devices to sequester narratives: Hegemony and harassment. *Communication Monographs, 60*(2), 113–136.

Clair, R. P., Chapman, P. A., & Kunkel, A. W. (1996, November). Narrative approaches to raising consciousness about sexual harassment: From research to pedagogy and back again. *Journal of Applied Communication Research, 24*(4), 241–259.

Clemetson, L. (2006, February 9). Work vs. family, complicated by race. *The New York Times*, pp. 1–2.

Cohen, S. B. (2003). *The essential difference: The truth about the male and female brain*. New York: Basic Books.

Collins, G. (2009). *When everything changed: The amazing journey of American women from 1960 to the present*. New York: Little, Brown & Co.

Correll, S. J., Bernard, S., & Paik, I. (2007). Getting a job: Is there a motherhood penalty? *American Journal of Sociology, 112*, 1297–1338.

Crabtree, R. D., Sapp, D. A., & Licona, A. C. (2009). *Feminist pedagogy: Looking back to move forward*. Baltimore: Johns Hopkins University Press.

Crittenden, A. (2001). *The price of motherhood: Why the most important job in the world is still the least valued*. New York: Henry Holt.

Crittenden, A. (2004). *If you've raised kids, you can manage anything: Leadership begins at home*. New York: Gotham.

Croll, P. (1985). Teacher interaction with individual male and female pupils in junior-age classrooms. *Educational Research, 27*, 220–223.

Daffin, L., & Anderson, G. L. (2009). Diversity and educational leadership: Democratic equality and the goals of schooling. In S. R. Steinberg (Ed.), *Diversity and multiculturalism: A reader* (pp. 438–447). New York: Peter Lang.

Davis, F. (1992). *Fashion, culture and identity*. Chicago: University of Chicago Press.

de Beauvoir, S. (1953). *The second sex* (H. M. Parshley, Ed. & Trans.). New York: Alfred A. Knopf.

de Marneffe, R. (2004). *Maternal desire: On children, love, and the inner life.* New York: Little, Brown, & Co.

Dean, C. (2005, February 1). For some girls the problem with math is that they're good at it. *The New York Times*, p. F3.

Delmeiren, C. (2009, October 22). Rape troubles nearly all in South Africa. The Gallup Poll. Retrieved October 22, 2009, from http://www.gallup.com/poll

Desmond-Harris, J. (2010, February 22). My race-based Valentine. *Time, 175*(7), 99–100.

Deutsch, M. (2000). Justice and conflict. In M. Deutsch & P. T. Coleman (Eds.), *The handbook of conflict resolution: Theory and practice* (pp. 41–64). San Francisco: Jossey-Bass.

DeWine, S. (1987, August). Female leadership in male dominated organizations. *Association for Communication Administration Bulletin, 61*, 19–29.

Dexter, B. (2004). *The case for diversity: Attaining global competitive advantage.* New York: Hudson Highland Group.

Dickens, W. T., & Flynn, J. R. (2006). Black Americans reduce the racial IQ gap: Evidence from standardization samples. *Psychological Science, 17*, 913–920.

DiMaria, F. (2006). Working-class students: Lost in a college's middle-class culture. *Education Digest, 72*, 60–65.

Dobrzynski, J. H. (1996, November 6). Somber news for women on corporate ladder. *The New York Times*, pp. D1, D9.

Docan-Morgan, T., & Docan, C. A. (2007, August). Internet infidelity: Double standards and the differing views of women and men. *Communication Quarterly, 55*, 317–342.

Douglas, S. J. (2010). *Enlightened sexism: The seductive message that feminism's work is done.* New York: Henry Holt & Co.

Douglas, S. J., & Michaels, M. W. (2004). *The mommy myth: The idealization of motherhood and how it has undermined women.* New York: Free Press.

Dow, B. J., & Wood, J. T. (2006). *The Sage handbook of gender and communication.* Thousand Oaks, CA: Sage.

Doyle, J. A., & Paludi, M. A. (1985). *Sex and gender: The human experience.* Dubuque, IA: Wm. C. Brown.

Duckworth, A. L., & Seligman, M. E. P. (2005). Self-discipline outdoes IQ in predicting academic performance of adolescents. *Psychological Science, 16*, 939–944.

Dweck, C., Davidson, W., Nelson, S., & Enna, B. (1978). Sex differences in learned helplessness: The contingencies of evaluative feedback in the classroom—an experimental analysis. *Developmental Psychology, 14*, 268–276.

Eagly, A. H. (1987). *Sex differences in social behavior: A social-role interpretation.* Hillsdale, NY: Lawrence Erlbaum.

Eagly, A. H., & Johnson, B. T. (1990). Gender and the emergence of leaders: A meta-analysis. *Psychological Bulletin, 108*(2), 233–256.

Eakins, B. W., & Eakins, R. G. (1978). *Sex differences in human communication.* Boston: Houghton Mifflin.

Eccles, J. S., Barber, B., & Jozefowicz, D. (1999). Linking gender to educational, occupational, and recreational choices: Applying the Eccles et al. model of achievement-related choices. In W. B. Swann Jr., J. H. Langlois, &

L. A. Gilbert (Eds.), *Sexism and stereotypes in modern society: The gender science of Janet Taylor Spence* (pp. 153–191). Washington, DC: American Psychological Association.

Ehrenreich, B. (2005). *Bait and switch: The (futile) pursuit of the American dream*. New York: Henry Holt & Co./Metropolitan Books.

Eisler, R. (1987). *The chalice and the blade: Our history, our future*. San Francisco: Harper & Row.

Eliot, L. (2009). *Pink brain, blue brain: How small differences grow into troublesome gaps—and what we can do about it*. New York: Houghton Mifflin Harcourt.

Ekman, P., & Friesen, W. V. (1969). The repertoire of nonverbal behavior: Categories, origins, usage, and coding. *Semiotica, 1*, 49–98.

Eveland, W. P., Jr. (2002). The impact of news and entertainment media on perceptions of social reality. In J. P. Dillard & M. Pfau (Eds.), *The persuasion handbook: Developments in theory and practice* (pp. 691–727). Thousand Oaks, CA: Sage.

Evelyn, J. (2002). Community colleges start to ask: Where are the men? *Chronicle of Higher Education, 48*, A32–A34.

Fagot, B. (1978). The influence of sex of child on parental reaction. *Developmental Psychology, 10*, 554–558.

Faludi, S. (1991). *Backlash: The undeclared war against American women*. New York: Doubleday.

Farrell, W. (2005). *Why men earn more*. New York: American Management Association.

Fausto-Sterling, A. (1985). *Myths of gender: Biological theories about women and men*. New York: Basic Books.

Feliciano, C., Robnett, B., & Komaie, G. (2009, March). Gendered racial exclusion among white Internet daters. *Social Science Research, 38*, 39–54.

Fels, A. (2004). *Necessary dreams: Ambition in women's changing lives*. New York: Pantheon.

Fennema, E., & Sherman, J. (1977, Winter). Sex-related differences in mathematical achievement. *American Educational Research, 14*, 51–71.

Ferris, S. P., & Roper, S. (2002, Summer). Same and mixed gender identity in a virtual environment. *Qualitative Research Reports in Communication, 3*, 47–55.

Fine, C. (2010). *Delusions of gender: How our minds, society, and neurosexism create difference*. New York: W. W. Norton.

Fisch, H. (2005). *The male biological clock*. New York: Free Press/Simon & Schuster.

Fisherkeller, J. (2002). *Growing up with television: Everyday learning among young adolescents*. Philadelphia: Temple University Press.

Fitzpatrick, M. (1987). *Between husbands and wives: Communication in marriage*. Newbury Park, CA: Sage.

Flynn, J. R. (2007). *What is intelligence? Beyond the Flynn effect*. New York: Cambridge University Press.

Fonow, M. M., & Marty, D. (2009). The shift from identity politics to the politics of identity: Lesbian panels in the women's studies classroom. In R. D. Crabtree, D. A. Sapp, & A. C. Licona (Eds.), *Feminist pedagogy: Looking back to move forward* (pp. 159–170). Baltimore: Johns Hopkins University Press.

For young earners in big city, a gap in women's favor. (2007, August 3). *The New York Times*, p. A3.

Foucault, M. (1982). The subject and power. In N. Dreyfuss & P. Rabinow (Eds.), *Michel Foucault: Beyond structuralism and hermeneutics* (pp. 208–226). Chicago: University of Chicago Press.

Foucault, M. (1985). Sexuality and solitude. In M. Blonsky (Ed.), *On signs* (pp. 365–372). Baltimore: Johns Hopkins University Press.

Franken, B. (1995, October 16). An emotional celebration for thousands of black men. Retrieved from http://www.cnn.com/US/9510/megamarch/10-16/wrap/index.html

Franklin, C. W., II. (1984). *The changing definition of masculinity*. New York: Plenum Press.

Freedman, R. (1986). *Beauty bound*. Lexington, MA: D.C. Heath.

Freire, P. (2004). *Pedagogy of indignation*. Boulder, CO: Paradigm.

French, J. (1984). Gender imbalances in the primary classroom. *Educational Research, 26*, 126–127.

Friedman, T. L. (2007). *The world is flat 3.0: A brief history of the twenty-first century*. New York: Picador.

Galvin, K. M. (1993). Preventing the problems: Preparing faculty members for the issues of sexual harassment. In G. L. Kreps (Ed.), *Sexual harassment: Communication implications* (pp. 257–266). Cresskill, NJ: Hampton Press.

Galvin, K. M. (2006). Gender and family interaction: Dress rehearsal for an improvisation? In B. J. Dow & J. T. Wood (Eds.), *The Sage handbook of gender and communication* (pp. 41–55). Thousand Oaks, CA: Sage.

Garden, K. (2006, January). Real men read—fact not fiction. *Times Educational Supplement, 4668*, Special Section 4.

Gardner, H. (1983). *Frames of mind: The theory of multiple intelligences*. New York: Basic Books.

Geidner, N. W., Flook, C. A., & Bell, M. A. (2007, April). Masculinity and online social networks: Male self-identification on Facebook.com. Paper presented at the annual meeting of the Eastern Communication Association, Providence, RI.

George, J. F., & Robb, A. (2008, July–December). Deception and computer-mediated communication in everyday life. *Communication Reports, 21*, 92–103.

Gettleman, J. (2009, August 5). Latest tragic symbol of unhealed Congo: Male rape victims. *The New York Times*, pp. A1, A7.

Gherardi, S. (1995). *Gender, symbolism and organizational cultures*. London: Sage.

Gibbs, N. (2009, October 16). What women want *now: A Time* special report. *Time*, 25–33.

Glater, J. D. (2006, December 3). Straight "A" student? Good luck making partner. *The New York Times*, sec. 4, p. 3.

Goffman, E. (1979). *Gender advertisements*. New York: Harper & Row.

Gold, D., Crombie, G., & Noble, S. (1987). Relations between teachers' judgments of girls' and boys' compliance and intellectual competence. *Sex Roles, 16*, 351–358.

Goldin, C., Katz, L. F., & Kuziemko, I. (2006). *The homecoming of American college women: The reversal of the college gender gap*. Cambridge, MA: National Bureau of Economic Research.

Goleman, D. (1998). *Working with emotional intelligence*. New York: Bantam.

Goleman, D. (2006). *Social intelligence: The new science of human relationships*. New York: Bantam Dell.

Goleman, D., Boyatzis, R., & McKee, A. (2002). *Primal leadership: Learning to lead with emotional intelligence*. Boston: Harvard Business School Press.

Good, T., & Slayings, R. (1988). Male and female student question-asking behavior in elementary and secondary mathematical and language arts classes. *Journal of Research in Childhood, 3*, 5–23.

Gornick, V., & Moran, B. K. (1971). *Woman in sexist society: Studies in power and powerlessness*. New York: Signet Book/New American Library/Basic Books.

Gowdy, E. A., & Robertson, S. A. (1994). Postsecondary learning assistance: Characteristics of the clientele. *Community College Journal of Research and Practice, 18*, 43–55.

Graddol, D., & Swann, J. (1989). *Gender voices*. Cambridge, MA: Basil Blackwell.

Granell, A. (2009, April). What men and women call sex. *Men's Health, 24*(3), 34.

Graves, L., & Powell, G. N. (1993). An investigation of sex discrimination in recruiters' evaluations of actual applicants. In G. N. Powell (Ed.), *Women and men in management* (2nd ed.). Newbury Park, CA: Sage.

Guerrero, L. K., Farinelli, L., & McEwan, B. (2009, December). Attachment and relational satisfaction: The mediating effect of emotional communication. *Communication Monographs, 76*(4), 487–514.

Guinness World Records. (2008). BBC world visionaries: Madonna vs. Mozart. Retrieved May 12, 2008, from http://www.visionariesdebate.com/visionaries.php?id=3

Gumpert, G., & Cathcart, R. (1979). *Inter/media: Interpersonal communication in a media world*. New York: Oxford University Press.

Gumpert, G., & Cathcart, R. (1982). *Inter/media: Interpersonal communication in a media world* (2nd ed.). New York: Oxford University Press.

Gumpert, G., & Cathcart, R. (1986). *Inter/media: Interpersonal communication in a media world* (3rd ed.). New York: Oxford University Press.

Gurian, M. (2002). *The wonder of girls: Understanding the hidden nature of our daughters*. New York: St. Martin's.

Hackman, M. Z., & Johnson, C. E. (2009). *Leadership: A communication perspective* (5th ed.). Long Grove, IL: Waveland Press.

Hall, E. T. (1981). *The silent language*. New York: Anchor.

Hall, J. (1984). *Nonverbal sex differences: Communication accuracy and expressive style*. Baltimore: Johns Hopkins University Press.

Hall, R. M., & Sandler, B. R. (1984). *The classroom climate: A chilly one for women?* Project of the Status and Education of Women. Washington, DC: Association of American Colleges.

Hall, S. (1993). *Negotiating Caribbean identities: Walter Rodney memorial lecture*. Centre for Caribbean Studies: University of Warwick.

Hamre, B. K., & Pianta, R. C. (2001). Early teacher-child relationships and the trajectory of children's outcomes through eighth grade. *Child Development, 72*, 625–638.

Han, M. (2003, Spring). Body image dissatisfaction and eating disturbance among Korean college female students: Relationships to media exposure, upward comparison and perceived reality. *Communication Studies, 54*(1), 65–78.

Han, S. (2000). Asian American gay men's (dis)claim on masculinity. In P. Nardi (Ed.), *Gay masculinities* (pp. 206–223). Thousand Oaks, CA: Sage.

Harding, S. (1991). *Whose science? Whose knowledge?* Ithaca, NY: Cornell University Press.

Harker, R. (2000). Achievement, gender and the single-sex/coed debate. *British Journal of Sociology of Education*, *21*, 203–218.

Harlan, A., & Weiss, C. L. (1982). Sex difference in factors affecting managerial career advancement. In P. A. Wallace (Ed.), *Women in the workplace* (pp. 59–100). Boston: Auburn House.

Hart, B., & Risley, T. (1995). *Meaningful differences in the everyday experience of young American children*. Baltimore: Brookes.

Harter, S. (1992, May 17). Is your child caught in the beauty trap? *First*, 54.

Haste, H. (1994). *The sexual metaphor: Men, women, and the thinking that makes the difference*. Cambridge, MA: Harvard University Press.

Haswell, J., & Haswell, R. H. (1995). Gendership and the miswriting of students. *College Composition and Communication*, *46*, 223–254.

Hatfield, E., & Sprecher, S. (1986). *Mirror, mirror: The importance of looks in everyday life*. Albany: State University of New York Press.

Heath, S. B. (1982). What no bedtime story means: Narrative skills at home and school. *Language in Society*, *11*, 49–79.

Helfand, J. (2009). Teaching outside whiteness. In S. S. Steinberg (Ed.), *Diversity and multiculturalism: A reader* (pp. 77–96). New York: Peter Lang.

Helsper, E. J. (2010, June). Gendered Internet use across generations and life stages. *Communication Research*, *37*, 352–374.

Herndon, S. (1994). Gender and communication. In R. L. Ray (Ed.), *Bridging both worlds: The communication consultant in corporate America* (pp. 125–136). Lanham, MD: University Press of America.

Herrnstein, R. J., & Murray, C. (1994). *The bell curve: Intelligence and class struggle in America*. New York: Free Press.

Hewlett, S. A. (2002). *Creating a life: Professional women and the quest for children*. New York: Talk Miramax Books.

Hewlett, S. A. (2007). *Off-ramps and on-ramps: Keeping talented women on the road to success*. Boston: Harvard Business School Press.

Hewlett, S. A., Luce, C. B., West, C., Chernikoff, H., Samalin, D., & Shiller, P. (2005). *Invisible lives: Celebrating and leveraging diversity in the executive suite*. New York: Center for Work-Life Policy.

Hinshaw, S. (with Kranz, R.). (2009). *The triple bind: Saving our teenage girls from today's pressures*. New York: Ballentine Books.

Hitsch, G. J., Hortacsu, A., & Ariely, D. (2004, October). What makes you click: An empirical analysis of online dating. Unpublished paper, Graduate School of Business, University of Chicago.

Hochschild, A. (1997). *The time bind: Where work becomes home and home becomes work*. New York: Henry Holt & Co.

Hochschild, A. (with Machung, A.). (1990). *The second shift*. New York: Avon Books.

Hoffman, M. F., & Cowan, R. L. (2008, August). The meaning of work/life: A corporate ideology of work/life balance. *Communication Quarterly*, *56*(3), 227–246.

Hofstede, G. (1998). *Masculinity and femininity: The taboo dimension of national cultures*. Thousand Oaks, CA: Sage.

Holland, K. (2006, December 3). When work time isn't face time. *The New York Times*, sect. 3, p. 1.

hooks, b. (1984). *Feminist theory: From margin to center*. Boston: South End Press.

hooks, b. (1994). *Teaching to transgress: Education as the practice of freedom*. New York: Routledge.

hooks, b. (1996). *Bone black: Memories of girlhood*. New York: Henry Holt.

Howe, N., & Strauss, W. (2000). *Millennials rising: The next great generation*. New York: Vintage Books.

Huang, C. C., & Pouncy, H. (2005). Why doesn't she have a child support order? Personal choice or objective constraint. *Family Relations: Interdisciplinary Journal of Applied Family Studies, 54*, 547–557.

Hudson, J. B. (1988). The University of Louisville tutoring program: 1986–1987 operations and outcomes. University of Louisville, ERIC document: ED334915.

Hulse, C. (2009, October 9). House votes to expand hate crime definition. *The New York Times*, pp. A1, A18.

Hyde, J. S., Fennema, E., & Lamon, S. J. (1990). Gender differences in mathematics performance: A meta-analysis. *Psychological Bulletin, 107*(2), 139–155.

Hyde, J., & Linn, M. C. (1988). Gender differences in verbal ability: A meta-analysis. *Psychological Bulletin, 107*, 53–69.

Hymowitz, C. (2006a, November 20). View from the top: Leading women executives talk about how they got where they are—and why their ranks are so thin. *The Wall Street Journal*, p. 6.

Hymowitz, C. (2006b, November 26). Women tell women: Life in the top jobs is worth the effort. *The Wall Street Journal,* p. B1.

Hymowitz, K. S. (2009, July 3–5). Losing confidence in marriage. *The Wall Street Journal*, p. W11.

Hyun, J. (2005). *Breaking the bamboo ceiling: Career strategies for Asians*. New York: HarperCollins.

International encyclopedia of communications. (1989). Volume 3. New York: Oxford University Press.

Internet World Stats News. (2009, December 31). Internet ends 2009 with 1,802 million. Retrieved April 4, 2010, from http://www.internetworldstats.com

Itzkoff, D. (2009, November 28). CBS is criticized for blurring of video. *The New York Times*, p. C2.

Ivy, D. K., & Backlund, P. (1994). *Exploring genderspeak: Personal effectiveness in gender communication*. New York: McGraw-Hill.

Ivy, D. K., & Backlund, P. (2008). *Genderspeak: Personal effectiveness in gender communication* (4th ed.). Boston: Allyn & Bacon.

Jablin, F. M. (1987). Organizational entry, assimilation, and exit. In F. M. Jablin, L. L. Putnam, K. H. Roberts, & L. W. Porter (Eds.), *Handbook of organizational communication* (pp. 679–740). Newbury Park, CA: Sage.

Jackson, R. (2004). My life as a housewife. In D. Jones (Ed.), *The bastard on the couch* (pp. 133–145). New York: HarperCollins.

Jackson, R. L., II. (2006). *Scripting the black masculine body: Identity, discourse and racial politics in popular media*. Albany: State University of New York Press.

Jackson, R. L., II, Warren, J. R., Pitts, M. J., & Wilson, K. B. (2007). "It is not my responsibility to teach culture!": White graduate teaching assistants negotiating identity and pedagogy. In L. M. Cooks & J. S. Simpson (Eds.), *Whiteness, pedagogy, performance: Dis/placing race* (pp. 67–86). Lanham, MD: Lexington.

Jacobs, J. A., & Steinberg, R. J. (1995). Further evidence on compensating differences and the gender gap in wages. In J. A. Jacobs (Ed.), *Gender inequality at work* (pp. 93–124). Thousand Oaks, CA: Sage.

Jamieson, K. H. (1995). *Beyond the double bind: Women and leadership.* New York: Oxford University Press.

Johnson, F. L., & Young, K. (2002, December). Gendered voices in children's advertising. *Critical Studies in Media Communication, 19*(4), 461–480.

Johnson, W. B., & Ridley, C. R. (2004). *The elements of mentoring.* New York: Palgrave Macmillan.

Jones, G. M., & Wheatley, J. (1990). Gender differences in teacher-student interactions in science classrooms. *Journal of Research in Science Training, 27*(9), 861–874.

Jones, M. (1989). Gender issues in teacher education. *Journal of Teacher Education, 40,* 33–44.

Jones, S., & Dindia, K. (2004, Winter). A meta-analytic perspective on sex equity in the classroom. *Review of Educational Research, 64*(4), 443–471.

Jordan-Jackson, F. F., Lin, Y., Rancer, A. S., & Infante, D. A. (2008, July–September). Perceptions of males and females' use of aggressive affirming and nonaffirming messages in an interpersonal dispute: You've come a long way baby? *Western Journal of Communication, 72*(3), 239–258.

Jurgensen, J. (2010, January 29). The lessons of Lady Gaga. *The Wall Street Journal,* pp. W1, W12.

Kadaba, L. S. (2010, March 21). Girls abandon dolls for web-based toys. *Inquirer.* Retrieved from http://www.philly.com/Inquirer/magazine/20100331-Girls-abandon-dolls-for-web-based-toys.html

Kahn, J. S. (2009). *An introduction to masculinities.* Malden, MA: Wiley-Blackwell.

Kakutani, M. (2010, March 21). Texts without context. *The New York Times,* pp. AR1, AR22–AR23.

Kanter, R. M. (1995). Numbers: Minorities and majorities. In S. R. Corman, S. P. Banks, C. R. Bantz, & M. E. Mayer (Eds.), *Foundations of organizational communication: A reader* (2nd ed., pp. 298–322). White Plains, NY: Longman.

Kantrowitz, B., & Peterson, H. (2007, October 16). Women and power 2007. *Newsweek,* 46.

Kaplan, A. G. (1976). *Beyond sex-role stereotypes: Readings toward a psychology of androgyny.* Glenview, IL: Scott Foresman.

Kay, K. (2000). Introduction. In K. Kay, J. Nagle, & B. Goulds (Eds.), *Male lust: Pleasure, power, and transformation* (pp. xvii–xxi). Binghamton, NY: Harrington Park Press/The Haworth Press.

Keen, S. (1991). *The fire in the belly: On being a man.* New York: Bantam Books.

Keenan, K., & Hipwell, A. E. (2005). Preadolescent clues to understanding depression in girls. *Clinical Child and Family Psychology Review, 8,* 89–105.

Kessler, L. T. (2007, January). Keeping discrimination theory front and center in the discourse over work and family conflict. *Pepperdine Law Review, 34,* 313, Westlaw, 1–15.

Kilborn, P. T. (1995, March 16). Women and minorities still face glass ceiling. *The New York Times,* p. C11.

Kim, L. M. (2009). "I was (so) busy fighting racism that I didn't even know I was being oppressed as a woman!": Challenges, changes, and empowerment in teaching about women of color. In R. D. Crabtree, D. A. Sapp, & A. C. Licona (Eds.), *Feminist pedagogy: Looking back to look forward* (pp. 195–208). Baltimore: Johns Hopkins University Press.

King, J. L. (with Hunter, K.). (2004). *On the down low: A journey into the lives of "straight" black men who sleep with men*. New York: Harlem Moon.

Kirby, E. L., & Krone, K. J. (2002). "The policy exists but you can't use it": Communication and the structuration of work-family policies. *Journal of Applied Communication Research, 30*(1), 50–77.

Knapp, M. L., & Hall, J. A. (2009). *Nonverbal communication in human interaction* (7th ed.). Belmont, CA: Wadsworth.

Kotulak, R. (1985, April 7). Researchers decipher a powerful "language." *Chicago Tribune*, sec. 6.

Kristof, N. D., & WuDunn, S. (2009, August 23). The women's crusade. *The New York Times Magazine*, pp. 28–39.

La France, B. H., Henningsen, D. D., Oates, A., & Shaw, C. M. (2009, September). Socio-sexual interactions? Meta-analyses of sex differences in perceptions of flirtatiousness, seductiveness, and promiscuousness. *Communication Monographs, 76*(3), 263–285.

Lake, C., Conway, K., & Whitney, C. (2005). *What women really want: How American women are quietly erasing political, racial, class, and religious lines to change the way we live*. New York: Free Press.

Lang, I. H. (2010, April 15). Have women shattered corporate glass ceiling? No. *USA Today*, p. 11A.

Lareau, A. (2003). *Unequal childhoods: Class, race, and family*. Berkeley: University of California Press.

Larson, C. (2006). The penny pinch. In P. J. Dubeck & D. Dunn (Eds.), *Workplace/women's place: An anthology* (3rd ed., pp. 77–82). Los Angeles: Roxbury.

Lauzen, M. M., Dozier, D. M., & Horan, N. (2008, June). Constructing gender stereotypes through social roles in prime-time television. *Journal of Broadcasting & Electronic Media, 52*, 200–214.

LaVoie, J. C., & Andrews, R. (1976). Facial attractiveness, physique, and sex role identity in young children. *Developmental Psychology, 12*, 550–551.

Lax, J. (2007, Spring). Do employer requests for salary history discriminate against women? *Labor Law Journal, 58*(1), 47–52.

Lea, V. (2009). Unmasking whiteness in the teacher education college classroom. In S. R. Steinberg (Ed.), *Diversity and multiculturalism: A reader* (pp. 57–75). New York: Peter Lang.

Leaf, R. (2007, April 23). *Pay gap exists as early as one year out of college, new research says*. American Association of University Women Educational Foundation Report. Retrieved from http://www.aauw.org/newsroom/pressreleases/042307_PayGap.cfm

Leahey, E., & Guo, G. (2000). Gender differences in mathematical trajectories. *Social Forces, 80*, 713–732.

Leathers, D. (1986). *Successful nonverbal communication: Principles and applications*. New York: Macmillan.

Lederman, L. C. (2001). The impact of gender on the self and self-talk. In L. P. Arliss & D. J. Borisoff (Eds.), *Women and men communicating: Challenges and changes* (2nd ed., pp. 78–89). Long Grove, IL: Waveland Press.

Lee, D. (2005, March). Androgyny becoming global? Retrieved from http:// uniorb.com/RCHECK/RAndrogyny.htm

Lee, E. J. (2006, December). When and how does depersonalization increase conformity to group norms in computer-mediated communication? *Communication Research, 33,* 423–447.

Lee, P. C., & Gropper, N. B. (1974). Sex-role culture and educational practice. *Harvard Educational Review, 44,* 369–407.

Lenhart, A., Purcell, K., Smith, A., & Zickuhr, K. (2010, February 3). Social media & mobile Internet use among teens and young adults. Pew Research Center. Retrieved February 5, 2010, from www.pewresearch.org/millennials

Lewin, T. (1996, March 2). Child care in conflict with job. *The New York Times,* p. 8.

Lewin, T. (2010, January 20). If your kids are awake, they're probably online. *The New York Times,* pp. A1 and A3.

Lin, C. A. (1997). Beefcake versus cheesecake in the 1990s: Sexist portrayals of both genders in television commercials. *The Howard Journal of Communication, 8*(3), 237–249.

Lindesmith, A. R., Strauss, A. L., & Denzin, N. K. (1999). *Social psychology* (8th ed.). Thousand Oaks, CA: Sage.

Lindgren, S., & Lelievre, M. (2009, December). In the laboratory of masculinity: Renegotiating gender subjectivities in MTV's *Jackass. Critical Studies in Media Communication, 26,* 393–410.

Lipman-Blumen, J. (1994). The existential bases of power relationships: The gender role case. In H. L. Radtke & H. J. Stam (Eds.), *Power/gender: Social relations in theory and practice* (pp. 108–135). Thousand Oaks, CA: Sage.

Lipsman, A. (2010, May 13). Americans received 1 trillion display ads in Q1 2010 as online advertising market rebounds from 2009 recession. ComScore.com. Retrieved May 15, 2010, from http://news@comscore.com

Lorber, J. (Ed.). (1998). *Gender inequality: Feminist theories and politics.* Los Angeles: Roxbury.

Lorenz, K. (2007, June 14). Survey: Working dads want more family time. CNN. Retrieved from http://www.cnn.com/2007/US/Careers/06/13/dads.work/ index.html

Luo, M. (2009a, December 1). In job hunt, even a college degree can't close the racial gap. *The New York Times,* pp. A1, A4.

Luo, M. (2009b, December 6). "Whitening" the resume. *The New York Times,* p. 3.

Lytton, H., & Romney, D. M. (1991). Parents' differential socialization of boys and girls: A meta-analysis. *Psychological Bulletin, 109,* 267–296.

MacKinnon, C. (1979). *Sexual harassment of working women.* New Haven: Yale University Press.

Macoby, E. E., & Jacklin, C. N. (1974). *The psychology of sex differences.* Stanford, CA: Stanford University Press.

Magni, M., & Atsmon, Y. (2010, February 24). China's Internet obsession. *Harvard Business School, 88*(2). Retrieved March 11, 2010, from http:// blogs.hbr.org/cs/2010/02/chinas_internet-obsession_html?utm_so...

Mahar, M. (1993, April). The truth about women's pay. *Working Woman,* 72–75, 100–102.

Mainiero, L. A., & Sullivan, S. E. (2006). Kaleidoscope careers: An alternate explanation for the "opt-out" revolution. In P. J. Dubeck & D. Dunn (Eds.), *Workplace/women's place: An anthology* (3rd ed., pp. 324–339). Los Angeles: Roxbury.

Major, B. (1987). Justice, and the psychology of entitlement. In P. Shaver & C. Hendrick (Eds.), *Sex and gender* (pp. 124–148). Newbury Park, CA: Sage.

Malandro, L. A., Barker, L., & Barker, D. A. (1989). *Nonverbal communication* (2nd ed.). New York: Random House.

Marcus, J. (2000). Colleges urged to give men a break. *The Times Higher Education Supplement, 1461*, 11.

Marcus, S. S. (2009, December 13). Women want to want. *The New York Times Magazine*, p. 16.

Marini, M. M., & Brinton, M. (1984). Sex typing in occupational socialization. In D. F. Reskin (Ed.), *Sex segregation in the workplace: Trends, explanations, remedies*. Washington, DC: National Academy Press.

Marsh, H. W., & Rowe, K. J. (1996). The effects of single-sex and mixed-sex mathematics classes within a coeducational school: A reanalysis and comment. *Australian Journal of Education, 40*, 147–162.

Martínez, K. Z. (2008). Real women and their curves: Letters to the editor and a magazine's celebration of the "Latina body." In A. N. Valdivia (Ed.), *Latina/o communication studies today* (pp. 137–159). New York: Peter Lang.

Matias, A. (2001). Women in the legal profession: Challenges and changes. In L. P. Arliss & D. J. Borisoff (Eds.), *Women and men communicating: Challenges and changes* (2nd ed., pp. 254–267). Long Grove, IL: Waveland Press.

Mattioli, D. (2010, March 23). More men make harassment claims. *The Wall Street Journal*, p. D4.

McCann, D., & Delmonte, H. (2005). Lesbian and gay parenting: Babes in arms or babes in the woods? *Sexual and Relationship Therapy, 20*, 333–347.

McCroskey, J. W. (2006). An introduction to rhetorical communication: A Western rhetorical perspective (9th ed.). Boston: Pearson/Allyn and Bacon.

McIntosh, P. (1988). *White privilege and male privilege: A personal account of coming to see correspondences through work on women's studies* (Working Paper No. 189). Wellesley, MA: Wellesley College, Center for Research on Women. Retrieved March 4, 2008, from http://www.feingberg.northwestern.edu/diversity/uploaded_docs/UnpackingTheKnapsack.pdf

McIntyre, S., Mohberg, D. J., & Posner, B. Z. (1980). Preferential treatment in preselection decisions according to sex and race. *Academy of Management Journal, 23*, 738–749.

McKinley, J. C., Jr. (2009, December 13). Houston is largest city to elect openly gay mayor. *The New York Times*, p. A34.

McLaren, P. (2003). Critical pedagogy: A look at the major concepts. In A. Darder, M. Baltodano, & R. Torres (Eds.), *The critical pedagogy reader*. New York: Routledge Falmer.

McLuhan, H. M. (1964). *Understanding media: The extensions of man*. New York: McGraw-Hill.

McLuhan, H. M., & Fiore, Q. (1968). *War and peace in the global village*. New York: McGraw-Hill.

McNeil, D. G., Jr. (2004, September 19). Real men don't clean bathrooms. *The New York Times*, p. 3.

Mehrabian, A. (1968, September). Communication without words. *Psychology Today*, 2(4), 52–55.

Meisenbach, R. J., Remke, R. V., Buzzanell, P. M., & Liu, M. (2008, March). "They allowed": Pentadic mapping of women's maternity leave discourses as organizational rhetoric. *Communication Monographs*, 75(1), 1–24.

Meyer, E. (2009). Creating schools that value sexual diversity. In S. R. Steinberg (Ed.), *Diversity and multiculturalism: A reader* (pp. 173–192). New York: Peter Lang.

Mikulecky, L. (1996). *Family literacy: Parent and child interactions*. Washington, DC: U.S. Department of Education.

Miller, C. C. (2010, April 16). Out of the loop in Silicon Valley. *The New York Times*, pp. BU1, BU8.

Miller, S. A. (2010, April). Making the boys cry: The performative dimensions of fluid gender. *Text and Performance Quarterly*, 30, 163–182.

Millett, K. (1970). *Sexual politics*. Garden City, NY: Doubleday & Company, Inc.

Mindlin, A. (2008, October 20). For men, stronger online connections. *The New York Times*, p. B4.

Mindlin, A. (2010, March 7). Rapid rise of children with cell phones. *The New York Times*, p. B2.

Mohan, E. (2009). Putting multiethnic students on the radar: A case for greater consideration of our multiethnic students. In S. R. Steinberg (Ed.), *Diversity and multiculturalism: A reader* (pp. 131–141). New York: Peter Lang.

Montaresky, R. (2005). Studies show biological differences in how boys and girls learn math, but social factors play a big role too. *The Chronicle of Higher Education*, pp. A1, A12–19.

Moore, E. G. J. (1986). Family socialization and the IQ test performance of traditionally and trans-racially adopted children. *Developmental Psychology*, 22, 317–326.

Morin, R., & Cohen, D. (2008, September 25). Gender and power: Women call the shots at home; on the job, leadership preferences are mixed. Retrieved from http://pewresearch.org

Morin, R., & Taylor, P. (2008, September 15). Politics, gender and parenthood. Pew Research Center. Retrieved September 15, 2008, from http://pewsocialtrends.org

Morrison, A. M., White, R. P., Van Velsor, E., & The Center for Creative Leadership. (1992). *Breaking the glass ceiling: Can women reach the top of America's largest corporations?* Reading, MA: Addison-Wesley.

Moss, P., & Tilly, C. (2001). *Stories employers tell: Race, skill and hiring in America*. New York: Russell Sage Foundation.

Mouw, T. (2002). Are black workers missing the connection? The effect of spatial distance and employee referrals on interfirm racial segregation. *Demography*, 39(3), 507–528.

Murphy, B. O., & Zorn, T. (1996). Gendered interaction in professional relationships. In J. T. Wood (Ed.), *Gendered relationships* (pp. 213–232). Mountain View, CA: Mayfield.

Myers, S. L. (2009, December 28). A peril in war zones: Sexual abuse by fellow G.I.'s. *The New York Times*, pp. A1, A10.

National Science Foundation. (2010). ADVANCE at a glance. Retrieved May 24, 2010, from http://www.nsf.gov/erssprgm/advance/index.jsp

Navai, R. (2007, July). Welcome to Tehran: Nose job capital of the world. *Marie Claire,* 139–141.

Newsome, M. (2005, December). Empty inside: For older women the quest for perfection leads increasingly to eating disorders. *American Association for Retired People,* 13–14.

Nielsen SoundScan. (2010, January 7). Nielsen SoundScan lists Taylor Swift as the top-selling digital artist in history. *PR Newswire.* Retrieved January 11, 2010, from http://www.prnewswire.com/news-release/nielsen-soundscan-lists-artist-in-history-80965892.html

Nisbett, R. (2009). *Intelligence and how to get it: Why schools and cultures count.* New York: W. W. Norton

Noddings, N. (2002). *Starting at home: Caring and social policy.* Berkeley: University of California Press.

Nossiter, A. (2009, October 6). In a Guinea seized by violence, women as prey. *The New York Times,* pp. A1, A3.

Obama, B. (2009, June 21). We need fathers to step up. *Parade,* 4–5.

O'Brien, T. L. (2006, March 19). Up the down staircase: Why do so few women reach the top of big law firms? *The New York Times,* sec. 3, pp. 1, 4.

Onishi, N. (2002, October 3). Globalization of beauty makes slimness trendy. *The New York Times,* p. A4.

Orenstein, P. (1994). Shortchanging girls: Gender socialization in schools. In P. J. Dubeck & D. Dunn (Eds.), *Workplace/women's place: An anthology* (2nd ed., pp. 38–46). Los Angeles: Roxbury.

Ozden, Y. (1996). Have efforts to improve higher education opportunities for low-income youth succeeded? *The Journal of Student Financial Aid, 26,* 19–39.

Paetzold, R. L., & O'Leary-Kelly, A. M. (1993). Organizational communication and the legal dimensions of hostile work environment sexual harassment. In G. L. Kreps (Ed.), *Sexual harassment: Communication implications* (pp. 63–77). Cresskill, NJ: Hampton Press.

Pager, D. (2003). The mark of a criminal record. *American Journal of Sociology, 108,* 937–975.

Paglia, C. (2010, June 27). No sex please, we're middle class. *The New York Times,* p. WK12.

Paglin, C. (1993). *Girls face barriers in science and mathematics, Northwest report: The challenge of sex equity.* Portland, OR: Northwest Regional Educational Laboratory.

Palmer, K. (2010, May). Getting back in the game. *U.S. News and World Report,* 29.

Papa, M. J., Daniels, T. D., & Spiker, B. K. (2008). *Organizational communication: Perspectives and trends.* Thousand Oaks, CA: Sage.

Parker, P. S. (2002). Negotiating identity in raced and gendered workplace interactions: The use of strategic communication by African American senior executives with dominant culture organizations. *Communication Quarterly, 50*(3&4), 251–268.

Parker O'Neal, L. (2005). *I'm every woman: Remixed stories of marriage, motherhood, and work.* New York: HarperCollins.

Parker O'Neal, L. (2006). The Donna Reed syndrome. In L. M. Steiner (Ed.), *Mommy wars* (pp. 62–69). New York: Random House.

Parker-Pope, T. (2010, April 6). Surprisingly, family time has grown. *The New York Times,* p. D5.

Parks, M. R., & Roberts, L. D. (1998). "Making MOOsic": The development of personal relationships online and a comparison to their off-line counterparts. *Journal of Social and Personal Relationships, 15,* 517–537.

Pauley, P. M., & Emmers-Sommer, T. M. (2007). The impact of Internet technologies on primary and secondary romantic relationship development. *Communication Studies, 58*(4), 411–427.

Pearson, J. C., Child, J. T., Carmon, A. F., & Miller, A. N. (2009, November). The influence of intimacy rituals and biological sex on relational quality and intimacy among dating couples. *Communication Research Reports, 26*(4), 297–310.

Pearson, J. C., & West, R. (1991). An initial investigation of the effects of gender on student questions in the classroom: Development a descriptive base. *Communication Education, 40,* 22–32.

Pew Internet & American Life Project. (2010, January 6). Demographics of Internet users. Retrieved May 13, 2010, from http://www.pewinternet.org

Pew Internet & American Life Project Infographics. (2009a, January 28). Generational differences in online activities. Retrieved February 3, 2010, from http://wwwpewinternet.org/Infographic

Pew Internet & American Life Project Infographics. (2009b, October 9). Social networking site users younger than overall Internet population. Retrieved February 2, 2010, from http://www.pewinternet.org/Infographics

Pew Research Center. (2006, February 13). Not looking for love. Retrieved February 12, 2010, from http://pewresearchcenter.org

Pew Research Center. (2007, July 12). Fewer mothers prefer full-time work. Retrieved from http://pewresearch.org

Pew Research Center. (2008, August 25). Men or women: Who's the better leader? Retrieved from http://pewresearch.org/pubs/932/men-or-women-whos-the-better-leader

Pew Research Center. (2010a, January 19). Women, men and the new economics of marriage. Pew Research Center's Social and Demographic Trends Project. Retrieved January 21, 2010, from http://pewsocialtrends.org

Pew Research Center. (2010b, July 1). *Gender equality universally embraced, but inequalities acknowledged.* Washington, DC: Pew Research Center, Global Attitudes Project.

Philipson, I. (2002). *Married to the job: Why we live to work and what we can do about it.* New York: Free Press.

Pinker, S. (2002). *The blank slate: The modern denial of human nature.* New York: Viking Penguin.

Pinker, S. (2008). *The sexual paradox: Men, women, and the real gender gap.* New York: Scribner.

Pollack, W. S. (1998). *Real boys: Rescuing our sons from the myths of boyhood.* New York: Henry Holt & Co.

Pope, H. G., Phillips, K. A., & Olivardia, R. (2000). *Adonis complex: The secret crisis of male body obsession.* New York: The Free Press.

Potter, W. J. (2008). *Media literacy* (4th ed.). Thousand Oaks, CA: Sage.

Powell, G. N. (1993). *Women and men in management* (2nd ed.). Newbury Park, CA: Sage.

Press, A. L. (1991). *Women watching television: Gender, class, and generation in the American television experience*. Philadelphia: University of Pennsylvania Press.

Preston, J. (2006). Gender and the formation of a women's profession: The case of public school teaching. In P. J. Dubeck & D. Dunn (Eds.), *Workplace/women's place: An anthology* (3rd ed., pp. 233–250). Los Angeles: Roxbury.

Putnam, L. L. (1983). "Lady you're trapped": Breaking out of conflict cycles. In J. J. Pilotta (Ed.), *Women in organizations: Barriers and breakthroughs* (pp. 39–53). Long Grove, IL: Waveland Press.

Putnam, L. L., & Kolb, D. (2000). Rethinking negotiation: Feminist views of communication & exchange. In P. Buzzanell (Ed.), *Rethinking organizational and managerial communication from a feminist perspective* (pp. 76–104). Thousand Oaks, CA: Sage.

Rabby, M. K. (2007, September). Relational maintenance and the influence of commitment in online and offline relationships. *Communication Studies, 58*, 315–337.

Rabinow, P. (1984). Introduction. In P. Rabinow (Ed.), *The Foucault reader* (pp. 3–29). New York: Pantheon Books.

Rainie, L., Horrigan, J., Wellman, B., & Boase, J. (2006, January). The strength of Internet ties. Pew Internet & American Life Project. Retrieved May 20, 2010, from http://www.pewinternet.org

Rakow, L. F., & Wackwitz, L. A. (Eds.). (2004). *Feminist communication theory: Selections in context*. Thousand Oaks, CA: Sage.

Ralston, S. M., & Kinser, A. E. (2001). Intersections of gender and employment interviewing. In L. P. Arliss & D. J. Borisoff (Eds.), *Women and men communicating: Challenges and changes* (2nd ed., pp. 185–211). Long Grove, IL: Waveland Press.

Ralston, S. M., & Kirkwood, W. G. (1995, February). Overcoming managerial bias in employment interviewing. *Journal of Applied Communication Research, 23*(1), 75–92.

Ramasubramanian, S. (2010, March). Television viewing, racial attitudes, and policy preferences: Exploring the role of social identity and intergroup emotions in influencing support for affirmative action. *Communication Monographs, 77*, 102–120.

Ramirez, A., Jr., & Zhang, S. (2007, September). When online meets offline: The effect of modality switching on relational communication. *Communication Monographs, 74*, 287–310.

Rebeldad.com. (2009, July 8). Stay-at-home dad statistics. Retrieved from http://www.rebeldad.com/stats.htm

Recording Industry Association of America. (1999). The American Recording Industry announces its artists of the century. Retrieved January 30, 2008, from http://www.riaa.com/newsitem.php?news_year_filter=1999& resultingpage=2&id=3ABF3EC8-EF5B-58F9-E949-3B57F5313DF

Recording Industry Association of America. (2010, June). Top selling artists. Retrieved June 15, 2010, from http://www.riaa.com/ goldandplatinumdata.php?table=tblTopArt

Reinard, J. C. (2002). Persuasion in the legal setting. In J. P. Dillard & M. Pfau (Eds.), *The persuasive handbook: Developments in theory and practice* (pp. 543–602). Thousand Oaks, CA: Sage.

Remick, H. (1984). Major issues in *a priori* applications. In H. Remick (Ed.), *Comparable worth and wage discrimination: Technical possibilities and political realities* (pp. 107–147). Washington, DC: National Committee on Pay Equity.

Reuters. (2009, December 24). U.N. website details peacekeeper sex abuse claims. *The New York Times*. Retrieved December 24, 2009, from http://query.nytimes.com/search/query

Rich, A. (1993). Compulsory heterosexuality and lesbian existence. In H. Abelone, D. Halperin, & M. A. Barale (Eds.), *The lesbian and gay studies reader* (pp. 227–254). New York: Routledge.

Richmond, V. P., & McCroskey, J. C. (2000). *Nonverbal behavior in interpersonal relations* (4th ed.). Boston: Allyn & Bacon.

Richmond, V. P., McCroskey, J. C., & McCroskey, L. L. (2005). *Organizational communication for survival: Making work work* (3rd ed.). Boston: Pearson.

Riddell, S. (1989). Pupils, resistance and gender codes: A study of classroom encounters. *Gender and Education*, *1*, 183–197.

Rideout, V. J., Foehr, U. G., & Roberts, D. F. (2010, January). *Generation M²: Media in the lives of 8- to 18-year-olds*. Menlo, CA: Henry J. Kaiser Family Foundation.

Rimer, S. (2005, April 15). For women in the sciences, the pace of progress at the top universities is slow. *The New York Times*, p. A15.

Roberts, S. (1995, April 27). Women's work: What's new, what isn't. *The New York Times*, p. A18.

Rochlin, M. (1977). The heterosexual questionnaire. Retrieved March 2, 2008, from http://www.advocatesforyouth.org/lessonplans/heterosexual2htm

Rochman, B. (2009, March 23). Economoms: Many who opted out of the rat race are scrambling to get back in. *Time*, 69, 70.

Rock, M., Stainback, S., & Adams, J. (2001). Women in news: Television and new media. In L. P. Arliss & D. J. Borisoff (Eds.), *Women and men communicating: Challenges and changes* (2nd ed., pp. 310–328). Long Grove, IL: Waveland Press.

Rock and Roll Hall of Fame. (2009). Madonna. Retrieved October 11, 2009, from http://www.rockhall.com/inductee/madonna

Rohter, L. (2007, January 14). In the land of bold beauty a trusted mirror cracks. *The New York Times*, sect. 4, pp. 1, 3.

Rosen, E. (2006, February 12). Derailed on the mommy track? There's help to get going again. *The New York Times*, sect. 10, pp. 1, 3.

Rosenfeld, L. B., & Jarrard, M. W. (1986). Student coping mechanisms in sexist and nonsexist professors' classes. *Communication Education*, *35*, 157–162.

Rosenthal, R., & Jacobson, L. (1968). *Pygmalion in the classroom*. New York: Holt, Rinehart & Winston.

Ross, C. (1972). Sex-role socialization in picture books for preschool children. *American Journal of Sociology*, *77*(6), 1125–1150.

Roth, L. M. (2006). Selling women short: A research note on gender differences in compensation on Wall Street. In P. J. Dubeck & D. Dunn (Eds.), *Workplace/women's place: An anthology* (3rd ed., pp. 207–215). Los Angeles: Roxbury.

Rubin, J. Z., Provensano, F., & Luria, Z. (1974). The eye of the beholder: Parents' views on sex of newborns. *American Journal of Orthopsychiatry*, *44*, 312–319.

Rubin, L. B. (1983). *Intimate strangers*. New York: Harper & Row.

Rushton, J. P., & Jensen, A. R. (2005). Thirty years of research on race differences in cognitive ability. *Psychology, Public Policy and Law, 11*, 235–294.

Russo, G., & Ommeren, J. (1998). Gender differences in recruitment outcomes. *Bulletin of Economic Research, 50*, 155–167.

Ryback, D. (1998). *Putting emotional intelligence to work*. Boston: Butterworth-Heinemann.

Sadker, M., & Sadker, D. (1985, March). Sexism in the schoolroom in the '80s. *Psychology Today*, 54–57.

Sadker, M., & Sadker, D. (1986). Sexism in the classroom: From grade school to grad school. *Phi Delta Kappa, 67*, 7.

Sadker, M., & Sadker, D. (1994). *Failing at fairness: How America's schools cheat girls*. New York: Charles Scribner's Sons.

Sahlstein, E. D., & Allen, M. (2002). Sex differences in self-esteem: A meta-analytic assessment. In M. Allen, R. Preiss, B. Gayle, & N. Burrell (Eds.), *Interpersonal communication research: Advances through meta-analysis* (pp. 59–72). Mahwah, NJ: Lawrence Erlbaum.

Salomone, R. C. (2003). *Same, different, equal: Rethinking single-sex schooling*. New Haven, CT: Yale University Press.

Sandberg, D. E., Ehrhardt, A. A., Mellins, C. A., Ince, S. E., & Meyer-Bahlburg, H. F. L. (1987). The influence of individual and family characteristics upon career aspirations of girls during childhood and adolescence. *Sex Roles, 16*, 649–668.

Sandler, B. R., & Hall, R. M. (1986). *Out of the classroom: A chilly campus climate for women*. Washington, DC: Association of American Colleges.

Sax, L. (2005). *Why gender matters*. New York: Doubleday.

Schoenemann, P. T., Budinger, T. F., Sarich, V. M., & Wang, W. (1999). Brain size does not predict general cognitive ability within families. *Proceedings of the National Academy of Science, 97*, 4932–4937.

Sennett, R. (1998). *The corrosion of character: The personal consequences of work in the new capitalism*. New York: W. W. Norton.

Shannon, M., & Kidd, M. P. (2003, December). Projecting the U.S. gender wage gap, 2000–40. *Atlantic Economic Journal, 31*(4), 316–329.

Shapiro, L. (1990, May 28). Guns and dolls: Nature or nurturance. *Newsweek*, 56–65.

Sheehy, G. (1998). *Understanding men's passages: Discovering the new map of men's lives*. New York: Random House.

Signorielli, N. (2009, November). Minorities representation in prime time: 2000 to 2008. *Communication Research Reports, 26*, 323–336.

Silva, H. (2010, February 28). Makeup's dream team. *The New York Times*, p. ST3.

Simonds, C. J., & Cooper, P. J. (2001). Communication and gender in the classroom. In L. P. Arliss & D. J. Borisoff (Eds.), *Women and men communicating: Challenges and changes* (2nd ed., pp. 232–253). Long Grove, IL: Waveland Press.

Simpson, A. W., & Erickson, M. T. (1983). Teachers' verbal and nonverbal communication patterns as a function of teacher race, student gender, and student race. *American Educational Research Journal, 20*, 183–198.

Simpson, J. S., Causey, A., & Williams, L. (2007, March). "I would want you to understand it": Students' perspectives on addressing race in the classroom. *Journal of Intercultural Communication Research*, *36*(1), 33–50.

Singer, N., & Wilson, D. (2009, December 13). Menopause, as brought to you by big pharma. *The New York Times*, pp. BU1, BU7.

Smithers, A., & Robinson, P. (2006). *The paradox of single sex and co-educational schooling*. Buckingham, England: Carmichael Press.

Solomon, D. (2009, December 13). Questions for Martha Nussbaum: Gross national politics. *The New York Times Magazine*, p. 22.

Southard, B. A. S. (2008, May). Beyond the backlash: *Sex & the City* and three feminist struggles. *Communication Quarterly*, *56*, 149–167.

Spender, D. (1985). *Man made language* (2nd ed.). London: Routledge & Kegan Paul.

Stake, J. E., & Katz, J. F. (1982). Teacher-pupil relationships in the elementary school classroom: Teacher-gender and pupil-gender differences. *American Educational Research Journal*, *19*, 465–471.

Steele, C. M. (1997). A threat in the air: How stereotypes shape the identities and performance of women and African Americans. *American Psychologist, 52*, 613–629.

Steele, C. M., & Aronson, J. (1995). Stereotype threat and the performance of African Americans. *Journal of Personality and Social Psychology*, *69*, 797–811.

Steinberg, R. J. (1990). The social construction of skill. *Work and Occupations*, *17*, 449–482.

Steinberg, S. R. (Ed.). (2009). *Diversity and multiculturalism: A reader*. New York: Peter Lang.

Steiner, L. M. (Ed.). (2006). *The mommy wars*. New York: Random House.

Stephens, B. (2010, March 30). Lady Gaga versus Mideast peace. *The Wall Street Journal*, p. A17.

Stern, M., & Karraker, K. H. (1989). Sex stereotyping in infants: A review of gender labeling studies. *Sex Roles, 20*, 501–522.

Stewart, L. P., Cooper, P. J., & Friedley, S. A. (1986). *Communication between the sexes: Sex differences and sex-role stereotypes*. Scottsdale, AZ: Gorsuch Scarisbrik.

Stewart, L. P., Cooper, P. J., & Stewart, A. D. (with Friedley, S. A.). (2003). *Communication and gender* (4th ed.). Boston: Pearson Education.

Stockard, J., & Johnson, M. (1980). *Sex roles: Sex inequality and sex role development*. Englewood Cliffs, NJ: Prentice-Hall.

Stone, P., & Lovejoy, M. (2006). Fast-track women and the "choice" to stay home. In P. J. Dubeck & D. Dunn (Eds.), *Workplace/women's place: An anthology* (3rd ed., pp. 143–156). Los Angeles: Roxbury.

Story, L. (2005, September 20). Many women at elite colleges set career path to motherhood. *The New York Times,* pp. A1, A18.

Strauss, N. (2010, July 8–22). The broken heart & violent fantasies of Lady Gaga. *Rolling Stone*, *1108/1109*, 66–74.

Sturm, S. (2001). Second generation employment discrimination: A structural approach. *Columbia Law Review*, *458*, 465–474.

Suddath, C. (2010, May 17). Music pop star 2.0: The Internet-fueled rise of Justin Bieber. *Time*, *175*(19), 49–50.

Surowiecki, J. (2005). *The wisdom of crowds*. New York: Anchor Books.

Swiggers, P. (1989). Linguistics. In G. Gerbner & E. Barnouw (Eds.), *International encyclopedia of communications* (vol. 2, pp. 431–436). New York: Oxford University Press.

Tannen, D. (2006). "Put that paper down and talk to me!": Rapport-talk and report-talk. In K. M. Galvin & P. J. Cooper (Eds.), *Making connections: Readings in relational communication* (4th ed., pp. 116–127). Los Angeles: Roxbury.

Tarvis, C. (1992). *The mismeasure of woman*. New York: Simon & Schuster.

Teachout, T. (2009, July 25). Does Broadway need women? *The Wall Street Journal*. Retrieved July 27, 2009, from http://online.wsj.com/home-page

Teven, J. J., & Gorham, J. (1999). A qualitative analysis of low-inference student perceptions of teacher caring and non-caring behaviors within the college classroom. *Communication Research Reports, 15*, 288–298.

Teven, J. J., & McCroskey, J. C. (1997). The relationship of perceived teacher caring with student learning and teacher evaluation. *Communication Education, 46*, 1–9.

Thompson, T., & Ungerleider, C. (2004). *Single sex schooling: Final report*. Canadian Centre for Knowledge Mobilisation. Retrieved from http://www.cckm.ca/pdj/ss%20Final%20Report.pdf

Thorne, B. (1993). *Gender play: Girls and boys at school*. New Brunswick, NJ: Rutgers University Press.

Toma, C. L., & Hancock, J. T. (2010, June). Looks and lies: The role of physical attractiveness in online dating self-presentation and deception. *Communication Research, 37*, 335–351.

Tong, R. (1984). *Women, sex, and the law*. Savage, MA: Rowman & Littlefield.

Trebay, G. (2008, February 7). The vanishing point. *The New York Times*, p. G1.

Turkle, S. (1984). *The second self: Computers and the human spirit*. New York: Simon & Schuster.

Twenge, J. M. (2001, July). Changes in women's assertiveness in response to status and roles: A cross-temporal meta-analysis, 1931–1993. *Journal of Personality and Social Psychology, 81*(1), 133–145.

Tyre, P., Murr, A., Juarez, V., Underwood, K. S., & Wingert, P. (2006, January). The boy crisis: At every level they are falling behind. What to do? *Newsweek, 5*, 42–52.

U.S. Department of Education. (2005). *Single-sex versus coeducational schooling: A systematic review*. Office of Planning, Evaluation, and Policy Development. Retrieved from http://www.ed/gov/rschstat/eval/other/single-six/pdf

U.S. Department of Labor. (2010a). *Current population survey*. Washington, DC: Bureau of Labor Statistics.

U.S. Department of Labor. (2010b, April 15). *Usual weekly earnings of wage and salary workers: First quarter 2010* (USDL-10-0468). Washington, DC: Bureau of Labor Statistics.

U.S. Department of Labor. (2010c, May 27). *Employment characteristics of families* (USDL-10-0721). Washington, DC: Bureau of Labor Statistics.

Valentine, G. (1997, March). "My son's a bit ditzy." "My wife's a bit soft": Gender, children and cultures of parenting. *Gender, Place and Culture, 4*(l), 37–62.

Vavrus, M. D. (2007, March). Opting out moms in the news: Selling new traditionalism in the new millennium. *Feminist Media Studies, 7*(1), 47–64.

Wallace, P. (2004). *The Internet in the workplace: How new technology is transforming work*. New York: Cambridge University Press.

Wallis, C. (2004, March 22). The case for staying home: Why more young moms are opting out of the rat race. *Time*, 50–59.

Walther, J. B., Van Der Heide, B., Hamel, L. M., & Shulman, H. C. (2009, April). Self-generated versus other-generated statements and impressions in computer-mediated communication: A test of warranting theory using Facebook. *Communication Research, 36*, 229–253.

Warner, J. (2005). *Perfect madness: Motherhood in the age of anxiety*. New York: Penguin Group.

Watson, C. (1994). Gender differences in negotiating behavior and outcomes: Fact or artifact? In A. Taylor & J. Bernstein Miller (Eds.), *Conflict and gender* (pp. 191–209). Cresskill, NJ: Hampton Press.

Watzlawick, P., Beavin, J. H., & Jackson, D. D. (1967). *Pragmatics of human communication: A study of interactional patterns, pathologies, and paradoxes*. New York: W.W. Norton & Co.

Weaver-Hightower, M. (2003). The "boy turn" in research on gender and education. *Review of Educational Research, 73*, 471–498.

Webster's New Collegiate Dictionary. (2003). Springfield, MA: G. & C. Merriam Company.

Weil, E. (2008, March 2). Teaching to the testosterone. *The New York Times Magazine*, 39–45, 84–87.

Welch, S-A, & Rubin, R. B. (2002, Winter). Development of relationship stage measures. *Communication Quarterly, 50*(1), 24–40.

West, P. (1999). Boys' underachievement in schools: Some persistent problems and some current research. *Issues in Educational Research, 9*, 33–54.

Whittaker, Z. (2010, February 26). Facebook profiles: Society is beyond "male" and "female." Retrieved February 27, 2010, from http://blogs.zdnet.com/igeneration/

Wildermuth, S. M., & Vogl-Bauer, S. (2007, September). We met on the Net: Exploring the perceptions of online romantic relationship participants. *Southern Communication Journal, 72*, 211–227.

Wilden, A. (1987). *Man and woman, war and peace: The strategist's companion*. New York: Routledge and Kegan Paul.

Wilkins, B. M., & Anderson, P. A. (1991). Gender differences and similarities in management communication: A meta-analysis. *Communication Quarterly, 3*, 6–35.

Williams, J. C. (2010). *Reshaping the work-family debate: Why men and class matter*. Cambridge, MA: Harvard University Press.

Williams, D., Consalvo, M., Caplan, S., & Yee, N. (2009, December). Looking for gender: Gender roles and behaviors among online gamers. *Journal of Communication, 59*, 700–725.

Wolf, N. (1991). *The beauty myth: How images of beauty are used against women*. New York: Morrow.

Wood, J. T. (1982, Spring). Communication and relational culture: Bases for the study of human relationships. *Communication Quarterly, 30*, 75–83.

Wood, J. T. (1993). Naming and interpreting sexual harassment: A conceptual framework for scholars. In G. L. Kreps (Ed.), *Sexual harassment: Communication implications* (pp. 9–26). Cresskill, NJ: Hampton Press.

Wood, J. T. (2009). *Gendered lives: Communication, gender, and culture* (8th ed.). Boston: Wadsworth.

Wortham, J. (2010, March 12). Facebook helps social start-ups gain users. *The New York Times*, p. B3.

Wu, F. (2002). *Yellow: Race in America beyond black and white*. New York: Basic Books.

Yee, D. K., & Eccles, J. S. (1988). Parent perceptions and attributions for children's math achievement. *Sex Roles, 19*, 5–6.

Young, M., & Willmott, P. (1973). *The symmetrical family*. New York: Pantheon.

Zahn-Waxler, C., & Polanichka, N. (2004). All things interpersonal: Socialization and female aggression. In M. Putallaz & K. L. Bierman (Eds.), *Aggression, antisocial behavior, and violence among girls*. New York: Guilford.

Zamani, E. M. (2000). *Aspiring to the baccalaureate: Attitudes of community college students toward affirmative action in college admissions* (Unpublished doctoral dissertation). University of Illinois at Urbana-Champaign.

Zernike, K. (2010, January 3). Career U.: Making college relevant. *The New York Times: Educational Life*, pp. 16–17, 25.

Zhang, Q. (2010, February). Asian Americans beyond the model minority stereotype: The nerdy and the left out. *Journal of International and Intercultural Communication, 3*(1), 20–37.

Zweigenhaft, R. L. (1984). *Who gets to the top?* New York: Institute of Human Relations, American Jewish Committee.

Index